EIGHTYSIXED

A memoir about unforgettable men, mistakes, and meals.

BY EMILY BELDEN

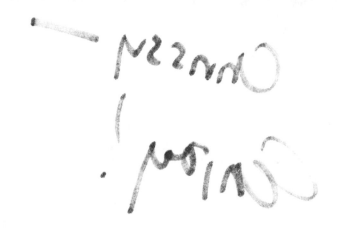

Dedicated to my mom and dad, who always encouraged me to be my true, authentic self.

PART ONE

CHAPTER ONE/LESSON ONE

- Facebook news is the worst kind of news

"Hey, this is just a friendly text to see if you're dealing okay with the whole Layla situation."

That's the text message that popped up on my phone at 4:55 PM on June 13th. It came from a guy named Geoffrey, a coworker from my previous ad agency gig a few months back. Mapping out our mutual friends, I could only assume he was talking about the one Layla we both knew. She was our quiet graphic design intern—a flannel-wearing hipster, who didn't say much and could probably benefit from eating a carb once in a while. In other words, a skinny bitch who knew her way around Photoshop. Those girls, and the ones who make six-figure salaries doing makeup tutorials on YouTube, are my enemies.

With the "who" pinpointed, it was now time to address the

"what"—i.e., "the whole situation." I could only assume Geoffrey knew better than to allude to something grotesque like an untimely death in a text message, but then again, how much social etiquette can a guy who sits alone all day in a darkroom editing B-roll footage really have? About as much sex as he was having. That's how much.

Regardless of his social shortcomings, the message warranted a reply. Whether she was dead, pregnant, promoted, or wanted for a triple homicide, I needed to write back. Knowing I was minutes away from powering down for the day, the best I could come up with was: "???"

Sent.

Geoffrey's response came back immediately, like he already had it loaded in the cannon.

"Just…check her Facebook. Alright?"

Did she create an album dedicated to her refurbished Schwinn bicycle collection? Switch employers and take a job with our old agency rival? Declare she was interested in women like I had suspected all along?

Five minutes from Happy Hour, I had all but closed out of the Internet tabs on my work computer. Magically, Facebook was still open so it was easy to navigate to her page on my 20-inch monitor. And once there, it didn't take long to see what was going on. My eyes shot directly to a photo of a bouquet of bright red bushy roses.

Ok, so what?

They were pretty, but why was this breaking news?

I scrolled down to read the caption: "Overjoyed!"

Oh, so this is good news.

But just before I clicked the "like" button, I saw her next update pop up on my newsfeed: "Layla is in a Relationship."

With my most recent ex-boyfriend, whom I thought I was going to marry.

With her "overjoyed," and me "overwhelmed," there I had it: the whole Layla situation.

~ ~ ~

Before you write this off as just another glorified college-entrance essay about a time some twenty-something had to overcome bad luck with men, let me assure you two things. 1) Admissions counselors could care less about guy problems, and 2) this story is quite the opposite. It's one about good luck—the best, in fact. It just took me a while to see that and I want to explain how.

This is actually the story of a girl (I know her well) who attempted to take control of things that were a wee bit beyond her. After all, isn't that what all twenty-something women are encouraged to do—take control? Get your finances in order, nab a career, lock down a love life, take over the world—there's a Suze Orman book for them all, I'm sure. Sorry you're stuck with this Rated-R memoir for now.

But truth be told, these pie-in-the-sky pillars were more like the limbs of a baby deer for me after graduating college. My finances were feeble. My career, wobbly. My love life, weak. And despite the many times I tried to patch up my fails with a reconnaissance plan or a bootleg prescription for painkillers, I learned that there sometimes is no other choice but to let it all crumble. To cut the balloon on whatever you're worrying about and let it fly. To let it all just run out. In the restaurant industry, this is called "eighty-sixing" something; it's what they say to indicate an item is no longer available.

Patience, single good-looking men, vodka, hope—these were all "eightysixed" for me at one point or another.

When it comes to love—finding it, losing it, having it, making it, whatever—I once was convinced that all of our stories were basically the same; iterations of bad break ups, evil exes, and delusional happiness that someday culminates in a marriage that may or may not last longer than that of Kim Kardashian and Kris Humphries. But that view eventually changed for me. I know how, and I will share that with you throughout this book. But I do not know why. Why I was chosen to learn these life lessons, especially in the order in which they were received. Why I was taken to the trenches, only to be pulled from them and given a true chance to become a believer in something much bigger than myself. And no, I'm not talking about the storyline of Stranger Things.

As a non-practicing half-Jew, who lived and sinned in the city of Chicago, during the entire time this story took place, I know calling my lessons "a gift from God" would be borderline offensive. But I really believe I was subject to something special. That being said, I'll resolve to circle back to what I called it all before—good luck. Really good luck.

Now here's the story.

~ ~ ~

I grew up in suburb of Chicago with dreams as big as the city itself to make it in the advertising industry as a copywriter. For those of you who don't know, "making it" in the ad industry as a writer means pulling a salary of about $28,000 (after taxes), exhausting yourself by coming up with brilliant copy for products like baby formula, accepting said taglines will never see the light of day because the client is a conservative Christian, and working well into the evenings on most nights, including weekends and holidays to come up with a diluted, generic tagline that the FCC won't take issue with.

That being said, "making it" meant also saying goodbye to my creative soul, as well as my disposable income, and being OK with occasional free lunches from my boss and having Casimir Pulaski Day off as my only real employee benefits. I must not have been totally clear as to what the American Dream was when I decided this was my life's calling.

But before I committed to a life of that level of grandeur, I accepted an academic scholarship at a four-year, private Jesuit university located a few states over in Nebraska. I'm not sure what influence I was under when I made this choice, but before I knew it, this never-been-to-church, childhood-kleptomaniac soon found herself, and all of her life belongings, packed into a 1998 Toyota Camry with a dorm assignment in hand. The next thing I knew, I was sitting in the passenger seat cruising down the not-so-scenic I-80 West for the first time in my life wondering what the hell I had just gotten myself into.

Alas, I was going away to college as a delusional virgin donned in an Abercrombie polo shirt, a flounce skirt, and knock-off UGG boots. Cringe-worthy? Yes. But also, the perfect uniform for such an occasion.

~ ~ ~

The university I went to wasn't exactly the hub for anything creative (or anything besides corn stalks and devout republicans). So I spent the next four years trying to "figure myself out" at a school that didn't really do it for me, earning credits from mandated theology classes, and spending way too much money on textbooks that would inevitably become irrelevant and digitized by the time I turned in my cap and gown. If I only knew then that getting a job in the real world would ultimately come down to leaving the top button undone on a blouse and stalking the hiring manager on social media, I probably would have just taken classes online and lived off my parents for four more years.

By the second semester of my senior year, I could feel the ride winding down. I was in the home stretch. So much so, I had already started researching my future walk-up Chicago apartment on Craigslist. Neighborhood and price didn't matter. I just wanted a 312 area code, a professional sports team (or five), and a slice of edible pizza at my everyday disposal.

So, with just one semester left, I did what anyone with a New Year's resolution would do. I stopped binge drinking and joined a gym on the first of January. If there was one thing I wanted to leave behind in Nebraska, it was the "Freshman 15" that came along with cheap alcohol, sugary mixers, and an unlimited meal plan in a shitty cafeteria. Soon, though, through hard work, a dedicated personal trainer, and an on-again off-again relationship with anorexia, I was able to drop a substantial amount of weight in preparation for my big date with Summer in the City.

After ten personal training sessions, I did the cliché thing: I fell in love with my newfound quads, and the fine-as-fuck coach, Dave, who helped put them there.

I don't know if it was the way he held his stopwatch, or the fact that he didn't need real food to survive—just protein bars and juice cleanses—but I was infatuated with this man who I had only ever seen in running shorts and who always smelled faintly of B.O. But regardless of his hygienic shortcomings, I eventually asked him out the way any aspiring copywriter would—I slipped him an ultra-cute, seriously-who-does-that note that looked just like the brochure he gave me on the first day of training sessions. I could only hope that his brain was as developed as his six-pack, and that he would get the point of the gesture.

Eight hours of photo editing, two hours of copywriting, and a pair of balls later, I had my answer from Dave: no.

I wish he had been just getting out of a bad break-up. I wish he had a thing where he didn't date attractive brunettes who looked like Sandra Bullock's hotter, younger sister with a brand-new banging body. I wish he were a half-gay unicorn.

Seriously, any reason would have been better than what came out of his mouth next: "You are the most adorable girl I've ever met, but I have a girlfriend."

How did I miss that? Maybe if my college wasn't so busy jamming biblical studies down my throat, they would have taught me how to adequately Google someone. I was nearly four years into journalism school and my investigative tactics were nowhere near ready for the real world. Such a waste.

Regardless, it was a swing and a miss that took more courage than total calories consumed in an entire month for me to do and I was rejected all in an instant. Had I eaten anything that day, I would have easily vomited—not because he was seeing someone else, but because of the continued awkwardness that ensued after his initial explanation.

"Look, I may not be single…but my roommate is. Would you want to meet him?"

Oh, fantastic. A consolation prize for the runner up. The only thing worse would be him physically writing me a rain check to come back and see him when things with the current girl didn't work out.

Seriously, though. A participation ribbon? It was as if Dave was standing in one of those wind cylinders where cash is just whipping around and you have only ten seconds to clench as many dollar bills as you can. Except, instead of money flying around, they were random responses written on sheets of paper, all options for how you can turn down a girl who just asked you out. The one he ended up grabbing read: "Defer her to the roommate."

Obviously the combination of my subsequent, "Sure, yeah, that sounds great," and his "Okay, great, I'll set it up," sent any ounce of an appetite running for the hills, as I bolted out the gym's door wondering what in God's name just went down. I went in to sweep my trainer off his feet and I wound up scoring a "maybe" date with his "could-be-ugly" roommate. All I could do was get back in my trusty Camry and head home, where I'd pull out my reserve copy of He's Just Not That Into You and contemplate what kind of wine goes best with humiliation and defeat.

A few days later, I was putting some clothes away when my phone rang with an unidentified Nebraska number. Although I typically sent those straight to voice-mail because they were usually someone trying to send me on a free 10-day cruise with the purchase of new Kia Soul, I for some reason answered this one. And that ten-digit number would become one I would, unfortunately, always remember.

It was Trent, Dave's "single roommate." Trent: the runner up, the beta version, the back-up plan. Trent: my (and also Layla's) future boyfriend.

I realize it's a little early to introduce him as the villain that he inevitably became, so I'm going to hold on and preserve his character a little longer before I fly this plane straight into the ground. After all, it wouldn't have hurt so badly if I didn't wind up loving him. And I wound up loving him because he had a killer six-pack and some redeeming qualities (emphasis on some).

Trent asked me out for dinner on a nothing-else-going-on Wednesday night in February. He told me he'd pick me up in a "white truck" at 8:00 PM Based purely on the description of his vehicle, I knew he was a thoroughbred Nebraskan.

It had been over a month since I had been out on the town and about as long since I had eaten a solid meal. You see, attempting to lose weight eradicates any ounce of being social since calorie-counting pulls of Irish whiskey on dollar-shot night isn't exactly kosher in the dieting world. As such, I'm sure you can imagine the anxiety that began brewing when I knew "out for dinner" meant having to eat in front of a total stranger.

Nonetheless, I accepted his offer and hoped ingesting something other than a Fiber One bar with peanut butter smeared on it for dinner wouldn't send my digestive system into shock. Not to mention, I'd never been picked up for a blind date by someone in a "white truck" and I was kind of looking forward to buckling up next to a bumpkin.

Wednesday night arrived, and according to a right-on-time text, he was waiting for me outside. I tell you, he could have been ugly as sin, but he definitely earned points for being punctual. So, with a few swipes of blush and a silent prayer that my body would behave in the presence of real food, I trotted down the stairs with standard pre-date jitters.

Busting out of my apartment doors, I had my eyes peeled for a roaring Ford F-150 and was listening for a muffled track off of an Alan Jackson Christmas album. But the only car in sight on this deserted winter night was a Cadillac Escalade. A white Cadillac Escalade.

Process of elimination, and a much-too-peppy person emerging from a descending driver's side tinted window, told me that the driver was Trent, and that the pearlescent, luxury SUV was his "white truck." As he flagged me over, nothing about this reality synced up with the picture I had painted in my head. Let's be clear, though, I wasn't complaining.

"Emily!" he exclaimed with wide eyes and impeccable hair, opening the door for me.

"Trent . . ." I subtly responded in a questionable tone.

Everything about him—from his excitement to see me, to the striped cardigan he was sporting, to the heated-leather passenger's seat I was sitting in—was a total surprise and delight. Well I'll be damned, I thought. The could-be-ugly roommate was exactly the opposite: a total hottie. Six-foot-something, toned, tan; with Madonna's tooth gap and Tom Ford's wardrobe. This was one case of sloppy second I didn't mind.

He began talking right as we pulled away. He was exuberant and bubbly, but I had no idea what he was saying. I was too busy silently thanking God I had been rejected by his meathead roommate who suddenly didn't seem all that great anymore. As Trent jabbered on, for the first time in my young, often-intoxicated adulthood, I was somewhat speechless—scared even. I was so thrown off by my instant attraction I began to doubt what I was bringing to this party for two. Sure, my jeans were fitting better than they ever had, my dark brown hair had recently been highlighted to show off my cheekbones, and I was this-close to clinching my degree at the best university in the state. But would all that be enough to hook the-enigma-known-as-Trent?

Arriving at the small dare-I-say-romantic wine bar, my inability to act like a functioning human being continued once seated. We were the only ones in the quiet restaurant, but I still couldn't focus on anything other than this person's unexplainable, instant likeability. It was as if the lead singer of Coldplay had a tall, dark, and handsome lovechild. That's with whom I was having dinner.

Clearly, I was not the only one who liked him. Moments later, the server came over and greeted my date by name, "Trent, my man. What's happening?" he said, giving him that little slap-then-snap thing that men do with their hands in social situations. Next thing I knew, the server said he'd throw in "two filets for us." It was apparent from the royal treatment that Trent was either one of their regulars, or he owned the place.

Both turned out to be the case.

About a half-hour later, the plates were dropped. I was looking at the first slab of meat I'd seen in weeks—euphemisms not excused. But longer than it had been since I'd eaten a real meal, was how long it had been since I enjoyed being on a date. My philosophy had always been to tolerate-it-for-the-free-meal but this time, it was different. In this situation, I thanked whatever half-Jew god was looking out for me that my personal trainer was the perfect combination of incredibly unavailable and totally awkward, because without those two qualities, I would never have found myself sitting across from such a spectacular guy.

A few more dinner dates ensued just like this. Several hours and calories would go by, and the conversation, laughs, and compatibility racked up. But it wasn't the time together that led us to be exclusive and give this relationship thing a real go, it was something else entirely.

Ever since I phased out of my gym membership, I started to feel sick. At first, I attributed it to the butterflies that came along with seeing someone new and exciting, but eventually I realized my stomach was no longer playing nice with my yo-yo dieting. Out of desperation, I drove myself to the emergency room on an otherwise routine night and crossed my fingers it wasn't a baby.

It was just moments after I had seen the doctor and been diagnosed with ulcers (phew) that Trent had texted me.

"What's up cutie pie?"

Oy vey. He was going to think I was a hypochondriac. A wimp. An attention whore. Diseased. Damaged. Dramatic.

I should probably just say, "Nothing, reading a book. You?"

But instead, I answered truthfully: "I'm in the emergency room, actually. I've been feeling bad lately and they are running some tests. It's looking like some ulcers."

"Oh my god. Are you okay? What hospital are you at? Can I come down there?" he responded immediately.

"No, no. It's fine. I appreciate that though. I really do," I answered hoping to deflect any and all chances of him seeing me draped in a white tarp drinking a Pepto-cocktail next to a room full of stabbing victims with Whooping Cough.

"Well, just so you know, we are there."

"Meaning?" I asked for clarification.

"Meaning…I would come there for you. Gladly. In an instant. I want to be with you. So just say the word and I'm there."

I instantly smirked. I got a good one, I thought.

"I will let you know, Trent. Thanks."

"And while you are on the subject of keeping me informed, would you also let me know if you'd like to be my girlfriend?"

Finally, and for the first time that night, I was going to take him up on an offer. Trent was going to get a resounding "yes" out of me. I wanted to be his girlfriend, and I was going to be his girlfriend.

From then on, our relationship took off. It soared. And it wasn't his money. It wasn't his car. It wasn't the wine shop he owned on the side, or that he was the vice president of his dad's company at age 24, or the fact that he still talked to me after the first time we had sex. It was something about his joyful spirit and the way it oozed out of his beady, brown eyes. Every time I looked at them, I just knew. I knew I had been led straight to my person. And when you find your person, you don't let them go. At least,

I think that's what the post on Thought Catalog said.

So, with four months until college graduation, I decided to abandon my plan to move back to Chi-Town—all for a boy who lived in, and couldn't move away from, Nebraska. With Trent's successful, six-figured career cemented in Omaha, I had no choice but to loosen the vice grip I had on my dreams of being a poor Chicagoan with a useless college degree. My visions of radiator heat and expensive rent had disseminated as I racked my brain over the best way to break the news to the masses—or at least to my parents who had already cleared out my old room in preparation for my homecoming.

Their initial reaction was to stage an intervention, as they thought I was abusing drugs and wasn't in my right mind choosing voluntarily to live my life in Nebraska. Unfortunately, I was stone sober when I made that decision, something I wish I hadn't been when breaking it to my mom.

No one took it harder than her, my native New Yorker mother, who 35 years prior had moved away from her family, city, and career to be with my dad 700 miles away in the Midwest. Perhaps her vehement disdain was an omen I should have paid more attention to at the time, but after taking her word and guidance on everything for twenty-two years straight, I figured there wasn't much harm in doing things my way just this once.

Hindsight: LOL

So, I went rogue on this one and was reaffirmed about my decision when Trent proved to be at my side the entire way. He helped me move into my first apartment, which wasn't too far from the architectural masterpiece he lived in. Once I got my degreee, he threw me a graduation party and even had a cake decorated especially with my name on it. He brought me to his parents' mansion for a traditional family dinner every Sunday, where I pretended to mumble Grace under my breath and practiced being the best future-daughter-in-law ever amongst his very-catholic mom and dad.

When I wasn't busy envisioning our married life, Trent and I traveled with one another frequently. We shared a lot of expensive luggage and earned a lot of mileage points during our time together. From weekend trips that spanned the coasts to week-long romantic stints below the border, he was my very own Bachelor and I was just waiting to accept the final rose.

But like any ebb and flow, the closer we got, the further away we'd inevitably grow. It was hard to believe, but one day I realized that a whole two years of trading in skyscrapers for cornhuskers had come and gone. Just like that, "the time of my life" was slipping away and I was still living in an apartment down the road with no ring on my finger.

Trent and I had gone through thousands of experiences together, both good and bad. From pregnancy scares to paradise getaways, I'll never forget—or regret—the roster of things we got ourselves into. But when I stopped to take inventory of our two-year relationship, I realized something that stabbed me in the gut. He was scared of me. He was scared of us.

I was coming to the end of my apartment lease term and gently bridged the topic of moving in together with Trent. After all, Trent and Dave were still the only people living in his sprawling, four-bedroom house. I would have been more than happy to lower their mortgage and chip in on a room for myself. But the thought of making a spare key and giving it to someone with a vagina sent Trent into the biggest tailspin he'd experienced since realizing NFL 360 didn't come standard with his cable package.

"I'm not going to abandon Dave like that," Trent put his foot down. I could hear the aggravation in his voice. "I won't just kick him out."

Don't roll your eyes, don't roll your eyes.

"You don't have to, Trent. I'm saying I'll move into one of the spare rooms. There's room for all of us."

"No. And I'm not making you a key either," he fired back, pacing and refusing to make eye contact.

"What? Why not?" I asked, knowing he'd had my spare since day-one.

"Because. What if—what if . . ." Trent struggled to find an excuse. "What if—Dave is watching TV in the basement and you just come in unannounced—and—you scare him."

"What if I scare Dave? Is that a real question? He's an almost-30-year-old man who's own girlfriend has a key to your house. I'm sure he's familiar with the concept of someone walking into a house."

"It's not happening. Not yet. I'm sorry," he said.

With a defense like that, I chose to lay my prosecution to rest. Potentially startling Dave in the middle of Shark Week was not the reason Trent and I weren't going to be sharing an address. It was Trent's fear that this was it: that a spare key was the nail in the coffin. That his single-life was over as he knew it.

I bet you can guess how that made me feel.

After nearly 730 days of being boyfriend and girlfriend, I had to accept that living down the block and being perpetual neighbors was as good as it was going to get with Trent—indefinitely. Would that be enough for me? Would that be okay with me?

To this day, it still hurts to think that all Trent looked at was what moving in together would have taken away from Dave versus what it could have done for us. Fucking idiot.

Beneath his amazing wardrobe and his ridiculously good body, I finally found a fault. I picked someone whose ability to commit was broken, paralyzed in fact. Every passing milestone only made it worse. Anniversaries were treated like the redheaded stepchild: ignored and unspoken about. I'd of course grab booze for those special days—not to celebrate, but to ease the pain of passing them alone.

Eventually it got to the point where he avoided me on weekends in an effort to put a real stake in the ground and define his bachelor life. As most of you know, for any couple that works a 9-to-5, the weekend is the chance to catch up. To talk. Hang out. Have sex. I can confidently say that none of those things—not even a text, sext, or smoke signal—happened between Friday and Sunday nights.

Clearly he was seeing another girl, right? Wrong. He simply was out drinking with the boys. Going out and getting wasted was his theme song and he had it on repeat for about a year of our relationship.

One time, I decided to counter his bro-time with a girls' night out. It was going well until one of friends returned from the bathroom.

"Oh my god, you guys," she began. "There is this homeless man outside who is so drunk, he can't even grab the handle of the door to get in here. He's just grasping at it and falling. It's actually hilarious. Come look."

Of course, we all jumped up from our seats to catch a glimpse of this wasted loser struggling to comprehend the concept of "Pull." Laughing and pointing ensued until I realized it wasn't a homeless man—it was Trent.

His hair was disheveled, clothing ripped, knuckles bloodied. Clearly, he had just been in a fight in a nearby bar and was in no shape to get himself home. It was pure coincidence that he wound up at the bar where I was trying to wind down. Completely humiliated, I threw down a twenty and grabbed my purse. I had to clean up this mess before someone called the cops on him or he walked into traffic.

"So this is what you're up to on the weekends?" I shouted at him while driving his alcohol-infused body back to my place. After all, we couldn't go to his. It wasn't like I had a key of my own or anything and God only knows where his was. Probably with his lost cell phone and wallet.

"Babe, what are you talking about?" he mumbled. Clearly, this wasn't the time for any earth-shattering conversation, but I was so heated, I just couldn't stay quiet.

"It's like you're a frat boy gone wrong. You can't let go of your college years. You realize that, right? Tell me I can't be the only one who sees that…" I demanded.

"I guess you're right," he whispered vulnerably. "I do act that way."

Whether he was agreeing with me for the free ride home, or just completely unaware of anything going on, it seemed I had my answer. There was no denying reality as I dragged his lifeless body by his ankles through my doorway before rolling him on his side and finally covering him with a blanket.

"Fuck this shit," I said as I shut off the lights. The end was near. I could feel it.

But just when I didn't think I could get any more pissed and fed up, he'd make up for it. No matter what debauchery went on over the weekend, he would spend the week smoothing things over with nice dinners and lots of quality time. We would have deep conversation, a glass of expensive wine, meaningful sex. And lo and behold, things were great again. So I renewed my lease on a month-to-month basis.

This ridiculous cycle repeated for over a year and the sad—or rather, the sick part was, I barely even noticed it.

So, instead of seeing this as a red flag, I started to look at it as the new normal. I was convinced that eventually he'd see the sacrifice I had made to take a chance on our relationship. A sacrifice that would warrant some form of reciprocation, or perhaps even just basic gratitude, or a date on an otherwise blocked-off Saturday night. I didn't necessarily need a ring, although that would have been a really nice gesture, I just needed to somehow know I was more than a geographically convenient hook-up, with whom he played keep-away on the weekends unless he needed a sober driver.

One day, when I was paying rent, it suddenly dawned on me what I was actually doing. I was submitting my monthly dues; the fee I had to fork over in order to continue seeing my commitment-phob boyfriend on a regular basis. Maybe it would have been a different story if I had a killer apartment, a dog to come home to, or a neighbor who baked me awesome goodies—but I didn't. This was not the life I had imagined having with the man who picked me up in a "white truck" on a cold winter night two years before. This was a perpetual man-child struggling to accept he wasn't 18 years old anymore. Unfortunately, his girlfriend who "wanted more" was a constant reminder of that and regular David Yurman jewelry boxes weren't squashing my intentions to legitimize this relationship like he'd hoped.

Whether or not he'd eventually be capable of marriage—or even giving me a spare key to his home—was irrelevant at this point. I didn't want to waste anymore time being the leading lady in a love story that was going nowhere. So, with every single-girl anthem ever made playing in the back of my head, I researched the logistics of moving back home and outlined them on a piece of paper. My plan was to show him I was serious about quitting my sorry-excuse for an advertising job and packing my bags if he couldn't make a change and move us forward.

And I'd do it all in under thirty days.

To my surprise, the shock therapy didn't work. The day after I presented him with my Venn diagram, I found myself quitting my job, adjusting my relationship status on Facebook, and tackling step-one of my plan.

The relationship was over.

My breakup was equal parts abrupt and sucky: not an exception to the rule by any means. But what made it worst was that I couldn't run to a girlfriend's house, I couldn't cry on my mom's shoulder, I couldn't throw myself into the job I'd just quit—I was in purgatory. I had a lease I was committed to for thirty more days in a state that was four hundred miles away from my family and friends. I had no health insurance anymore and I couldn't afford the pain medication I so badly wanted to be abusing in the privacy of my quiet, little apartment. All I could do was vacillate between total numbness and sob attacks as I put each piece of furniture up for sale online.

And so it began: the countdown to living back with my parents, a place where flushing the toilet while someone was showering was off limits.

~ ~ ~

Twenty-seven days went by and I had heard nothing from him. Nothing. He knew I was still here, waiting out my lease, and never once an apology, a come-to-Jesus, a drunken "I love you" text—nothing. Then one night, there was a knock at my door. You know where this is going. But even more cliché than it being him standing there in the doorway, was the fact that he was literally holding a cardboard box with my various belongings sticking out of it. Was this a collection of props from every break-up movie ever made? Did I really leave a tennis racket at his place? Regardless of the irony, and the additional shit I would have to pack up and bring home, Trent had unexpectedly come to say goodbye to me in my almost-empty apartment, just three days before I was set to hit the open road.

Not only was it the first time I had seen him in a few weeks, it was the first time I had seen raw emotion from him—pretty much ever. He walked into my apartment, now the blank product of several Craigslist transactions, and took a moment to look around. It was the same space he had helped me move into not that long ago. He broke down at the lack of evidence proving we ever had a life together.

"You're really leaving, huh?" he asked in the echoey room.

"Yup. I'm really going," I confirmed.

At that, he cracked like an egg and tears started flowing. His emotion was contagious and I broke down too, but I still remained confident in my decision to leave. After all, Trent was in sales—and he was damn good at it, so good that he made it to the top of his company before he was a quarter of a century old. His job, quite literally, was to make deals day-in and day-out. He knew how to make things happen. And if he couldn't get me to buy into a relationship with him at this point, then it was clear he wasn't really selling me one. I had to swallow that pill and keep moving forward.

But I will say this: that sneak-peek of emotion was just what I needed to really bank on him pulling up in a cab within six months, walking up my brownstone's decrepit steps, and begging for me back. At that, I hugged him goodbye, and placed my bet: he'll be back for me.

A few days later, I merged onto I-80 East for the first time in six years.

~ ~ ~

Fortunately, a job opportunity in downtown Chicago had surfaced during the month I had nothing else to do besides eat my feelings, neurotically check my phone for missed calls and texts, and hang out with my mom.

It wasn't the downtown ad agency gig I had imagined, but it was my ticket to no longer sleeping on a twin mattress in the room I grew up in. So when an offer came through for a position in the hotel industry, I accepted it. Was it the perfect fit for me? Probably not. Was I qualified? Definitely not. But if anything, it would give me a reason to move out and start living the life I was two years behind on.

At the time, my friends from high school were looking for a third roommate and I was looking for a reason to get excited about something other than polishing off a pint of ice cream by myself. Needless to say, I checked the next item off my list and co-signed a lease with them. We would move into our Lincoln Park walk-up in just one week.

Folding clothes and getting situated, I heard an instant message ding come through from my laptop. It was Trent on Skype. Ironic how he always made crucial contact with me during laundry hour, right? Also ironic? It had been 27 days—the magic number with him—since I moved home.

"Hello," it said.

I knew saying "hi" back would have been the appropriate response, but for the moment I couldn't think of a valid reply. All I could see from my screen was a little pen icon moving (meaning he was typing), then an eraser (meaning he was deleting), then the pen icon again, and the eraser. I stared in silence at the madness waiting for him to spit it out, God dammit.

"I'm on a guys' trip in Mexico," he wrote.

What an ass, my inner dialogue replied. Did he really feel it necessary to remind me I no longer had access to his luxury timeshare?

The pen icon was moving again.

"I came here to clear my head and get over you."

Again, good for him, I thought. Had I been the one with an exorbitant amount of disposable income for any person my age, I too would have indulged in a weeklong tequila-fest with my besties.

The pen icon continued to dance on the screen and I had yet to type anything. I was somewhat paralyzed by the fact he was chatting with me from another country while he should have been slamming margaritas and procuring Mexican hookers. And to be real, I should have been packing and getting ready for my move. But, apparently, I was hardwired to come running whenever he called—or Skyped—no matter the circumstances. I believe this is known as: failed-relationship prison.

"I've been doing some thinking and I really miss you."

"I miss you, too," I wrote back.

A wave of butterflies came over me as I broke my silence. The Holy Grail was within my reach, I knew it.

"When I get back home," he typed. "I'm going to concentrate all my powers on us."

Where were my Cliff's notes, because honestly, I had no idea what that meant, but it seemed like some superhero shit and I liked the sound of it.

Before I could peg for details, he fired off a hasty goodbye. " Sorry, my Internet keeps crashing. I'll get in touch with you after I'm back. I promise."

Trent is offline.

Abrupt and ambiguous. Just like our relationship. And just like our relationship, I took that as good enough for me for the millionth time.

I saved this "conversation" and reread it a thousand times until I could recite it all by heart. Perhaps I was putting the cart before the horse, but I was excited. I had a small piece of proof that miracles did exist and it brought tears of joys to my eyes. All was going to plan, we were going to hit the reset button and get back together.

To perpetuate this idea, right when he got back to the States, I started to receive "I miss you" texts from him on the regular—especially later on in his lonely nights. It was obvious his bed was just a little too cold, his house, just a little too quiet, his heart, just a little too lonely. You don't know what you've got until it's gone, they say.

After five months since breaking up, and just thirty days short of my six-month plan coming to fruition, he started calling me on the phone during the day to chat about nothing, just like when we were dating and I was 15 minutes or less away from him at all times.

But one day, he called to talk about something very specific: a trip to Chicago in the next two weeks with the sole mission of "figuring things out."

Bingo-bango. My power to predict the future was scary-good. And at that moment, I gave myself a pat on the back for my psychic qualities. You know, I knew this kid better than he knew himself and I was impressed that he was finally seeing the light—that there was more to life than just getting blackout drunk on the weekends in an effort to evade your girlfriend's texts. It was evident that he missed me and not only was he coming to his senses, he was coming to get me.

I needed to purchase a teeth-whitening kit and start cutting out carbs immediately.

In just a couple of weeks, my prince charming was going to arrive on his white horse (err, Escalade?) and bring me back to the life I left in good old Omaha. Sure, leaving the city after just getting my bearings would be difficult, but I was convinced that things were happening for a reason, and that he was my person after all.

And when you find your person, what do you do? You don't let them go.

So, I embraced the impending change and assessed the situation. Here's how the lay of the land was looking: my life as a "single lady" had about two weeks until it expired and I needed to "put my hands up," as Beyoncé would say. Essentially, I was on the market for a limited time only and for the last time of my life, as I was sure Trent was planning on making a comeback in a big, sparkly way. Therefore, I needed to open up this narrow window and let in a little fresh air.

On one hand, I was a typical hopeless romantic in hot pursuit of my happily ever after. On the other, I was a typical twenty-three-year-old girl who felt like she needed a break from being on her best behavior. And with a free fourteen-day trial to do what I wanted, and with whom, it was time get it in shape. Clearly, I wasn't going to commit to anything with anyone, but that wasn't going to stop me from doing a little circuit training in the meantime.

I know this sounds less-than-ladylike, but nonetheless, I was proud that men other than Ben & Jerry were getting my oral attention for the first time in half a year. And even in hindsight, I wouldn't have changed a thing. It's a delicate balance, satiating your sex life while preparing for the vow of commitment every girl hopes to get from the man of her dreams, and I was nailing it (among other things/people).

For this short time, I felt like Chicago's very own Carrie Bradshaw, just younger and with a less glamorous wardrobe. I bought a pack of condoms for the first time since college and went on the prowl. Channeling my inner wild-child, I managed to cap my random hookups at exactly three exceptionally good-looking species, and staggered them perfectly apart— bros with benefits, one might say. Regardless, like a walk-up doughnut bar, they were swiftly in and out and on their way with their goodies.

A day before his rumored trip, it had dawned on me that I had yet to receive any sort of tangible plans from him: no airline info, no hotel reservation, no arrival times, no nothing. However, I quickly talked myself off the ledge. Reuniting was his idea; his gesture. I trusted that his travel was in order. After all, I saw the kid cry before I left. I had the Skype conversation printed and tucked under my mattress. My call log didn't lie and neither did my text inbox. This was all proof that he had real emotions, which in my mind was just as good as confirming his flight number.

It was now the day-of his rumored arrival and I had to break the radio silence. I called. I texted. I e-mailed. I punched his name into the county jail's inmate search box. But when my inquiry produced zero hits, it was only logical to deduce one thing: I had been blown off in a big way.

God fucking dammit! What was it about me that gave him the coldest cold feet ever? Why was I sitting on the floor of my shower, watching my tears, and a myriad of other shitty feelings, swirl down the drain when we were supposed to be cuddling on my couch, ordering half the menu from my favorite take-out place, and making out. Why, half-Jew god? Why the torture?

The harshness was in the reality. And the reality was that that morning when I woke up, there wasn't a single part of me that didn't fully believe my Say Anything moment was merely hours away. I know I had just finished self-medicating by getting frisky with enough people to form a small kickball team, but I didn't think that was enough to fuck with the karma fairy. And although I had been devoid of any true emotion for the last couple weeks, please believe me when I say—I was hurting. Badly.

The weekend we were supposed to be deliriously happy together came and went. I instead spent it alone. And in my solitude, it had dawned on me that for as excited as I was about Trent's visit, I never told anyone about it—not my roommates, not my friends, not my mom. This wasn't like me. I'm a sharer of juicy gossip and this had the potential to be big. But, like I said, I knew this kid better than he knew himself, and I wondered if deep down I was aware this whole time that he wasn't going to actually show. Perhaps, my intuition led me to stay silent as a way to save myself from having to break the embarrassingly bad news to the masses: that I had been stood up for no reason whatsoever.

Good call, intuition. Good call.

Flash forward to the Tuesday after he was supposed to be with me and that's when I received the "friendly" text from my old pal, Geoffrey, and learned layer-by-layer about the "Whole Layla Situation". And now, you too, have learned about it, aka., the painful explanation of why Trent never showed up for me in Chicago.

CHAPTER TWO/LESSON TWO

- Make a gay best friend, choose your break-up booze wisely, and keep a drawer of loose-fitting clothes

Seeing the roses on Layla's wall was a thorn straight to my heart, as it truly was a picture worth a thousand words—several of them being iterations of "fuck those motherfuckers." The roses represented twelve, freshly-cut reasons precisely why Trent never showed. He found a new girlfriend down the block, which was apparently much more convenient than resurrecting things with his old one four hundred miles away. I guess he deserved points for efficiency.

Now I could accept that just under six months might not have been enough time for him to travel across the country and declare true love. I could not, however, deal with my ex-boyfriend moving on to my former coworker (and friend, for that matter) sometime in the last two weeks. That serious? That fast? That girl? Bitch, please.

Layla was my former intern-turned-friend. Professionally, she was a talented graphic designer, and I had nothing but the utmost respect for her and the way she made rocked typeface on a print ad. Personally, she was a fabulous drinking buddy who could make a mean Cosmopolitan and host a girls' night so good, you wouldn't remember it the next day. She was a trusted confidant who knew all of the highs and lows of my relationship with Trent. She never failed to be there for me and prior to my departure, she never missed an opportunity to "admire my strength" or say "you go girl" when I told her I was leaving to pursue a more rewarding, albeit single, life.

To throw even more salt on the wound, she was the very person who arranged my going-away party before I left Omaha. I'll never forget the meaningful night among work friends that she coordinated at our favorite sushi spot. Furthermore, I'll never forget the hand-written letter she sent to wish me well, and thank me for my mentorship, my friendship, and to promise to stay in touch through e-mails and visits. I somehow missed the fine print that mentioned we'd also remain close by sharing boyfriends. I believe that's called Eskimo Sisters, but I could be wrong. Needless to say, I never in a million years thought that in this lifetime, both Trent and I would end up calling Layla "one of our good girlfriends."

So, on one hand, we had an ex-boyfriend who strung me along by dangling rumors of a romantic visit in front of my face three months after he let me go easier than a fart on an airplane. And on the other hand, we had his new girlfriend, Layla, who was someone who in the past had repeatedly told me that I deserved someone better than her now-boyfriend, but who ultimately ended up being a two-faced shit stirrer.

Between the two of them, I couldn't tell you who the bigger asshole was. I honestly couldn't.

Immediately, a million questions and thoughts raced through my mind: how did this courtship transpire? How long was this going on? What did he see in her? Where were their consciences? How big were their balls? What the hell was up with the roses? I hate to out the kid, but if it wasn't a bag of weed, there wasn't anything plant-based that this commitment-phob felt comfortable giving to a female: not for anniversaries, Valentine's Days, or even the times (yes, times) I caught him lying about getting a lap dance from a stripper. And now, suddenly, my Facebook feed is indicating that he had become the man I wanted to date all along? Well, I'll be damned.

Seeing that news was like my love life's version of 9/11. I will always remember where I was, and what I was doing, at the moment of impact—you know—right before everything burst into flames and crashed to the ground. I'll probably even tell my grandkids about the great tragedy of Tuesday June 13th and in my old age, I'll deliriously wonder why people don't get the day off from work to commemorate it.

For real, that moment went down in the Emily Almanac as the worst homeland attack my heart had ever endured—and for good measure. It was a surprise ambush, led by two legit terrorists—one, an ex-lover, and the other, an ex-coworker. The causalities (my ego, appetite, sense of trust, wasted Brazilian bikini wax, etc.) tallied up by the minute. Every aspect of my planned future fell to the ground and instantly dissolved into undetectable, powdery debris. Worst of all, I had no choice but to stand among the rubble in a state of shock and wait until the dust settled before I could begin to take inventory of what, if anything, was left of me.

You know, it's kind of scary not knowing how you really feel about something in a given moment. Life is about responding to stimuli. We all know what to do when we're bored (mindlessly snack), thirsty (pour a sauv blanc), tired (stay up reading Buzzfeed), etc. But what about when you've been royally fucked over by not just one, but two people who you thought would be in your life forever—then what do you do? Not that I've ever been lost at sea between living in Omaha and Chicago, but I imagine the blankness and numbness was something like that. I just had to drift and wait, wait and drift. But thankfully, there to pull me into a lifeboat was my new-and-improved co-worker, a beautiful gay man who I'll forever wish was straight, named Justin.

Because we shared adjacent cubicles, we also shared stories—most of which were about the good hookups and even better margaritas we each had over the weekend. He was abreast of my life, and I was up on his. And even though our Fridays would indicate that I was mundane and he was fabulous, when we scooted our ergonomic office chairs within feet of each other to gossip, we were both just two twenty-something Chicagoans out looking for love.

On this fateful June day, Justin looked over to see if I was ready to get my Happy Hour on and saw that I was knee-deep in a staring contest with my news feed. He must have caught on to my crazy, as he whispered from across the cube, "Hey, Em. You okay?" I couldn't muster words to respond because I didn't have any. So, I just kind of frowned and shook my head, like an American Idol hopeful being rejected at her audition.

Even though we were both working in the hospitality business, we obviously were in the wrong industries. I, for one, should have been a producer of 16 & Pregnant so I could wake up each day to a nice dose of "someone has it worse than you," whereas Justin should have been Britney

Spears' publicist during her hot-mess phase. Why? Because he had crisis control down to a science.

In true mom fashion, Justin saw me moments away from a total meltdown and sprung straight into action. He wanted me out of a bad situation and knew that if the new, hot IT guy (talk about an oxymoron) saw me whaling, it'd ruin my chances of a little system reboot with him on a future weekend. So, within seconds, Justin shot out of his chair, shut down my computer, and packed up my things for me. The next thing I knew, he grabbed me by the arm and whisked me out of our office. I couldn't quite tell if he was using his other hand to block the paparazzi's flashbulbs, but for a short moment, I kind of felt like I was a popstar being shuttled into a courthouse to face her DUI charges.

"Do NOT let them see you like this," Justin demanded as we took a sharp right and headed down the back access stairwell in true A-lister fashion. "There's no reason to cry. We're going to the bar."

Even though that had been our plan from the moment we realized the coffee machine did not, in fact, dispense vodka, the purpose for our boozing had sharply changed—and for that, I felt somewhat guilty. I'm sure Justin wanted to slam some back while talking about the backs he most recently slammed, but we were now about to find ourselves playing a new drinking game called, "Take-a-shot-every-time-Emily-looks-likeshe's-gonna-lose-it." Don't get me wrong, this was still bound to be a great way to get hammered, but the mood had become so grim, I pitied Justin for being close enough to become collateral damage as I sat there and suffered another wave of real heartbreak from the master of disaster, Trent.

When we had finally navigated our way through the bellies of our building and out to the receiving alley, it was pouring rain. I of course had no umbrella to shield me from the unexpected, mammoth drops that were pelting us left and right. I couldn't help but feel like the weather was mocking my situation a little bit, but regardless, Justin and I continued to beeline it to the bar at the Hard Rock, a hotel we were quite familiar with through our line of work. Although this seemed slightly unprofessional in hindsight, drinking for free, and then submitting our receipts under the expense category "competitive research," felt completely ethical at the time.

Nonetheless, I propped my soaking wet self up on a bar stool and ordered my first drink—a vodka cranberry. I realize now that is a cocktail you should only order on an airplane or when you're a forty-five-year-old cougar on the prowl in a sports bar, but I felt like my chances were slim in getting what I really wanted: a pack of cigarettes and an entire bottle of Jameson.

With my pink drink in hand, I could finally form sentences about my feelings, to which Justin would respond things like, "Utterly dis-GUS-ting" or "What assholes!" My favorite? "It's Nebraska. Don't they inbreed there?"

Between the two of us bantering and bitching, it didn't take long for the bar manager to overhear excerpts from my love life. Perhaps she knew how to deal with crisis better than I, or perhaps she just wanted to provide an example of how the Hard Rock's hospitality goes above and beyond, but out of nowhere the manager-on-duty swooped in and swapped out my glorified Shirley Temple for a pitcher of house-made sangria, saying, "This one's extra strong, and from all of us, honey."

With that generous gift from the Lonely Hearts Club, I figured I should probably shoot my roommates—Andrew and Katie—a quick text foreshadowing this fresh Hell. After all, with a kiddie-pool of liquor in front of my face, I knew right then I wouldn't be sleeping alone that night: at some point later during that rip-roaring Tuesday evening, prior to me plowing in drunk through the front door, a designated puke bucket needed to be placed on my nightstand.

To be expected, my two roommates passed the initial "good-friends" test, responding that they were happily preparing for my arrival and sanitizing the bowl. To go the extra step, they purchased a magnum of red wine, a package of frozen cheese tortellini, and a pint of hazelnut ice gelato from the corner store for whenever I decided to barrel back in. As their food and beverage selections indicated, I was officially in "fucked-over-by-a-dude" mode.

Despite their ominous grocery list, I truly did appreciate those two stepping up to prepare for my arrival. It's amazing to see who in your life is willing to cancel their sand volleyball practice, or date with the DVR, all in the name of being there for you—especially when I was on-track to remember about one percent of what I was actually upset about the following day. Nevertheless, all that was left to hope for was that they'd manage to center the "Congratulations! You didn't throw yourself in front of a train!" banner over our mantle before my homecoming.

At the bar, only an hour had gone by and already my blood-alcohol content level was heading into Layla Lohan territory. I wondered if I should have slowed down, not because anyone was judging me, or that I had to function at work the following morning, but because I started to feel disappointed: I had done the most cliché thing possible. Got dumped and then got drunk. With that, I pictured my future daughter, and I cringed at the thought of her at some hotel bar, wasted before most people have even finished going through their e-mails for the day.

After a few rounds, I excused myself to the restroom. This was the first moment I had to myself, and I wondered if I'd use it to punch a wall, send a few drunken hate-texts, or share my life story with the bathroom attendant. Proudly, I did none of that. Instead, I locked myself in the bathroom stall and sat down on the seat with my pants still on. I felt a kind of clarity that usually doesn't come with exorbitant amounts of hard alcohol. Yet, I realized that maybe I wasn't boozing in an effort to drown my sorrows. Maybe it was more like I was raising a glass (or four) to celebrate the end of an ambiguous era in my life. After all, I didn't have to wait, wonder, or watch for anything anymore. As crappy as things were, I was finally free from all the bullshit. And even though the slave days are over, we all know that emancipation didn't come easy. This was no different.

I returned to my seat at the bar and plopped down. Justin put out his hand—and let me tell you, it wasn't for a high-five that I had successfully made it up and down a flight of stairs while tipsy without falling on my face. I opened up my purse and dug around for my phone. It was time for him to extract a number that had been saved in my contacts since the day, two and a half years ago, that it had shown up on my screen while I was putting laundry away in my college dorm room. Though I remembered all the digits by heart, not having it in my phone made it a step or two harder to text something I'd inevitably regret.

The time was approaching to trade in Tanqueray for some tortellini and head home to be with my roommates. At that, Justin put his hands on my shoulders and looked me drunkenly in the eye before saying: "Emily, I know it feels like you got him at his absolute worst—and now he's some knight-in-shining-armor sending some skinny hipster flowers and swooping her off her Converse-One-Star-laden feet—but remember, you paid it forward, and karma will come back for you."

I paid it forward? Call me crazy, but when did I sign up to be the stepping stone in someone else's love story? Sure, I got what he was saying about karma, and I wanted to believe it. Because if things that go around really do come around, then it would only be a matter of time before someone ripped the side-view mirrors off Trent's Escalade while Layla developed a thyroid problem and got fat. But even those punishments didn't offer the big-picture comfort I was seeking. I'm all about things happening for a reason, but I still saw no reason for this. Regardless, I thanked Justin for his mama-bear hospitality, and left the bar without spending a dime of my own money. Perhaps this was karma already getting to work.

By now, the steady rain had turned into a total downpour, complete with flashes of lightning and the occasional wave of golf-ball-sized hail. There wasn't a cab unoccupied by a pretentious woman and her giant purse in all of downtown Chicago and Uber was surging like a motherfucker. So I ducked under an awning and waited until the weather let up a bit.

Prior to this night, I had never drunk dialed my mom; at least never before 7 PM on a weekday. But this was a day of many firsts, so I stayed on-trend with the theme and decided to phone home. When she answered, I immediately started sobbing. I'm pretty sure she thought I was going to tell her I was pregnant.

I'm not sure what she was able to gather from that initial call, as it was a combination of inaudible words and incoherent injections of: "That BASTARD!" Regardless, my mom fired off a string of typical suburban, maternal one-liners, including: "Don't give your power away" and "Honey, be the bigger person!"

Realizing I wasn't going to get her to use profanity in this conversation, I sort of tuned her out and wondered how bad my eyeliner was running. Right then, a homeless person came under the awning and asked if I was okay. Let me repeat: a homeless person asked me if I was okay. Like I said, it was a day of many firsts.

I gave the man the "one-moment" finger and mouthed to him that I was on the phone with my mom. He whispered back: "Okay, I'll wait" as he crept further under the awning and pulled out a pack of cigarettes. I wasn't a smoker, and I knew that that ten-dollar pack probably took him at least two weeks to hustle, but I wanted one—two if he was feeling generous. And on that note, I rushed the woman who gave birth to me off the phone, citing "spotty service," as I proceeded to mooch a much-needed cigarette off a man of poverty.

His name was Eric, and as he lit my cigarette, he wasted no time getting into his life story. He was a 27-year-old Detroit native rocking a giant, oversized Lion's hoodie. He wasn't exactly bad looking, but by no means was he gorgeous either (I think this is how I'd describe myself at that moment, to be honest). Every word he spoke, mainly about the trouble he ran into along the way, sounded like it was going to segue into a freestyle rap session. Clearly, he didn't fit the bill for your standard toothless bum with shit-stained sweatpants, but his lack of repulsion was okay with me. Especially if it meant I could hang around him long enough to score that second cigarette.

In between drags, I started to find out a little more about how Eric wound up under this awning next to me. A few weeks ago, he had caught his best friend screwing his wife. Due to the fact they had five kids together, he found her actions unforgivable and immediately filed for divorce with plans to take the wee ones with him. She fired back in the courtroom, citing his history with drugs and alcohol (shocker) as means to seek full custody. The judge granted her wish, finalized the divorce, and the next thing Eric knew, he was kicked to the curb with nothing but his cubic zirconia earrings and a bus pass to Chicago. Side note: even in my slightly boozy haze, I was confident I could provide a solid police report for this guy if he decided to try anything.

"Yeah, so that's that," he said after chronicling his series of unfortunate events.

"Sucks man," I said as I took a drag. Really, what else could I say?

"So, why were you crying?" he bravely asked.

Flicking my cigarette butt to the curb, I blew out the smoke and said, "It's stupid, really." Knowing full well there was nothing bashful about the rant that would ensue, I at least thought it polite to give him one last chance to bail if he didn't want an incoherent earful about a breakup that, in perspective, wasn't half as bad as his. But, apparently, misery truly does love company, because he stuck around and begged me to continue.

After dishing out the abridged-for-a-bum version, Eric decided to take a "we've-all-been-there" approach and tell me a little more about his fucked up life. As much as I wanted to, I could hardly follow his meth-induced rant, so I let my mind wander as I soaked up the last few seconds of my only-when-I'm-drinking nicotine fix.

Staring off into the street and watching the water rush down the sewer, I took comfort in the fact that I was sharing cigarettes with a homeless man underneath an awning in the pouring rain. It was such a stark contrast to what I'd normally be doing after work—exercising, microwaving dinner, unwinding, and catching up on The Bachelor—but desperate times call for desperate measures. Regardless, it was time for me to let the curtain fall on this party for two.

I knew Eric was going to charge me for this therapy session in the form of asking for a few bucks before I headed to the train, so I took a proactive approach and lied. I told him I'd left my wallet at work in my disillusioned state.

"Oh," he said, flicking his cigarette to the curb. "Sucks, man."

I wondered how that white lie was going to sit with the karma fairy.

~ ~ ~

"Mazel!" my roommates shouted, as if I had walked into some sort of surprise bat mitzvah back at my apartment. Apparently, they were just excited I had made it home without passing out on the train or rebounding with the first guy I saw in a neon cardigan.

"Thanks guys," my soaking-wet self said as I took a bow and rung out my hair.

"Jesus, Em," said my roommate Andrew as he helped peel off my drenched (read: ruined) cardigan. "Did you go out?"

Clearly, Andrew was unfamiliar with how a twenty-three-year-old girl copes with heartache on a Tuesday night, so I simply replied with "Booze now. Talk later." in hopes that someone would uncork something, fast.

"Ten-four," Katie said, as she pried open a bottle of cheap red wine and directed Andrew to toss the frozen tortellini in the microwave for three minutes. I admired their collaborative effort to get me drunk and fat in the least amount of time possible.

I had known Andrew and Katie since high school.

Andrew and I fiercely competed against one another to be Editor-in-Chief of our school paper, but ultimately tied for second and were named co-managing editors. He was a loudmouth track runner known for being a bit of a Matt Damon look-alike. I was the five-foot-three-inch half-Jew who wore a lot of Hollister clothing. Together, we ruled the paper, printing our fair share of typos and libel; the stuff nerdy friendships—and future roommates—are made of.

Katie I met through Andrew. She was a year younger than us, but was way smarter and more adjusted to society. She was the type of girl that knew how to throw a dinner party, give good gifts, and fill out a W-2 correctly. Secretly, I believe Andrew has been in love with her this whole time. Nonetheless, they both were looking to move downtown and needed a third roommate to break up any residual sexual tension. That person would inevitably become me.

Without further ado, I found myself deep-diving into the wine and shoveling the pasta. "Didn't you guys say you got me ice cream?" I asked sending my roommates scattering to the freezer.

God, where was Jillian Michaels to call you a fat-ass loser when you needed her?

In between hundred-calorie swigs and bites, it dawned on me that I was heading down a road only the most broken girls had gone before. I was about to sink into a depression that was ten times worse than the reality of the situation, creating a funk that would surely render my appetite null-and-void for an indefinite period of time. As such, I vowed to enjoy my "last supper" so to speak, and stocked up in preparation for the famine. I had to hand it to myself: I absolutely loved the way my drunk-self was giving my anorexic-self a get-out-of-jail-free card on this one, and I found the way they were rallying in a time of crisis to be rather charming. If only my real-life relationships were half as compassionate.

The time had come to fill in Andrew and Katie, two of the Devil's biggest advocates. Both of them had heard me talk about Trent before: after all, I had to explain to them why I moved back to Chicago in the first place, right? Additionally, they—like everybody else—had seen enough photos of us vacationing in Mexico to put a face to the villain's name.

However, their take on life was far more rational than any twenty-something's should be, and I momentarily doubted my ability to turn them into bandwagon Trent haters. I was going up against a panel of judges who would most certainly deduct points for an ounce of exaggeration or unnecessary drama. Therefore, I gave it to them straight—just not totally sober.

I had gone a solid four minutes without once getting interrupted. Another six went by in order for me to complete the story and, still, there were still no comments from the peanut gallery. I rehydrated with a sip of wine and gestured a "come on" motion with my other hand, signaling that the floor was now open for their impending feedback. I braced for the blow.

Katie and Andrew are two of the most verbally aggressive individuals I've ever met. Whether it was how to properly cook bacon or what can or cannot be deleted on the DVR, there was no subject that wasn't worth debating to death between these two. Which is why when their initial response was silence, I was shocked—even scared. Quiet, pensive behavior was just not in their repertoire. They never listened to understand, they listened to retort, react, and rebut. I didn't know whether to close my eyes and brace for impact or celebrate the fact that I had finally earned some well-deserved sympathy points from my friends.

Moments later, however, they broke the silence. The first audible thing wasn't a spoken word, though, it was a swallow. Andrew could do nothing but take a gulp of his wine as he prepared for these words to exit his mouth: "Damn, that's some icy cold shit, Em."

Cold, indeed. So cold, it burned throughout my bones. I just never thought I'd have to round up my roommates, circle around a gigantic vat of wine, and have this conversation in my kitchen six months after the fact. This was the type of set up (best friends, lots of booze, fatty food) for celebratory, happy news. Not a bloody breakup.

When I was a teenager, whenever I was upset, my mom used to always tell me: "Don't be sad anymore. That's giving your power away." I never really knew exactly what she meant by that, but I think it meant: shut it down.

So, in her honor, I decided to call it a night: for if by nine o'clock on a weeknight I was blacked out in my bed, my power would be unavailable for the taking. Of that, I was sure.

Katie grabbed my arm, stabilized my wobbly body down our hallway, and escorted me to my bedroom. Once I was horizontal, she proceeded to tuck me in, wafting a boozy, smoky, wet-dog smell out from under the blankets. I knew right then this was a personal worst for me. I wasn't in college anymore. The fact that I still hadn't even washed the makeup off my face since coming home was simply unacceptable for someone claiming to be an adult.

I was uncomfortably drunk. I had never done drugs, but I could empathize with people who resorted to doing a line of blow just to sober up. Not willing to stimulate the Colombian economy, or do anything illegal, I just kept my eyes closed and tried to distract myself from the next round of nausea by thinking of random, vengeful things I could do to get back at Trent, because, hey, that's normal.

"I should call the police. Have them raid his place. I know he keeps a bunch of weed in there. It's got to be enough for a felony. I wouldn't even have to say who I am. I could do this totally anonymously and get away with it. His dad would take away his Escalade and demote him to an hourly wage, that is, if he would even want a drug addict criminal working in the office.

"And, of course, his mom would cut him off financially. Stop letting him use the timeshare in Mexico. Then what would Layla want with him? Not only would her weed hook-up be tapped, but she'd have nowhere to vacation with him and his receding hairline.

"That's it. I'm calling the police tomorrow. First thing in the morning, from a pay phone. I don't even care what happens to him. I'm doing it."

For the record: I never did it. It was a terrible idea, and it made no sense. God, I wonder how many brain cells were lost during this internal riot-fest.

Though I didn't open my eyes to confirm this, I heard Katie reenter my room at some point, tiptoeing toward my bed while I was knee-deep in this feisty coma. She quietly placed the freshly sanitized mixing bowl on my nightstand, just as I had requested much earlier in the night. Finally, someone had my best interest at heart. And with faith in humanity temporarily restored, I attempted to get some sleep on a good note after all.

Sadly, I wasn't able to drift off quite like I had hoped. In fact, I was experiencing the opposite, getting up every few minutes to clutch the bowl and dry heave into the bottom of it like I was bobbing for sober apples. I could tell I was coming down and my version of emotional Novocain was wearing off—fast. Consequently, real thoughts were settling in for the first time since Facebook fucked my day up. While I certainly wasn't dreaming, this was a total nightmare.

It's not that I didn't want him to be happy: everyone deserves that, no matter how douchey you are. It's just that I wanted to be responsible for his happiness. I wanted him to realize a dark cloud rolled in when I rolled out and he couldn't live without me. Isn't that the goal of everyone who has ever been in love with someone? But instead, he (not me), had the single-girl swagger, moving on and moving fast. If that doesn't make someone question fundamental things about life, love, and luck, then I don't know what does. Cue the quarter-life crisis, please.

While I admittedly had no clue how to move forward with things, I was at least able to accept the fact that a giant spatula flipping me off my sheets was not how I'd be getting out of bed the following morning. I needed to get some sleep, use mind tricks to avoid vomiting, and recharge my batteries just enough to make it to work the next day and cozy up in my cubicle. My only prayer was that when I finally got around to closing my eyes, I wouldn't automatically envision the happy couple, holding hands, skipping through the cornfields of Nebraska.

"God help me," I said out loud. And, in all honesty, I think he already had. After all, I didn't call my ex. I didn't leave a snide comment about the roses on Layla's Facebook wall. I didn't send a well-deserved hate text featuring some combination of the words "white trash motherfuckers." Divine Intervention had to be the only explanation for my dignity being still intact. My sobriety? Not so much. But they didn't have to know that.

In fact, they didn't have to know a lot of things. They didn't have to know that in my drafts folder on my phone were misspelled, belligerent messages along the lines of "You are such an asshole." They didn't have to know I basically recruited an entire pit crew, which included my mother, my roommates, the staff at the Hard Rock Hotel, my token gay coworker, and a homeless man with the body type of Skeletor, to help get me through the next few laps of my life.

There I had it: quality people. Several of them in fact, which made making the conscious decision to eradicate the worthless people from my life easy. I had to kick them off my door—Titanic style. If the relation "ship" was going down, then neither Layla nor Trent deserved to hold on to my buoyant piece of wood. I deserved some chance of being saved. When, by whom, and how? None of that really mattered. All I knew was that if a rescue boat passed by, it sure as hell wasn't going to pick me up if I was still hanging on to the frozen corpses of my failed relationship.

This was undoubtedly painful. Not necessarily because it meant I would never see or speak to them again, but rather because I had to instantly disseminate all the memories I had accrued and relinquish all the dreams I held. The fact that I had to do this all on someone else's terms was bogus.

I realize that I could have avoided all that by just giving them my blessing, and carrying on with my life as usual, but the reality was that I really hadn't known "a life as usual" in quite some time—maybe ever at all, actually. I was twenty-three-years old for crying out loud. I hadn't built up enough relevant life experience to scale just how big of a deal this whole thing really was. All I knew was that for the first time in two years, I had to completely stop caring about someone who I admittedly had put first in every single situation. My wishing, waiting, and wanting, was forced to come to a hard stop, and the only way I knew how to deal with a dream that I knew no longer could come true was to get under it and pluck it out like an unwanted weed.

Trent was a cancer that had been overtaking my body for several months. And Layla? She was it spreading to my lungs. As such, it all had to go—immediately and completely. Initially, I contemplated if this meant that I was heartless, but then I begged to differ with myself. In fact, it was because I had a heart that I was able to do this with the utmost conviction. After all, if I ever had plans of giving this old heart of mine to someone else in the future, I'd need it to be fully functioning.

So, scalpel please.

~ ~ ~

The next morning, the sun came up and so did a little bit of the tortellini-wine-gelato trifecta. But, alas, I was alive and life was going on. #HowBowDah.

In true mom fashion, Katie marched into my room to make sure I was up for work by 7:30am.

"Good morning, lovie," she said, pulling back the curtains and forcing me to accept that a new day had come. Next thing I knew, she swapped out the mixing bowl for a glass of coconut water, and slapped a cold washcloth over my eyelids. Truthfully, I don't know how she wasn't repulsed by the toxic spill going on behind my bedroom door, but I certainly commended her for braving the exposure and attempting to clean up the mess. It was evident that that was a true solver of the world's most common white-girl problems.

"Loose-fitting clothes," I muttered.

"Excuse me, dear?"

"I need loose-fitting clothes. I feel like a septic tank," I clarified.

"Got it. I have a tunic from my fat days with your name on it. Be right back," said Katie, a reformed bulimic.

Getting myself upright was a bit of a challenge. Slipping on the "fat tunic" was not. Seriously, it was like stepping into a potato sack, but I brought the extra five pounds on myself, so I couldn't really complain.

After cinching the tarp with a stylish belt, changing out my earrings, and slipping on some high heels, the only thing missing from my ensemble was a "HAZARDOUS WASTE" symbol sewn onto my back. Seriously, the only plus to my physical appearance was that the boozy stench radiating from my pores prevented people from taking the seat next to me on the bus, allowing me to enjoy my hangover in peace and quiet.

I can honestly say at that point, I was starting to really miss my clear head, and I wondered if people who were always high on drugs ever thought the same. I mean, sometimes it's okay to take a vacation from yourself and the crazy, but sometimes it feels good to just be "home", you know? And while I was in no position to turn down a Xanax if given to me, I simply longed for my feet to feel like they were firmly planted on the ground once again. I was more than ready to reclaim the old me. The one who existed before my heart and liver had both been tarred and feathered. The one before I got into the habit of sharing cigarettes with homeless people.

Undoubtedly, this process was going to take some research, some critical thinking, some hypothetical backspacing, and a little bit of storyboarding, to initiate the master reset I was after. It had been a while since college and I had a refreshed thirst for wisdom. Getting "back to basics" was a new and rare opportunity, one that would inevitably yield a very valuable life lesson: Who am I, and what do I want? Vague, I know. But these were precisely the questions I needed answers so I would never again "give my power away" to unworthy motherfuckers. For my intentions, not my eloquence, I'm sure my mother would have been proud.

The first order of business was to alter my mindset about this whole shit show. Instead of making "getting over it" my plan, I revised it just a bit. First off, I declared that a "goal" was more attainable than a "plan." And that "moving passed" things was more manageable than "getting over" them.

Here's the visual that put this into perspective for me: They say life is a journey. Right? As such, I equated the whole situation to a giant piece of roadkill laying in the lane directly ahead of me. So, yes, this meant imagining the former love of my life as a dead carcass, which isn't the most pleasant thought, yet a surprisingly accurate and comforting description of someone by whom you are freshly appalled. I digress.

With that as my mental image, it made strategizing a recovery easy. Put yourself behind the wheel in that situation for a minute, will you? There you see it: blood and guts oozing out and instantly you feel bad. But you've got to keep cruising along, there's no time to stop. So, you acknowledge it, keep focused on the road, move around it quickly, and then—that's it—you get back in your lane and go on toward your destination, making sure to give a quick courtesy wave to those who were kind enough to let you maneuver and move along.

Above all, I had to keep reminding myself that my situation, though a first for me, was not unique in comparison to all the other crazy shit that happens in this universe—a lesson I later learned first-hand, over and over.

I know I went into great detail painting a picture of just how bad I had it, but deep down I knew the world was not going to stop and have a moment of silence for my personal devastation. And sadly, no national holiday was going to be declared because I got screwed over. The banks were still going to be open and mail would most certainly get delivered in future years. What can I say, people? I tried to finagle us a three-day weekend out of this mess, but only came out with a two-day hangover. Life isn't fair.

~ ~ ~

A few days later, the alcohol bloat finally subsided and I was able to wear jeans again without looking like I was somewhere in my second trimester. I was making progress and slowly becoming a contributing member in society once again, despite the fact that this was still the first thing on my mind in the morning and the last thing on my mind when I went to bed. However, the sheer fact that I was getting in and out of the bed was a great sign. Along with the fact that I was showing up to work, making an effort to be social, and refraining from cutting myself in when alone in the bathroom. Did I mention I was even showering and brushing my teeth, too?

I was also eating again: the downside to nurturing myself obviously meant I wasn't going to lose any substantial amount of weight, but at least I was healthy. Not to mention, I hadn't smoked a cigarette since Eric had lent me those two, which means I hadn't gotten drunk enough since then to think coating my lungs in tar was cool. It was progress, not perfection. And that was alright with me.

What wasn't alright with me was the PowerPoint presentation my mom presented to me a few days later.

In an effort to become more employable, my middle-aged (and apparently bored) mother had recently enrolled herself in a Microsoft Office class at the local public library. For the practical part of the lesson, the students were tasked with putting together a series of five slides about a subject of their choice. Part of me was touched that she chose to make her daughter the topic of her presentation, but the other half wondered why she just couldn't have done it on something like stained glass windows or Zumba, as I now had a 50-year-old's electronic slide show rendition of how I had been dicked over.

With the lyrics to Michael Bublé's "I Just Haven't Met You Yet" plastered all over the title page of this thing, I had no one to blame but myself. Last she really heard from me, I had drunk-dialed her in a fit of hysteria on my way home from work. Had I realized that would be the precursor to a PowerPoint presentation with atrocious gradient backgrounds and inconsistent font choices, I probably would have had Justin delete her number from my phone that night along with Trent's. Alas, paging through the presentation, I saw giant, Times New Roman bolded, heroic words, such as "STRENGTH" and "POWER," coupled with images of things like thunderbolts and spider webs.

"This is a thoughtful gesture. This is a thoughtful gesture. This is a thoughtful gesture," I repeated out loud, as I dragged the document to the trash icon on my desktop and emptied it promptly after.

In other news, this singlehandedly ruined Michael Bublé for me.

CHAPTER THREE/LESSON THREE

- "Try" to be happy because lashing out is not lady-like

A few weeks had now passed and I hadn't yet "relapsed." So, to celebrate, I headed out to Long Island for the Fourth of July weekend with my family. Think: Adirondack chairs, nasally New York accents, bagels with lox, and you're practically there.

Considering the cast of characters included a bunch of yentas and their designer dogs, a few hormonal pregnant people, and a cousin or two who likely had a stash of recreational drugs in their thousand-dollar weekender bags, I was looking forward to tabling my crazy and letting some of the others have the spotlight.

One day, as a group of us sat down by the water and did the crossword puzzle from the Times, my mom took it upon herself to interrupt an otherwise peaceful moment, asserting that she had read something recently that reminded her of me. Glancing over at her beach bag, I saw some self-help book poking out from her tote and I knew something wretched was coming. My only salvation rested in the fact that it wasn't going to be an excerpt from Fifty Shades of Grey.

In an effort to be respectful and give her credit for being as committed as I was to constantly thinking about my miserable situation, I gave her the floor and let her share her piece.

Holding her book like she was about to recite a hymnal, she flipped directly to the dog-eared page and began reading: "'You can't always control what happens in life, but you can make the decision to not let it affect you.' That is so you, right?"

Yeah, that was "so me" like a thug-life tattoo on my face was "so me." Really, mom? Really? Where had I heard something like that before? A fortune cookie? Bumper sticker? On the book flap of Chicken Soup for the Teenage Soul? Was that actually the profound, hard-hitting advice my mom had highlighted specifically for me? I have to say, I expected better.

Absolutely no part of that resonated with me—and furthermore, I couldn't really imagine it hitting hard for anyone who wasn't in the post-menopausal phase of her life. At this point in the healing process my theory was that if Oprah, or one of her cronies, hadn't coined it, then, quite frankly, I didn't want to hear about it. And apparently, I was so hell-bent on that prerequisite, that my immediate reaction to this quip was sheer anger. Like, unexplainable, flip the table, Teresa Giudice-Real Housewives of New Jersey anger.

Perhaps I was just PMSing, but I was wildly offended. Sure, I had no real frame of reference as to who this character was and what had happened to her, but how could someone be making money off royalties by penning that feelings could be turned on and off like a light switch? If it were in fact that easy, clearly I would have taken a sledgehammer to the circuit breaker and stopped feeling shitty about Trent and Layla a long time ago. Trust me, I was ready to wake up in the morning somewhere other than what could be a set for a Cymbalta commercial.

In hindsight, I should have just thanked my mom for sharing, and then excused myself back to the house where I'd rifle through my cousin's Louis bag in search of a joint or unmarked pill container. But instead, I chose to respond with: "Mom, that's complete bullshit."

"I'm sorry?" she asked, surprised.

That's when I tossed in some bullets and spun the barrel. It was time for me to let off a few rounds.

"It's bullshit. You can't just decide when your feelings will go away. It's not like telling the dog to get off the couch. You don't just clap your hands and they go scampering off. Don't get me wrong, I'm not about wallowing away in misery, and God forbid I 'give them any more of my power,' but hell—don't you think I would have 'decided to be over this' a long time ago if I could? Can I get a damn break and just be a little pissed off for a while?"

I then channeled a thirteen-year-old girl who was just told by her parent she couldn't go to the movies wearing a tube top and stormed off to my bedroom, refusing to change. Unfortunately, there was no door within earshot that I could slam to drive home my point that I was definitely not coming down for dinner that night.

I felt bad after leaving my family on the beach like that, and knew I had probably caused some degree of post-traumatic stress disorder for everyone who was within a ten-foot radius of my freak-out. I was also sure my mother contemplated writing in to Maury Povich and requesting boot camp for her out of control daughter. Lord knows I was only one bad dye job and an illegitimate child away from being casted for that show.

Trust me, I was well aware that I had literally ripped the woman's face off with my cutting words, and I recognized that that wasn't an appropriate thing to do to the person who's responsible for giving me life, regardless of how fucked up it was at the moment. The beach was supposed to be a safe haven for us all. And there I went, turning my crazy into an oil spill and letting it overflow into the otherwise peaceful waters. Worst of all, my mom was just trying to help and I knew that. What the hell was I thinking arguing with my biggest ally? Especially considering I was still on her medical insurance and needed to keep that relationship tight if I ever wanted to make good on some pain meds.

But, in my defense, there really are only two things in this world that send me—and pretty much all women—straight into the red zone: when people call you crazy, and when someone tells you to calm down. The advice she so gleefully narrated implied both. Unfortunately, two wrongs didn't make a right in this case, which is all it took to convince me I needed to see a professional therapist or be locked in a cage.

Foregoing being held captive, I decided to step on the gas to get passed the road kill. I needed to snap out of it and quit playing the victim. Above all, I needed to progress my love story. As unwritten as it was by this point, I needed things to get weird, wild, or wonderful. Thankfully, it did all of those—big time.

Realizing I had let the two people who I'd previously decided to evict from my life live rent-free in the pit of my stomach for more than a month was unacceptable. They were baggage I'd hoped the airline would lose on my way to New York—but that didn't happen. An epiphany, however, did.

It had been half a year since I pulled the plug on my comatose relationship—since I had left him, that silly state of Nebraska, and every single fair-weathered-friend behind. It was time for me bring up the anchors and let this ship sail. More importantly, I needed to realize I didn't have it that fucking bad. Really, I didn't. In fact, it would be about a year later and a guy named Jacob before I had any idea what "that fucking bad" really was. More on that to come.

Long before I ever declared the official end to our relationship, it was evident that Trent had already packed up his things and moved out of my heart. For whatever reason, he just wasn't making it his home the way someone who wants to spend his life with you should. And call me crazy (actually don't, as it's one of the things that sends me into the red zone), but my heart was prime real estate, if you asked me. And it definitely deserved to be put back on the market for other potential buyers, not flakey renters. It just was up to me to make the necessary improvements that would increase its value over time.

At the end of the day, I wasn't a forty-eight-year-old divorcee. I was a twenty-something girl who was DTF and determined to prove that not every guy I encountered was a douche bag deep down.

To do this, I would have to shave my legs, get socially lubricated, and go fish for singles at the bar: uncharted territory for me, but completely normal for everyone else my age. There I had it: a tangible plan. I was going to get myself in front of someone new, preferably someone with a brain and a penis (but not necessarily in that order), and reclaim the life I had always meant to live in the fabulous, magical city of Chicago.

It was at this moment I decided to start a blog. Cliché? Maybe. But I needed somewhere safe that I could expel whatever was on my confused, little mind. Clearly, my expectations of life in my twenties did not jibe with reality, but I needed a place where I could figure it all out. I didn't care if anyone would read it or if it'd become the next Huffington Post. So, I hid behind a computer screen, instead of lashing out at friends and family, and created a Dear Diary On Steroids where I could chronicle the crazy, one entry at a time.

Maybe my mom's self-help book was right after all. The best way to move on would to be to make a conscious effort and try to be happy.

Keyword: try.

PART TWO

CHAPTER FOUR/LESSON FOUR

- It's ok to be scared of a new penis

Back from New York, I armed myself with a sun-kissed tan and a coupon for a four-pack of Schick razor blade refills right in time for my twenty-fourth birthday.

Little thing about birthdays when you have roommates: you have built-in friends who must acknowledge the fact that you've aged. That said, I had no doubts that Andrew and Katie would lead my blood-alcohol levels into familiar, saturated territory come the weekend when we had plans to celebrate another year of my so-called life.

As Saturday night came upon us, I restored order to my bikini line and my liver was ready to rumble, both for the first time in weeks. I was determined to head into the night with two personal goals in mind: no paying for drinks, and no puking up drinks.

Oh, to be twenty-four again.

"You look cuuuuute," said Katie, as I emerged from getting ready. Problem was, I couldn't tell if she actually thought I looked attractive, or if this was just an automated response to seeing me in something other than sweatpants for the first time since we signed our lease. Either way, I took the compliment.

Then, she asked me something that was more off-putting than the time my grandfather asked if Trent was a "nigro football player" the first time I mentioned to him that I had fancied myself a serious boyfriend.

"Are you ready to meet some boyssssss tonight?" she asked with big, battering eyes and an elbow nudge.

The emphasis on the word "boys" was giving my vagina stage fright. Perhaps if it were my first night on some all-inclusive, spring break, co-ed cruise ship, and I had just slapped on a neon wristband for an unlimited drink package, then I could have replied with a resounding "yes." But all I could do was cringe at the thought of being funneled into a situation that would inevitably put me in close proximity to strange men who were hoping to score a hookup along with their bar tab later that night. While I had been off the horse for a while, I knew how the rodeo went and I wasn't excused from the possibility of being corralled by an urban cowboy.

In fact, the more I thought about it, the more I believed infiltrating a new penis in my life was the scariest part about dating again. Penises are weird to begin with, so when you find one that you can actually stand to look at—let alone grant an all-access pass to—you want to hold on to it. Literally.

Clearly, this whole new penis thing was an issue for me, as seeing another man's junk for the first time represented just how far away I was from that turning point where the courting stops and the farting starts. I wished more than anything that I could just make a deal with the devil and bypass everything that most girls long to go through in the beginning with a guy. Save the cute texts, the butterflies in your stomach, the baseline manners, and skip straight to the land of sweatpants, pizza in front of the television, and little-to-no makeup ever again. But I knew that's not how it went in the real world. In the real world, you've got to put on some eyeliner, curl a few strands of hair, and at least attempt to converse with a guy in a way that doesn't overtly suggest his anatomy is utterly dreadful.

Alas, before I could trot down the stairs with my short skirt and giant purse, I had to answer Katie's question.

"Hell yeah. Let's do this," I replied emphatically, as I doused myself one final time in Calvin Klein perfume and drug-store hairspray, solidifying the facade that I was actually into her plan. Either way, I was ready for my night out, or a casting call for the Real World.

Walking to the bar, even the sound of our high heels clicking on the summer sidewalks made me nauseous. Aside from my feet already hurting, and my debilitating fear of the male genitalia, it hit me that I had also developed an unexplainable sense of entitlement when it came to whom I was going to date next.

With each person passing by us, I realized I had become noticeably pickier since dating Trent: a very handsome, wealthy, well dressed young man with respectable hygiene habits, and a knack for quality Italian leather goods. As such, I refused to date-down, and the mere thought of a bro with a gut and an overdue dental appointment made me sick to my stomach, even if he was a reigning beer-pong champ and had a framed certificate on the wall to prove it. I knew how this made me sound, trust me. And we all know I wasn't exactly a symbol of class myself during this period of my life. But for whatever reason, I continued to walk around like I was Miss July, whether I deserved the centerfold or not.

I wasn't always like that. In fact, I remember a time when I was legitimately interested in someone simply if he liked Kit-Kat bars as much as I did. Or if he knew the chorus to my favorite song for that particular summer. But after dating Trent, a Matthew McConaughey look-alike with just the right amount of inoffensive body hair, I couldn't help but find faults in just about everyone. And by "faults," I mean minor glitches, only detectable by an eagle eye, or a self-righteous single girl with a false sense of entitlement.

Unfortunately, no one was free from my cruel and unusual judgment. Not the butcher at the meat counter (doesn't make enough money, hands always smell like sausage), not the man who got on the bus in Lincoln Park (those dad jeans are a decade behind the times), and certainly not the guy next to me on the elliptical (shouldn't you be lifting weights?). Obviously, I made the rules up as I went along, handicapping myself from dating in the real world with each unrealistic filter I applied to the men in Chicago.

The worst part about this was that I was shooting myself in the foot well before giving myself the chance to have a walk of shame, and I couldn't even figure out why I was behaving like this. It wasn't like I was trying to find twelve, out-of-this-world, insanely flawless guys to photograph for a wall calendar. I just wanted a special friend. Someone tolerable, okay to look at even if I had my glasses on, good at texting, who knew the difference between "your" and "you're," and who liked making out. See? Not a tall order. But while on the subject of height, I should mention I refused to date anyone under five-foot-ten-inches.

Refused.

Snapping out of my list of do nots, must nots, and can't haves, we finally made it to the bar, where Katie immediately bolted to order her first drink. She was far too sober for 11:00 PM on a weekend and needed to survey the land through a pair of beer goggles. I didn't blame her. Upon first glance, I couldn't tell if we had walked into a bar or a frat house. I was overwhelmed, wondering if celebrating my birthday out in the wild was a big mistake dressed up as a good idea. How does the saying go? Put some lipstick on girl, and she's still just a socially awkward single lady in a dive bar full of wild animals in backwards hats? Yes, I believe that's it.

Big ones. Small ones. Tall ones. Smelly ones. Sweaty ones. They were everywhere. Men. Boys. Whatever you want to call them. And no matter what combo of khaki shorts and colored polos they wore, they all looked the same. I was in the midst of a complete bro-verlode. It was as if I had stepped into an Old Country Buffet.

By showing my ID and walking into this place, I had grabbed a hypothetical empty plate and proceeded to stare at endless options of mediocre food. Absolutely nothing was going to hit the spot, and all of it was quite nauseating.

The guys in this bar were all write-offs. From their carbon-copy plaid shorts, to their flipped up polo shirts, or their backwards hats with unsexy sweat stains, this was not what I'd call selection. This is what I would call a bro-based pigpen. And for as much as I wanted to see someone do a keg stand for the first time in three years, that wasn't exactly the reason I had applied twenty dollars worth of eyeliner and lip gloss before going out.

Clearly, I had wasted my pretty, but I was not going to waste anything else, especially not Katie's money. She had paid our cover for the night, and even though it was my party, and I could have left if I wanted to, I owed it to her (and to myself) to at least go through the motions: to test the water, to chug a beer, to give my number out. Let's not forget, I shaved my legs for this.

After about the fourth time Kesha came on the speakers, Katie was finally brave (read: drunk) enough to get this night going.

"See that cute guy?" she shouted in my ear from an inch away. In my opinion, he looked a little too much like Jim from The Office for my elitist tastes, but I commended her regardless. If anything, I was envious of her ability to see something in nothing.

"Yeah, I see him," I replied.

"Good, now come with me."

Where were we going? Better yet, where was this going? Little did I know, Katie was about to pull off one of the slickest moves that I have ever seen a girl throw down at a bar, and she was going to rope me into doing this along with her.

"Pick a guy," she ordered. "We're going to blow his mind in a sec."

A practical exam on the first night out? I wasn't quite prepared to pick my poison and attack, but I vowed to be a good sport. I know it seems like it couldn't be that hard. After all, it was a warm weekend night at a bar in one the most popular neighborhoods for young people in the third largest city in the country. I had bronzer on. I had lotioned up my legs. I had drank the Kool-Aid, okay? I had everything going in my favor, but this was actually very difficult for me, this scouting process. It was like having to pick out a piece of produce without being able to squeeze it, smell it, and touch it. Knowing my luck, I was going to grab a bad apple.

Plus, since I didn't know what exactly this poor gentleman was going to be the target of: it was hard for me to tell if I should go with the loud-mouth bro who just shot-gunned a beer and slammed the can flat on his forehead for no apparent reason, or the quiet dude who just nailed a bull's-eye on the dartboard by himself. All I knew was that I had to lock in my first-round pick fast, as Katie had just stepped up to the bar.

"Two shots of tequila—salt and lime, too," she ordered. Something told me these weren't for us.

"Here you go ladies, have fun," our endearing bartender said.

The shots were up and between the two of us girls we had two glasses, two limes, and our very own saltshaker. Had this been a road trip to Mexico, or a fiesta-themed bachelorette party, we would have been set. And yet, the reality was we were headed into unfamiliar territory with no proper documentation.

"Lick your hand," she demanded.

As if I already didn't like where this was going, bodily fluids were apparently now required. Great. However, since I wasn't violating the night's golden rules (no puking or paying), her strange request and up-to-something antics were technically fair game. As such, I salivated on the back of my hand and doused the spit with a dash of table salt. Even though there was no wound there, I could still feel the theoretical sting of whatever shameless thing I was about to do.

"Now follow me," she said before beelining it to the back of the bar. It was all-aboard the Katie Train. First stop: the Jim look alike.

Katie pumped the brakes about three feet away from him, locked eyes with him, and successfully diverted his attention from the sloppy conversation about fantasy football he was having with the other two average-looking guys next to him. She then pointed at him and did the whole "come hither" thing with her index finger. Though I had never seen it done in real-life, it was actually quite hot, and the whole scene resembled the beginning of a low-budget porno.

Jim probably shared the same physical reaction as I did, seeing that he took the bait in approximately half-a-second. Here's how it all went down: Katie held up her salt-covered hand to his mouth, and without ever having said a single word, he licked the granules from the little nook in between her index finger and thumb, took down the shot she fed to him, and finally sucked on a lime she held up with her other hand.

Game. Set. Match. At that point, I think he mentally climaxed, perhaps multiple times. Damn, girl! I mean, just like that, she had his attention in a big way. And all it took was one five-dollar shot of warm, bottom-shelf tequila. She didn't even have to speak, she just pointed at him, fed him booze, and for the rest of the night, no other girl came within an arms length of them two. She marked her territory and got what she wanted.

After canoodling with him for a moment, she looked back at me and pointed to a guy in a few feet away with a backwards baseball hat. Apparently, that was the only credential a guy needed in order to be "my type." I looked at him and decided that "not bad" was the best it was going to get for me. I proceeded with caution.

"Your turn," said Katie, as she spun me around and thrust me forward like we were playing a game of pin the tail on the donkey. I was entirely uncomfortable. Mama Bear had just forced me into the wild for the first time on my own. However, I couldn't ignore the fact that I was more inspired by what Katie had accomplished than any work of Mother Teresa's. With that, I proceeded to saunter over to backwards-baseball-cap boy. Every slow-mo step I took felt like Planet Earth was narrating it.

"Watch as the rare, beautiful, Emily walks with what appears to be two broken ankles as she approaches the underdeveloped, weak-minded Bro-licious Maximus in a novice attempt to mate," whispered Morgan Freeman.

I was about to seize my prey, and with the "come hither" motion that every guy dreams of creaming his jeans over at some point in life.

Every guy but him.

Zero reaction—unless, of course, you count "deer in the headlights" a reaction. What did I do wrong? Did I use my middle finger by accident? Did I overdo it on the eye makeup and look like a tranny? Were we in a gay bar? Was he blind? Clearly, I had hooked him. It was the reeling in that he was making unnecessarily difficult, and I had no idea why.

To explain my shortcomings was none-other-than his girlfriend, who I'd somehow managed to miss standing next to him just two feet away the entire time. Of all the guys in the bar, I zeroed in on the one who was in a relationship—with a very attractive girl, if you must know.

Coincidentally, when she finally turned toward me, she had two shots (presumably one for her, and one for her boyfriend) of tequila. I bet she wasn't going to make him jump through hoops to slam it, either.

The silver lining? My rejection came with a free shot of alcohol. Bottoms up.

Frustrated by this most recent swing-and-a-miss start, I scurried to the side and pulled out my phone, refusing to make eye contact with anyone else at the bar.

"Where you at?" I texted to our unfortunate-looking neighbor, Nick, testing the waters for a ride home. "Can you come get me at Shamrock's?"

"Sure. But it'll be via rickshaw. I'm boycotting Uber. You mind?" he replied.

I could only laugh at the irony. From being courted around in an Escalade with the sexiest man alive, to being picked up by a vegan-stoner-hippie with an aversion to health insurance, riding a bike with a bench attached to it.

"Yes, that's fine," I texted him back.

Ten minutes later, there we were: neighbor Nick and I sharing a seat and being peddled home by a guy with monstrous calves. It was the oddest and most unromantic of settings, which was enough to compel me to force a make out session upon Nick. I had no basis for this, other than to regain control of a situation that was an utter mess: my going-nowhere love life. Perhaps locking lips with a solid 3 was the morale booster I needed to get back on the field and try for a home run with someone whose physical appearance I could actually stomach. But after just a few seconds of what could possibly be the worst kiss of my life, I wanted to sideline myself for the rest of the season. I felt his tongue go where only a strep-test had gone before and it sent my inner dialogue into a tailspin.

Was this really what making out was like? Are the majority of people this bad at kissing? Am I expected to be turned on by this in any way, shape, or form? Would I like this better if I was drunk? How long do I have to do this? Does he think this is foreplay? Is how he kisses directly proportional to how good-looking he is? What do I have on my DVR? Do I taste buffalo sauce?

My questions snowballed into another round of crippling anxiety. It mounted at wondering whether it was me or him that needed to go back in the bullpen and warm up a little longer after this morbid make out session.

With the rickshaw pulling up to my place, I knew that both my friend, and our driver, were banking that Nick would be invited up. However, that couldn't have been further from my mind. I couldn't risk seeing his face under a streetlamp, let alone risk seeing it creep into my mind the next time I tried to masturbate, which let's face it, was the pinnacle of my romantic endeavors at the time.

"Well thank you sooooo much for rescuing me from Shamrock's. Have a good night, Nick!" I said, as I waved goodbye to him and his blue balls.

At that point, I didn't know if the devil wore Prada, but I could certainly confirm she shoots tequila and uses people for rides home on a rickshaw.

CHAPTER FIVE/LESSON FIVE

- Always be skeptical of the guy in a pink shirt

In an attempt to anonymously overeat, I ordered a giant cheeseburger the next morning from a bar down the block and headed over to pick it up in my uniform: sweatpants, no bra, giant hoodie. I wondered if people thought I was hiding a pregnancy, or if they just knew had zero fucks left to give about my physical appearance by Sunday.

As I waited for my impromptu add-on of sweet potato fries to come out of the kitchen, in walked a beautiful man. Far more beautiful than anything Lincoln Park could naturally produce.

"Pick-up for Mitchell," the man said. "Alexander Mitchell."

Not only did I have his full name (great for Facebooking purposes), but I had also confirmed my suspicion. He was not a Lincoln Park native. For that matter, he wasn't even American. From his accent, I could tell he was British.

I quickly took inventory of myself: gross oversized clothes, left-over hair and makeup, and a tinge of B.O. With absolutely nothing left to lose, I went for it—a symptom of shamelessness, I assume. That's right, I approached him with whatever gusto I had left from last night's dry run.

"You live around here, right? I recognize you—seen you around a few times," (lies). "I'm Emily."

I put out my hand and Alexander took it to give it a shake. Where was Morgan Freeman to narrate this mess?

"I'm Alexander, nice to meet you."

Alexander. Alexander. It was at that moment I decided there was something sexy about a guy with a three-syllable name who doesn't automatically insist I call him by his more common, casual alias.

The truth about Alexander was that I had actually never seen him prior to our chance burger rendezvous. But I wanted to see him again, if only to find out what he liked to put on his burger, or if he happened to be distant cousins with Prince William. And, somehow, the stars aligned just enough so that we could magically exchange contact information before leaving with our respective orders.

The following Thursday night we set a date (a real, bonfide date!) to have dinner at a small Italian trattoria in a quaint neighborhood called Old Town.

Alexander picked me up. In a Mercedes sedan. In a Prada blazer. And the best part? None of this looked as gay as it sounds because he was European and could get away with it! Finally, I was in my element and could feel good about the potential of seeing this man's penis at some point. Talk about relief.

As he pulled up, I quickly tucked my bus pass back into my purse and made sure to rip the Target tag off the tank top I had spent a whopping fourteen dollars on for this special occasion. I realized I had underdressed and underspent, as I tried to figure out how to turn down the air conditioning vents that were built into the passenger's seat. PS: Wow.

Evidently, he was older, and more established. As if I hadn't already figured that out from the fact that my vagina was being cooled through a highly intelligent vehicular HVAC system, it came out during the conversation we were having over ravioli and Chianti that Alexander was a thirty-year-old options trader (whatever that means) in the city, originally from London, and was hugely into soccer. While his day-job didn't resonate with me, I got the gist that he handled a lot of clients, a lot of power, and a lot of money. And in his free time, he worked on perfecting his best David Beckham impression on the field.

"So, what about you? I mean, are you ready for a relationship at this point in your life?" he asked in that cripplingly-sexy accent.

It was an odd question considering that, at that time, the lifespan of our courtship was about four days. But I understood where he was coming from. He was a thirty-year-old trapped in a sixty-year-old, high-powered CEO's body, with no time for the bullshit commonly known as "dating."

"I mean, if the right person comes along, then yeah, I'm all in. If you're asking me if I'm into you—or this—then the answer is yes. I like you, Alexander."

He smiled and held my hand as he sipped on his wine. It dawned on me: I liked these European businessmen. They smell good, they know how to close a deal, and they can wear a scarf in an unusually heterosexual way. If this were what a relationship would be like with him, then yes, I was ready, scarf and all.

Alexander invited me up to his place after dinner. He lived on the thirty-sixth floor in one of the only high rises in Lincoln Park. His toilet flushed itself and his garbage can lids were automatic. The unit had floor-to-ceiling windows and the expensive version of IKEA furniture throughout.

We made out for a few minutes, which I'm sure was the way people in Europe thank someone for treating them to dinner. But just as things were starting to get good, Alexander's phone buzzed. He looked at it, let out a big sigh, and began to escort me out.

"Looks like I'm flying to New York at four in the morning tomorrow," he said putting on his shoes. "I'm sorry, but I need to walk you out so I can pack and get some sleep."

"Not a problem," I said, bummed that the curtain was closing so early.

The elevator ride down to the lobby was long, silent, and awkward. In an attempt to break the mood, I intelligently asked, "What are you going to the Big Apple for?"

"Work."

Alexander's demeanor had clearly changed—tanked, rather. He obviously didn't want to elaborate so I didn't push. Well, not that hard at least.

"Big meeting?" I said with just a little sass.

"I just have to be present for a case with our legal team. That's all."

And that really was all. I got off the elevator, went home, and figured he'd tell me more about it when he got back in a couple of days.

But as fate would have it, I never heard from Alexander again. I tried texting and calling but his line was cut. I even asked the bartender at the burger place if they'd seen him. It was silence all around.

As off putting as I can be sometimes, I knew there was more to this. Relationships, at least the start of them, are often just a swirling mess of doubts and questions, wondering if you said or did something wrong. But just this once, it wasn't me. I replayed our evening over and over and I hit my marks. I was polite, attentive, honest, and hygienic. So, the crash and burn couldn't have been from any lack of deodorant on my end. That much I knew was true.

With the mystery burning inside me, I decided to put those four years of journalism school to good use and got my investigative reporting going. In other words, I Googled him.

The first hit back was a Chicago Tribune article. The second was from the New York Times. Alexander's name was big and bold in both search results.

"High-frequency trader convicted in fourteen-million-dollar scheme."

What the fucking fuck?! I clicked and read on.

"U.S. regulators claimed their first victory in a four-year-old effort to crack down on oil market manipulation on Thursday . . ."

So, that's why he didn't call me. He couldn't call me. I mean, not unless he wanted to use his one free call from jail to explain to me why there wouldn't be a second date.

After combing through all the articles, I collectively determined that Alexander was being deported and charged with participation in a ring of illegal oil trading schemes. I couldn't believe that at just thirty-years-old, his life (and our could-be relationship) was essentially over. All I could hope was that at thirty, the only things I'd be worrying about were my 401(k) and my house payment; not whether or not they served burgers in jail. God bless it.

~ ~ ~

Taking a break from the madness of the city, and all the embezzlers within it, I decided to spend a weekend in the suburbs where my parents lived. Every now and then, I liked to take forty-eight hours and enjoy the quiet of my childhood home. As a trade-off for having to post up in a twin bed, I gained access to a stocked refrigerator with fresh food, central air conditioning, and an inner peace from knowing that no one was going to stumble in drunk at 4 AM and leave a frozen pizza to burn in the oven until noon the next day.

This particular weekend, however, featured a shortlist of family get-togethers, which rendered the quest for a little R&R null and void. At the top of places to be and things to do was my brother's engagement party, where I would spend the afternoon chumming it up under a tent while I hoarded appetizers on a plate the size of an ashtray.

After about five hours of this, I had just about reached my limit of various foods atop toast points. Plus, I couldn't stand to see one more kiss from the happy couple, hear one more racist remark from my grandfather, or feel any more awkward that a committed relationship couldn't be further from my own future. Combine that with the intense heat, and this happy occasion was slowly evolving into my personal Hell. I needed to make a break for it.

Unfortunately, Elmhurst, Illinois, a town once ranked as the "number-one-most-livable-city-in-the-nation," didn't have quite the bar scene I needed to forget I had spent my day on the set of an eHarmony testimonial commercial. In fact, my watering hole selection included just two establishments and neither of them could guarantee me a dirty-bar make out with anyone I didn't go to high school with. Aside from that, I hadn't exactly packed any real bar-hopping attire with me, so the best that I could do in the way of wardrobe selection was to pair a semi-chic flannel shirt my dad ruined in the laundry with coral-colored cargo shorts from a second-hand shop. At least the summery pumps I had worn to the engagement party would give me the J.Crew flare I needed to fit in.

Somewhere between hodge-podge and hot mess, I walked into the bar. It was like a reunion of my tenth grade plant biology class, except with hard alcohol and a broken air conditioner. Seriously, it was the hottest day of the summer so far, and by process of elimination, I was wearing a flannel shirt. Regardless, I decided to stick—and sweat—it out at Fitz's Pub.

No sooner had I ordered a beer than it morphed into something that should only be served in a red Solo cup with weird things floating in it at the Kentucky State Fair. The heat was so unbearable I found myself making frequent trips to the bathroom just to blot the beads of sweat off my upper lip. If I didn't think I could lose five pounds of water weight simply by staying at this bar until closing time, I would have left before pitting out in record time. The things I did to fit into skinny jeans, I tell ya.

I was one white crewneck away from this turning into a wet t-shirt contest and I couldn't take it anymore. So, I went outside to join the smokers. The air sure as hell wasn't going to be fresh, but at least it'd be about ten degrees cooler, which is all I needed before returning to the sweat lodge.

As soon as the outside air hit me, I let out a gigantic sigh of relief. I guess it was audible enough for a group of guys nearby to turn and take notice. I instantly was attracted to one of them. He was dressed in a pink button-down shirt and tanned to perfection with a charming smile. From what I could tell, his wallet wasn't connected to anything else he was wearing by a chain and from that I knew he couldn't possibly be from the Midwest. I was right.

His name was Jax and he was in town from Scottsdale, Arizona, for a wedding. Considering I had come from my own bout with holy matrimony, we instantly found common ground and began talking. Apparently, he must have seen my bra through my sweat-soaked shirt, because the next thing I knew he was escorting me back into the bar and buying me a shot. Cheers to that, I thought.

Despite the fact that Jax lived in a world where Ed Hardy clothing reigned free, he was really, really pretty and our conversation was chemical. It wasn't long before both of us needed some air.

Heading back outside, we intruded on a cigarette break being shared by a couple of guys in Brazilian soccer jerseys.

"Excuse me," I said as I passed them to find a spot against a wall where I could catch my breath.

Upon cutting through, however, one of them muttered something along the lines of: "Damn, hot mami. You got an ass for days, chica."

Although it was true, Jax did not like this comment.

In just a few seconds, Jax had rounded up his Scottsdale posse and started to get mouthy with the south-of-the-border clan outside the bar. This was more excitement than Elmhurst had seen since a dog collapsed at the 15th Annual Pet Parade, and the police department was not going to let a scuffle laced with soccer jerseys and Affliction t-shirts tarnish the city's flawless rating. In just a few minutes, a squad car pulled up with its lights on and sirens blaring.

"Shit!" Jax said, shuffling me back into the bar.

"What? What's wrong?" I asked in somewhat of a panic, trying my best to keep up with his hustle.

"I've gotta get out of here. Quick, what's your number?" he said, phone in hand.

Without hesitation, I recited my digits as fast as I could. I sensed the urgency in his voice, though I couldn't identify the reason for it. Next thing I knew, he threw on his kinda-douchey blazer, headed towards the back of the bar with the rest of The Outsiders. I instinctively followed him, which is when he let me in on a little secret.

"Technically," he began, as he searched for a back exit, "I'm not allowed in this state. There's a warrant out for my arrest."

"Are you serious?" What was going on with my streak of hitting on criminals?

"Yes, I'm a felon."

Oh, but who isn't these days.

"I'm not supposed to be here right now but I wasn't going to miss my buddy's wedding. God damn, where the FUCK is the back door exit in this place?"

I was wondering the same damn thing.

"Well what'd you do?" I asked, and rightfully so.

"Long story."

Of course it was.

"Did you murder someone?" I just needed to know.

"Nah."

"Did you rape someone?"

It was a valid question.

"No. I gotta go. I'll text you later. Okay?"

And that was that. America's Most Wanted had vanished into the night out of the backdoor of Fitz's Pub by way of a black SUV with tinted windows. Who would have guessed that 15 minutes earlier, I was sitting there throwing back blueberry pancake flavored shots with a felon who wasn't legally allowed to be where we were?

Oh, but at least he didn't rape or murder someone though. So, I guess it was okay.

Back to myself, I immediately wondered what my mother would have thought of me giving out my number to an outlaw, but I couldn't dwell on that. In my defense, he reminded me very much of Leonardo DiCaprio in Catch Me If You Can. I had drinks with a modern-day Frank Abagnale, Jr. That's brag-worthy, right?

On my drive home, I contemplated what I'd wear to my interview with Dateline once the police caught Jax. After all, they'd probably want to speak with the last girl he would have been romantically connected to, had the cops not taken him down in a parking lot near the on-ramp to the interstate. I wondered if he'd use his one-free-call to follow up with me like he had promised. That'd be sweet.

CHAPTER SIX/LESSON SIX

- There's always a catch to making twenty-thousand dollars

I had just about enough suburbs excitement to last me through my twenties on that fateful night at Fitz's. After not hearing from Jax again, it was time to return to the city, where at least I was used to things always being somewhat of a jungle.

On an otherwise normal day at work, my phone buzzed with a text message sometime in the afternoon. It was a message from a familiar friend—a girl I went to college with, Mindy.

"Hey Em! I'm in town tonight! Short notice, I know—but dinner and drinks?"

Before I could get truly excited about reuniting with her, a part of me had to wonder if this was all a set up.

Mindy had been ahead of me in school: a senior while I was a freshman. We met while working on a project together in an advertising class, and many nights of studying at her house turned into cocktail hour and reruns of The Bachelor. You could say our friendship blossomed through Capitan Morgan and trashy TV, which I have to believe, is the foundation for most of life's greatest relationships. After all, it was enough to transcend our minimal age gap and for her to buy me booze while I was still under age.

Physically, she resembled a J.C. Penney Junior's department catalog model—plain face with chunky, Kelly Clarkson highlights and a good body. As a native Texan, she fit right in going to school in the middle of America and I was always impressed by the fact every single black guy at our school (all six of them) was infatuated with her. But despite the attention from a fourth of the basketball team, Mindy wasn't having any of it. She had a long-term, long-distance boyfriend named Mark, who was much older and very good looking, a la Rob Lowe.

She talked about him a lot and they were always in touch. To her, no other guy could cut it—and I didn't blame her. Mark was the catch of all catches, which is why she whittled down her social life to just me and her cat as she checked off the days until her graduation, when her and Mark could start living the life they had always imagined.

But until then, I kept her company and she became a solid friend, especially given the fact that I was some peon freshman riding her coattails so that all the older, black athletes would know my name. Regardless, she was always there to answer my texts, pick up my calls, take me to a party, invite me to a sleep over, and so much more. While I wanted to think she enjoyed my company, a part of me wondered if the real reason she was so readily available all the time had to do with the fact that she was bored out of her mind without Mark in Omaha.

But that changed when he came to visit Mindy and she still invited me to hang out. Even though I was third-wheel, I didn't mind. Mark was a stand-up guy, even traveling to cheer us on at a statewide collegiate advertising competition (yes, those exist) in Lincoln, Nebraska. As I saw him standing in the back of the room as we presented, it was evident he was irrefutably handsome, not to mention wonderfully supportive of his girlfriend. In that moment, I wanted to speed up time for them so that they could finally live in the same state, move in together, get married, and have multiple babies. I wanted that as much as I, myself, wanted to wind up with a man like Mark.

Until, I wound up with Mark himself.

Flash forward about four years, and Mindy and Mark were no more. I don't know why or how, but my source is my Facebook news feed, and as we know, it never lies. By this time, Mindy and I had fallen completely out of touch. I'm not sure if anyone was at fault. In fact, were I to guess, I would say a combination of time, distance, and alcohol unhinged the friendship we'd so easily built during her last year at school.

Just as I suspected, Mindy and Mark had moved in together after graduation. However, it was not back home to Texas to pop out a few kids. It was to South Carolina to take jobs at a ritzy country club—plot twist! I dug further and found out Mark was a golf caddy making nearly a thousand dollars per round at this exclusive course. In on it also was Mindy, who posted up as a cart-girl, driving around the place and serving people rich, old, white men booze, snacks, and cigars. While I was quick to judge this career choice, I realized she was probably collecting massive tips while working on her tan. I'm not sure if that's what her parents had in mind after spending $100,000 on her education, but she sounded smart as fuck to me! After sifting through their pictures, it appeared that everything really was all fine and dandy. How wrong I would end up being…

During another summer weekend in Long Island with my family (this was after my emotional meltdown on the waterfront) I received a Facebook message from Mark. He'd seen me post that I was in Greenport and wrote to say he was in Southampton, a town not far away where he just so happened to be caddying for an elite country club called Shinnecock (stop laughing) Hills. That's a long ways away from South Carolina, I thought. He then asked if I wanted to "hang out one of these days."

That was a weird question on so many levels: the first being that I had never brought a boy to Greenport. I had spent every summer since childhood in Long Island with my family, and I wasn't really sure anyone could fathom that I was actually at an age where boys didn't disgust me.

Secondly, I hadn't seen Mark since that time he visited Mindy in Omaha. The last time we were in the same room together, I was pitching a fake ad campaign to Coca-Cola executives in a pants suit, and he was dating Mindy.

Emphasis on "was" because with a little more social media sleuthing, I found out his relationship status was now set to single.

This news was equal parts interesting and tempting. But let's not forget that Mindy was my friend. Even though I hadn't heard from her in several years, we'd parted on good terms and therefore any girl code should have still been honored.

At the same time, I figured, what's the harm? I mean, really. If anything, Mark's presence would serve as a reminder to my family that I was no longer 12 years old. So, I had gone ahead and invited Mark, who was essentially a stranger, to make the 45-mile drive to Greenport.

When he arrived I was in another room in the house, and I had heard a rouse coming from the living room. Apparently, Mark had entered through an open screen door into a room full of ladies who must have thought I had ordered a stripper. I immediately rushed over and there he stood: handsome as ever with his crystal blue eyes, a golden tan, and a gift. Yes, he had brought me a present—wine and chocolate-covered raisins (a.k.a. the only items required for survival if I ever found myself deserted on an island).

"I hope I wind up with a man like Mark," I had once thought. And then, with an entrance like that, I could confirm everyone had thought the exact same thing.

Mark and I cozied up on a couch together. He smelled like a scented Ralph Lauren ad in the pages of a People Magazine. But not even his intoxicating smell or yummy blue eyes could distract me from the question that was on the tip of my tongue: what the fuck happened with Mindy? The love of his life? Sorry to be blunt, but she—or the lack of she—was the reason that there was a bottle of pinot noir and a box of chocolate three feet away from us, right?

The moment I brought up her name, he let out a big sigh and looked to the ground.

Uh-oh.

"Mindy went crazy," he said.

Mindy? Crazy? Doubtful.

"She let the country club life get to her a bit," he treaded lightly, as I sat in disbelief. "A little too much drugs, sex, and rock and roll, if you can believe it."

I couldn't. Clearly, Mark was just bitter about their break up and needed to paint Mindy in a bit of a less-than-flattering light to feel better about things. While I may have lost touch with her, I didn't lose sight of her. And, there was no way that Miss Junior Texas 1998 had turned to the dark side. Mark must have cheated. Mindy must have been a lesbian this whole time. Something, anything, other than the malarkey Mark was implying.

Regardless, I figured the truth would reveal itself in time, and it wasn't important to dwell on it. The takeaways were that she had moved on and he was in my summerhouse. So, if there was ever a time to make out with the elusive, temporarily single Mark, it was then. I proceeded to check him off my first-base bucket list, before sending him back solo to Shinnecock—innuendos not excused.

Now I'm not tooting my own horn here, but Mark, who must have been in his mid-thirties by this time, fell in love with me. He instantly wanted to move to Chicago to start a life together. I didn't know that my makeout abilities were that powerful, but apparently, they were the stuff cross-country moves were made of. The only caveat to his plan was that I wanted nothing to do with it. Sure, he was hot and he'd brought me wine, but I had a lot of life left to live as a single in the city. I wasn't ready to settle down with a man who couldn't see as anyone other than "Mindy's ex." So, I shot him down and kept him on the backburner where he belonged.

It wasn't long after that I received the text to get dinner and drinks from Mindy. So either karma had come back to haunt me after my mini-tryst with Mark, or Mindy was clueless I hooked up with her ex and actually really wanted to hang out with her former gal pal. From what I could tell, she was genuinely excited to see me—but whether that was to murder me, or share a cheese plate with me, I couldn't really tell.

"Sure, I'm around: how about this cafe in Lincoln Park by my house. You can crash here after," I cordially texted back to her, hoping for the best. I mean, I made out with her ex. The least I could do was open my home to potentially being strangled by her.

A few minutes later, my phone buzzed with her reply.

"Reservations are already at Gibsons at 7. I'll just meet you there! And, I have a hotel—so it's all good."

Gibsons? Really? Did Miss Mindy know that Gibsons was one of, if not the, most expensive steakhouses in Chicago? No joke, everything was served ala carte and a baked potato was $18. I couldn't even afford a side dish let alone an actual meal. I had to back out.

"Sorry, money is kinda tight. How about you just go to dinner, and I'll meet you after for dessert some pleace?"

I felt bad, but I was in no position to throw down a third of my rent on dinner when I had a Lean Cuisine with my name on it in the freezer. Granted, it would have made a hell of a last meal should she have really be trying to kill me.

"OMG don't even worry about paying. I'm sure as hell not. See you at 7!"

To say I was confused by her reply would be an understatement. But, apparently, I was good to go for a free meal in a few hours, so I let it slide, and headed home to see my roommates for what could have been the last time.

Andrew was home on the couch, per usual, when I walked in the door.

"What's up, Em? How was your day?" he said, not taking his eyes off of a riveting game of Halo 3.

"It was...interesting."

"Really? How so?" he asked, pretending to care.

"I got invited to a dinner by a girl I went to college with. I might not make it out alive," I said, sitting down next to him.

He paused the game.

"Umm, then don't go?" he suggested.

While many may believe that was the voice of reason, I begged to differ.

"No. I'm for-sure going. It's a free meal. But I'll probably write the girl's name and number on a Post-it and leave it in the kitchen. If I'm not back by midnight, give it to the cops."

"Fair enough," said Andrew, resuming his gaming.

And just like that, I got ready for (free) dinner at Gibsons.

It was 7 PM on the dot when I arrived wearing a strapless one-piece romper. Nothing said, "I hope you didn't find out I kissed your ex" like bare shoulders and clingy material. This whole night was already off to a bad start based purely on my wardrobe choice.

I assumed Mindy would be waiting for me outside the restaurant or in the lobby, which was not the case. I even walked into their bar, second floor ladies room, and the private dining room just in case, but I didn't see her anywhere.

"You're sure there's no reservation for Biltmore? Mindy Biltmore? Party of two?" I asked the hostess.

"No, nothing under that name. In fact, we have no parties of two at 7 PM on the books at all," she confirmed.

What the hell? This was starting to seem like an intro to a horror movie, but I didn't want to accept it. So, I stepped outside and called her. It would be the first time that I'd heard her voice in years...if she answered. Straight to voice-mail. Fuck.

Mindy's phone was either off or dead, and neither of those were very good options for locating my dining partner. So, I decided to give her ten minutes, which I equated to the amount of time it would take me to quickly browse the Urban Outfitters sale rack located directly across the street. If anything, maybe I could find something to replace this romper as hardest outfit to pee in.

Ten minutes went by and I was back at Gibsons hunting for Mindy (who was probably hunting me). And just when I was about to give up hope, I heard my name.

"Emily! Ohhhh my goddddd! How are youuuuuu?"

There she was. In a tight black Armani mini-dress, 4-inch Loubiton stilettos, and bleach-blonde hair. She was smoking a cigarette while texting with one hand and clutching a giant Fendi purse with other. She was dripping in money as she ashed her cig on the sidewalk.

"Oh my gosh, Mindy. You look so different," I sputtered out.

"Thank you," she said, assuming I was complimenting her.

Mindy took a final drag of her cigarette before tossing it to the curb.

"Sorry I was late, I had to run a quick errand. Did you find Bruce all right?" she asked.

Who the fuck was Bruce?

Before I could answer, she took my hand and brought me straight into the dining room, where, at a table for eight, sat six gentlemen not too far off from my father's age. The two empty spots were next to each other in the center of the rectangular table. We took our places.

"Bruce, this is Emily. Isn't she adorable? I told you she was attractive, didn't I? I wasn't lying!"

Bruce looked at me like a fat kid about to dive into this vanilla buttercream cake. He may have even licked his lips a little. Regardless, I immediately felt like I needed a shower.

"No you were not. Come here, my little brown-eyed girl," he said as he plopped a piece of filet in his mouth.

"Don't listen to him," she whispered in my ear. "Just stay by me."

I nodded and smiled as she ushered me into one of two empty chairs at the table.

As we sat down, a few things became clear. 1) Dinner started at six, not seven. 2) This party of two was a party of six. And 3) I was apparently the guest of honor, along with Mindy, at a gathering full of people I've never seen before.

It was as if I had stepped onto the scene of a soap opera, but no one had given me my lines. Too bad I was terrible at improvising and unable to piece together exactly what my role was supposed to be.

Bruce had ordered filets for us, and within five minutes of being seated, it was plated in front of me along with a bounty of fresh, hot side dishes. All of the other six guys were done eating, which left them to straight up stare at Mindy and I.

"So Mindy, how have you been?" I said, attempting to start some conversation.

"Good! You know, just working at the golf course, and playing golf with Bruce and the guys," she responded.

"I'm sorry. How do you all know each other again?" I asked, waving my fork in the general direction of these beastly men.

Silence—a lot of it.

"Well, I met Bruce when he was golfing one day. And then he took me on his plane with the guys, and we've been friends ever since," Mindy sputtered out.

Not only was that a feeble attempt at explaining herself, but like Donald Trump's press secretary, Bruce shot down any opportunity for follow-up questions.

"Hey, hey, hey. What did I say about not focusing on me, Mindy?" he said rather condescendingly.

"Sorry, I know. It's just that we haven't seen each other in a while." More silence.

"So, did you and Mark break up?" I whispered.

"Long time ago."

"Why?"

"It turned out we aren't into the same things. Like, at all," she said, chewing her steak and chasing it with a big gulp of cabernet.

"That's it," snapped Bruce. "Mindy, switch places with Tom and come sit next to me. I told you if you made this dinner all about girl time I'd split you two up."

"No! I'm sorry! Don't!" she said. "It won't happen again, Bruce."

Back to silence.

Without any talking, I took it upon myself to piece things together: Bruce was clearly the ringleader of this "golf group," which appeared to be an Old Man's Club. They all wore wedding bands (even Bruce), Mindy was exceptionally well dressed (beyond her means), and she obviously had dumped Mark to explore whatever lifestyle these guys could offer, which, apparently, included golfing around the globe, private jets, expensive steak dinners, and…big Fendi purses.

Just thing, it clicked how I could go about getting some much-needed answers.

"Cute purse," I said, as my journalism instincts kicked in.

"Thanks! Bruce got it for me. And this new gold iPhone," she said, pulling it out of her bag. "It's not on the market yet."

"Hey, careful with that," he said. "That's not for public use, you know."

"I know," she repeated.

"I certainly hope there's not more than one number saved in there, Mindy."

It was evident that Mindy was Bruce's mistress; and that the gold iPhone was his direct line to his much-younger escort.

Mindy rolled her eyes as Bruce chirped on.

"Emily, do you want to go to the ladies room with me?" asked Mindy.

At that point, there wasn't much I wouldn't do to leave that table, so I happily obliged leaving my barely-eaten steak to be cleared by our white-coat waiter. Normally, I'd have a huge problem parting with food like that, but realizing I was in the middle of a prostitution ring caused my appetite to suddenly escape me.

"Here, let's go into this one." Mindy grabbed my hand, walked me passed the bathroom attendant, and into the larger handicapped stall, before slamming the door shut and sliding the lock shut.

"Oh my god, he's so controlling, isn't he? Sometimes it's just so ridiculous," she said as she was fumbling around in her purse and setting things on top of the toilet paper dispenser.

"How exactly did you meet Bruce, Mindy?"

Mindy never turned to face me as she talked. She was still preoccupied with digging through her Fendi, but she opened up for the first time since 7:10 PM

"He was golfing one day with the guys. I pulled the cart around to offer him a drink and he ended up buying me one. Well, a few, actually. And we, just, we had a good time."

I nodded, not quite sure what to say.

"He's nothing like Mark. Bruce is a man. He owns a private jet company and makes, like, a bajillion dollars. He can fly wherever he wants, whenever he wants. He doesn't even live in South Carolina, he just likes to golf there. So he flies the guys up on Saturdays just to get a round in."

"Wow, that's pretty luxurious of him," I said. "Where does he live?"

"Him and his wife live in Miami. She's a stay-at-home-mom and watches their twin boys. They're so cute. Want to see a pic?"

Oh my god, how do I make it stop, I thought. But that was only the beginning. Things were about to go even more wrong.

"There it is. Found it," she said, taking out a baggie of cocaine. Mark was right. Mindy had lost her shit. Was this the same girl whose good times capped at Rum and Cokes just a few years ago?

"Please don't judge me," she said, as she scooped a little bit of cocaine onto a key. "This is called a bump."

Snort.

"Want one?"

"I don't do cocaine," I answered firmly.

"That's fine."

Snort.

I wondered if the bathroom attendant—or the girl who just slammed the stall door next to us shut—had any idea what was going on just feet away.

"God, that one burned. Woo!"

"Mindy, you done? We should get back to dinner."

Part of me was scared we'd get caught and part of me was scared Bruce was going to get angry we were taking so long and find some pervy way to punish us.

"Yup," she said, grabbing some toilet paper off the roll and wiping her nose. "That was why I was late, by the way. I had no idea it'd be this hard to score coke in Chicago."

My mind was as blown as Mindy's nostrils and just like that, we were back at the dinner table. The guys had ordered dessert and after-dinner drinks.

"So, Emily, are you golfing with us tomorrow? Mindy told us you're an excellent golfer."

Well Mindy told me you're a lying, cheating, scumbag, so…

"Oh, no. I can't. I haven't played in years and besides, I have to go to work."

Bruce and all of his friends laughed at my excuse.

"You have work?" he asked like it was some foreign concept.

"Yes. I have to go to my job tomorrow."

"Take the day off," Bruce suggested demanded.

"I can't do that. I have a lot of people who depend on me being there. I don't have any vacation racked up. I can't just...not show up."

Where was my wine? Why was it empty? God, help me.

"How much do you make a day, Emily?" asked Bruce as he sipped his port.

"Excuse me?" I haven't been to many dinner parties in my day, but I do know asking a stranger, a lady at that, how much they may isn't exactly kosher conversation for the table.

"You heard me. How much. Do you. Make. In a day?"

"I don't know—but it's not about the money. I simply ca . . ."

"$5,000?"

I didn't answer. And also: LOL, no.

"$10,000?"

I still didn't answer.

"Emily, how about this. Twenty-grand."

"Twenty grand what?" I asked.

"I will give you $20,000 to come with us tomorrow. A car will pick you up at 7AM. Our tee time is at 8. We'll finish around 2 PM Then, me and the boys will get on my private jet to New York, Mindy will be off to South Carolina, and I will have you flown back to Chicago all before the sun goes down."

"Twenty grand and you get to sleep in your own comfy bed by midnight? I would do it," said a coked-out Mindy.

Why was I not surprised?

"I can't, Bruce. I'm sorry. I just...can't."

"I seriously don't know how you're saying no to him, Emily," Mindy mumbled in disbelief as she swirled her wine glass. "This is going to be the biggest mistake of your life."

How was I saying no? She was acting like this was a matter of willpower. It wasn't. It was a matter of wanting to live to see another day. Sober or high as a kite, how could she not see that this had "bad idea" smeared all over it?

"Mindy...talk to you girl, please," Bruce demanded.

Mindy leaned in and pulled me close to her.

"This is how it all started for me. Bruce asked me to get on his plane after a round of golf with these guys, we flew to Miami, I made ten-grand, and I came home later on the same day. Now look. iPhone. Fendi. This dress. This hair. And that's only the start of it. Do your wardrobe a favor and say yes."

I sat back in my seat and looked at Bruce who was a little too eagerly waiting for my reply.

"Let me ask you this," I began. "What exactly do I have to do for twenty-grand?"

Let it be known that it wasn't like I was actually considering this. By no means was this a legitimate business endeavor. I just wanted to hear straight from the horse's mouth what he was looking for out of this deal.

Bruce took a slow sip of his drink and replied: "You just have to be your sweet, little self."

Why was I not buying that? Like, at all.

I was my "sweet, little self" every day at my job and the only thing I had to show for it was the chance to sneak out five minutes early if my boss just so happened to run to the bathroom at the same time I wanted to bolt. I wasn't dumb. I knew that twenty-thousand dollars didn't come that easily—not even if I scratched off a lotto ticket right in front of the 7-Eleven cashier himself.

At that point, I had to make a decision. The answer to his proposition was most certainly going to a no, but I didn't want my unfavorable reply to truncate this night before the bill was paid. Furthermore, just because I wasn't playing a round of golf and boarding a private jet the next day, did not mean that the night had to end. Let's be real. In the world of juicy gossip, this was a big, fat orange. We have Mindy—the former catholic school girl turned coke head—inviting me to a dinner with a pimp, Bruce, and his posse of middle-aged losers—asking me to board a private jet wherein I will most like have to strip or fellate someone, but in turn will receive the sum of one year's worth of my very-expensive college tuition. And to think I was worried that Mindy would be mad I made out with her ex-boyfriend. What was his name again? Oh, right. Irrelevant.

This was all too rich for words. So, I played my hand as follows:

"Look, the answer is no for tomorrow, although the offer sounds..."

"Attractive?" said Bruce.

"Intriguing. I'll give you intriguing," I bartered. "But, I'll say this: I would be delighted to attend an after-party, assuming you'll be having one this evening?"

Gently leading the witness was all I really needed to do in this situation, because the next thing I knew, Bruce had closed out our $3,500 tab (on his black American Express card) and asked the waitress to bag-up six bottles of Dom Pérignon and a handful of expensive cigars to go.

"Where are you staying, by the way?" I asked Bruce.

"Doubletree. Presidential Suite."

While I wasn't impressed with the first part of that response (the Doubletree? Really?), the second part meant something to me. Working in the hotel industry, it was somewhat ironic that I, myself, had never seen a "presidential suite" at any hotel, ever. If anything, this was research and development for my job. At least, that's what I told myself when I got into the stretch limousine that picked us up outside the restaurant.

A few minutes later, I knew something was wrong—terribly wrong. And while you might think it was because Mindy was now whipping her hair around, giving a lap dance to one of the guys, while chugging Dom P straight from the bottle like it was a sip of Ice Mountain, it was actually the fact that we were getting on the highway. The only Doubletree in the city that I knew of was a few blocks from the restaurant—no expressway travel required. We were now cruising at a swift 75 mph and heading west on I-290.

"Um, what hotel are you at again?" I shouted over the techno music Mindy had the driver put on.

"Doubletree…Schaumburg. Don't worry, we'll be there in about twenty, and then the party can really start."

Schaumburg? That was a western suburb even further away than where my parents lived. In fact, I could wave to them from the interstate as we passed their house. This was not going according to plan—not by a long shot. I went from "relax, I got this" to "totally fucked" in a matter of seconds. My heart began to race and my palms got sweaty. I felt like I was at my eighth grade dance again—except this time, there were all sorts of illegal activities going on, including prostitution and drug possession. Let me tell you, not as fun as it sounds.

Ok, Emily, think, I said to myself. I had to figure out something—namely, a way to get back home, fast. Bruce practically had a vice grip on me from across the table in a public restaurant, and now I was with him in a moving car that neither of us was driving. How did I lose control of this situation so badly?

Arriving at the hotel, we immediately took a private express elevator up to the 22nd floor. By this point, the other guys had dispersed to their rooms, so it was just the three of us: me, Mindy, and Bruce. I was convinced this would either end up in an orgy or a riveting game of Clue.

When we walked into the penthouse suite, my breath was somewhat taken away. I could see the whole city from miles away standing in the dining area of this apartment. I escaped the throws of Mindy and Bruce and took it upon myself to take a tour of the sweeping floorplan. One room led into the next until I was finally back at the entertaining area. And believe you-me, Mindy was taking full advantage of it.

In the amount of time it took me to walk the unit, she had managed to connect her phone into an MP3 player, put on some rap music, and strip. That's right. 50 Cent was on and Mindy's bra was off. I was convinced that this what Mark really meant when he'd said, "Mindy went psycho." At this point, I was more than willing to wave the white flag and admit that I was wrong. Mark was right. The Mindy we once knew was a goner. And at that, he wasn't being a bitter ex when he gave me the low down, he was being a heartbroken and flabbergasted individual (and rightfully so), who was just trying to get a grip on normality and score a make-out session with someone other than his ho-bag ex-girlfriend. Was this really happening?

As if you needed me to tell you, Bruce was completely infatuated with this whole song and dance (emphasis on dance) and I saw it as my chance to bail. I had no idea how I'd get home; determining that winding up on the other side of the door alone would be half the battle. Making my way to the foyer, Bruce caught me in his peripheral slithering out and chased after me. Fuck!

"Hey, hey, hey! Where are you going?" he asked.

Mindy sauntered over, topless, drunk, and high.

"I have got to get going. It's almost midnight. I'm getting tired,' I said.

"I have something for that," Mindy said, holding up a baggie of coke.

"I'm sorry, I have to go."

"Shit, girl. Then give me a hug," slurred Mindy, as she pressed her bare ta-tas into my chest. "Good seeing you."

"You, too," I said as her nipples pushed into mine.

Just when I didn't think my thin romper wardrobe choice couldn't get any worse, I was wrong.

"Bruce, give her a fucking fifty, okay? She's got to get going," demanded Mindy, the apparent voice of reason, before she walked back over to her makeshift stripper pole (a.k.a. a lamp in the living room).

I didn't want to wait around any longer, but I deemed the cash totally necessary considering an Uber back to the city at midnight wouldn't be cheap. So, I stood there as I watched Bruce dig through his wallet, searching for a fifty among a stack of crisp one hundreds.

Finally, he found one. I shamefully stuck out my hand to receive it, but instead of handing it to me like a normal person, he took it upon himself to pull out the top of my strapless romper and drop it down my shirt.

"Have a good night, brown-eyed girl," he said as he walked back to his play-thing.

I stood there numb for a good thirty seconds. Unscathed, but in complete shock at the reality I had just semi-voluntarily exposed myself to. And then...I fucking high-tailed it down the hallway, into the elevator, and got the fuck out of Dodge.

~ ~ ~

"I see you made it back alive," said Andrew when I returned home around 1AM He was in the same place where I left him: on the couch, playing video games, and eating something that smelled like it started as a powder before it was microwaved.

"Barely. Oh my god, you have got to hear what just happened. Pause that shit," I ordered as I obstructed his view of the television and proceeded to tell him the truth, the whole truth, and nothing but the truth.

His response?

"I would have taken the twenty-grand, Em."

CHAPTER SEVEN/LESSON SEVEN

- Online dating (a.k.a. free dinner with a side of shame)

Having passed on the most lucrative round of golf known to (wo)man-kind, survey said: I was still single. Not only that, but it was glaringly obvious that I hadn't met anyone close to suitable for my post-Trent match. What I had done, though, was build up the necessary momentum to keep trying. After all, I was firmly back on the wagon, which was half the battle. And in an unparalleled moment of positivity, I resolved that I couldn't let a series of epic failures keep me from trotting on.

From schemers, to terrible kissers, to felons, pimps, and everything in between—I came to accept that biting into a few bad apples was just part of the bargain. So, to make things easier, I decided to narrow-in on the locally grown goods. I decided to try it…a.k.a. online dating.

I have to admit, I never thought I'd try it, mostly because I never thought I would need it. In my not-so-humble opinion, I considered myself a fairly attractive person with an education, a sense of humor, and a nice family. I mean, how hard would it be to randomly meet a single guy who happened to be looking for normal stuff like that? Let's collectively answer this one together: hard. Very hard.

So, one day, I took inventory of the 30 internet browser tabs I had open and realized that 95 percent of my life was conducted online. I read gossip, I finalized shoe orders, I paid bills, and so much more. And most of this online activity, to the best of my knowledge, was done securely and instantly from the comfort of my kitchen counter.

That's when between scouring TMZ and finalizing my order on Rue La La, I decided to open a new browser window and pull up Match.com. After all, I knew some family, coworkers, and a handful of friends that had tried it out—many of whom wound up dating, engaged, or married. Not to mention, the god damn commercial for it came on every seven minutes when I had CNN on in the background. It was about time I gave in.

But really, the most alluring thing about trying Match was the fact that flirting with someone on this thing in no way, shape, or form, required blotting papers or pants, which was an excellent fit for my lifestyle at the time. And I figured that if I already did the majority of my shopping on the World Wide Web, then I'd probably be pretty good at picking out a new boyfriend and adding him to my cart.

Fuck it, let's do this.

Thankfully, in just a few short steps, and without any initial costs, had set up a quick-and-dirty "free" profile and was set to roam around the site and peruse the puppies in the window.

As one would expect, I felt like a bit of a voyeur at first, which coupled with Dr. Phil's "it's-okay-to-look" slogan plastered all over the page, made me feel as though this site was one step away from midget porn. But like anything that's taboo, I knew I couldn't look away just yet.

The sensory overload was undeniable and I quickly likened the whole thing to a Black Friday sale. The merchandise was perfectly fine, but in order for me to bring home something (someone) new and shiny, I'd have to brave the crowds, question American values, and be slightly uncomfortable the whole time.

Exploring this fetish a little further, I began to fill out some search fields and set some filters. The next thing I knew I was checking boxes to signify what type of body I desired, whether it was a deal-breaker, and how much money I wanted my potential mate to make—talk about a picky girl's dream! Though they didn't offer a check box for "can't have a criminal record," I could really appreciate the other criterion about which they were letting me have a say in. At that moment, I was sold on the concept. Sure, the right to vote was wonderfully empowering, but the opportunity to dictate a body type on a match-making website was LIFE.

It was a beautiful thing, to sit in the privacy of my own home and, with the simple click of a mouse, be as shallow as I wanted, without any judgment. For the first time in a long time, I felt completely stress-free and totally in control of the dating game. As I flew through the search options, creating parameters for my ideal match, I had no idea who would come back but I knew he sure as hell it would not be some "currently separated," "stocky," "bald" guy with "two kids" who "smoked" and "liked cats."

Moments later, page-one of my results had returned…and it was not as robust as maybe I had hoped.

For starters, from the looks of things, Joe Jonas was not on Match.com. Nor was Nick. Or their distant cousins.

Maybe finding a mate isn't all about outward appearances, but wouldn't it behoove the online dating CEOs to develop an algorithm that put their best faces forward? It's like Google search results. You've got the top three slots to speak right to me or I'm just going with whatever the first hit back from WebMD says—even if it suggests the redness around my eye could mean I'm pregnant.

Besides the looks department being slightly, shall I say, "understocked," there were other off-putting attributes, such as corny usernames and dating headline typos. Granted, usernames for anything other than a late 90s AOL Instant Messenger account seem ridiculous, "50ShadesOfLove" and "BetterThanACat" were borderline unforgivable.

Also, where was the "Fuck That" check box for ruling out guys with poor grammar? I mean, "I just want to be you're number one" or "their is never a bad time for love"—really? Really?

Who knew that a site meant to help me find exactly what I wanted would end up just giving me a whole slew of new things to pick apart? Dr. Phil never mentioned that.

To make matters worse, little did I know, my newly created profile was showing up in search results for men who had "paid" accounts with the site. And even though I did not have access to all of Match's features with my freebie set up, users who did were able to send me e-mails with their full access.

As the messages came through, I could only see who sent them (a little thumbnail accompanied the subject line of the note), but not what the message said. I wouldn't get to unlock that feature until I forked over some cash for a full-blown subscription.

It was like Prince Charming was ringing my doorbell and professing his love, but all I could do was stare through the peephole without hearing a single word he was saying…unless I gave up my credit card information.

As a few more dings came through (behold, the power of a photo from a time when I cared about combing my hair), my vulnerability, curiosity, and need for constant male attention was at an all-time high. Maybe these online dating CEOs were actually on to something because at that moment, I was convinced this company was functioning on one of the smartest business models ever.

I had to log off before I got sucked in.

~ ~ ~

My abstinence only lasted a few days, as later that week, in between completing a Yelp review for a Korean BBQ joint and paying my cable bill, I decided to log back into my Match profile and comb through a fresh round of search results. Lo and behold, a good-looking-on-paper guy appeared. He was everything I needed: brown hair and eyes, a straight smile, and tall enough to reach the things that I couldn't on shelves at the grocery store. Everything in his profile was spelled correctly, even the last sentence—a shout-out to his best friend, his mother. Sold.

I wanted to reach out to him with an e-mail right away, but the most I could do without a full-blown membership was just "wink" at him, the Match.com equivalent of a Facebook "poke." Even though it would be free to send, I refused to start this off on a creepy note. So instead, I pulled up the calculator app on my phone. It was time to see if my budget allowed room for boyfriend-hunting.

Though I hadn't done math since the 10th grade, I needed to figure out what my ROI would look like if I made the commitment to join the dating site—and for the first time since high school, I attempted to do some basic mathematics.

If I were to invest $60 in a three-month membership, and average one date a week, with a median food/drink bill of $50 for two people ($25 a head), that'd be approximately twelve dates and $300 in free food and beverage. Less the sign-on fee, I was looking at netting approximately $240 in waived nourishment costs.

So, whether I wound up wed, or just fed, I determined a three-month trial was worth it in the end. I pulled out my credit card and built a profile under the alias "Bel232", the exact letter-number combo printed on my college ID card from freshman year. I mean, why not pay homage to a time in my life when I gave the same amount of fucks (zero) as the version of me who was signing up for online dating?

Enter, Patrick.

Patrick was the name of the strapping young lad whose thumbnail-sized photo, and rather adorable profile, lured me into this monster of a dating site. He was a solid seven in the looks department, possibly more if I could figure out how to zoom, with a profile that indicated he had some grasp on how to properly use the words "their" and "there." And with that, we were well on the way to a first date.

Thanks to another half-stalkerish, half-useful feature of the site, I could tell that Patrick had viewed my profile and even marked me as a favorite. The kid obviously wanted to play ball, so I pitched him an e-mail. Of course I realized that my grandmother would roll over in her grave knowing that I made the first move, but I figured I had no other option. This was a like a Groupon deal: I had to act quickly if this special was going to be "on."

Hi there,

New to this, but wanted to toss you a line. I'm a writer, so even though e-mails are easy for me, I'd prefer a real, in-person date. Free on Tuesday?

-Emily

Sent.

And what a thrill it was! Might it wind up with my rape and murder? Sure, but what didn't those days…

Also, let's talk about Tuesdays.

I decided Tuesdays were the best for date nights, as it's an all-around, no-pressure day. Think about it: you're not juiced up for the weekend on a Tuesday, yet you aren't stranded in the middle of a workweek. You aren't dealing with a case of the Mondays and you aren't competing with Thursday night college football. You've respected Friday and Saturday as the prime real estate that they are, leaving Tuesday as your ultimate wingman.

"Tuesday works," Patrick confirmed. "Really looking forward to it," he added.

The best part? I was too.

Keeping things neutral, we decided to first meet at a very busy, very public coffee shop downtown before deciding where to go to eat and drink.

Even though the plan seemed easy going enough, so many thoughts were racing through my head as I sunk into an armchair at Starbucks and watched one person after the next walk through the doors.

Again, my inner dialogue went nuts. Was I ready for this? What if he doesn't look like his picture? What if we don't recognize each other? Oh, was that him? No, that was a woman. What if he sees me and isn't interested? What if he asks me what's wrong with me? Wait a minute. What's wrong with him? What if he doesn't show up at all? What if he tries to put something in my drink? How long is this gig supposed to last? Should I have told someone I was out with a stranger?

The noise in my head quieted when a man wearing an impeccable trench coat walked through the doors. Spending the last six years in Nebraska where the only men's style I was exposed to was either camouflage overalls or whatever Trent was wearing, I was blown away at this man's clear ability to dog-ear a page in GQ and follow up with a Neiman Marcus sales associate accordingly. Yes, his jacket was that unbelievable. Even better was the fact that this dapper-as-fuck individual didn't step up to the counter to place an order right away. He rubber-necked a bit, meaning: I just might have been the vanilla latte he ordered.

Moments later, he locked eyes with me and a smile crept into the sides of his lips. It was him. It was Patrick.

I wasn't quite sure just how to greet my mail-ordered date and we somehow ended up doing an estranged-uncle-side-hug. I deserved a penalty for letting that happen and prayed silently that weirdness would not to set the tone for the rest of the evening.

"So," he started, "I came up with a few places around here that we could go depending on what you're in the mood for."

Options. Pre-planning. Thought. Consideration. I liked it!

As it turned out, "what I was in the mood for" was going to have to wait until at least the third date and an appointment with my European waxer, but for the time being, we settled on a multi-level bar nearby that was known for its swanky drink menu and delicious after-work apps.

Things went well over the next few hours. The conversation was flowing and he asked a lot of smart questions, keeping the conversation mostly about me. I know they say it's rude to talk about yourself, but I crave the opportunity to paint a picture of myself to a total stranger. It's as if all of my memories, experiences, and opinions about life suddenly take the form of an à la carte menu and I can just pick and choose what mash-up of me this person will get. There's something very joyous about someone never having to know I didn't make out with a boy until I was seventeen, or that I had braces for a quarter of my life. Therapists, go ahead. Have a field day.

Anyhow, as the date wrapped, he wasted no time claiming the bill. It was nice to see a man aggressively handle a tab. Ours I imagine was around $120 for our few rounds of cocktails, fancy food, and generous tip. Though I would never consider myself a gold-digger, the thought did cross my mind that I was already ahead on my fiscal goals in regards to joining the site, which felt great. So did the fact that the gesture to pay for me indicated his financial assets were better than that of a fourteen year old.

It also felt great when Patrick walked me back to my train, held my hand, and asked to see me again soon. Could I really have struck gold on my first go at this?

Either way, it was Tuesday for the win. Good old Tuesday.

~ ~ ~

Date number two was scheduled about a week later. In the interim, several Match.com features were biting me in the ass. Patrick could tell when I logged on and how often, which I could imagine felt like a bit of a slap in the face even if I was simply signing on to devoid my inbox of creepy messages. Needless to say, the Jewish guilt that runs through my blood kicked in and I started to feel like real dick. "Dr. Phil said it was okay to look," I reminded myself ad nauseum.

A day or so later, Patrick shot me a text message telling me his Match membership was terming and he would not be renewing. I knew what he was implying. That he had found what he was looking for. His astute sureness, coupled with my crippling fear of missing out on other dates, made me feel uncomfortable and at a loss for words with how to reply. He knew I had just signed on for a three-month membership, I told him that. He also knew that he was my first date, so it seemed unreasonable that I would terminate my account in tandem just because.

Yes, Patrick was a win. But he didn't sweep the series despite that amaze-balls trench coat. For me, it was going to take more than just one date, two mini-burgers, and some strong-ass cocktails to be bought out of this contract. So, I ghosted on a reply and hoped he wouldn't bring it up again.

Our next date was planned for a Sunday afternoon. I wasn't entirely comfortable with this time slot. By no means was I religious, but a holy day? And by that, I mean a day reserved for nursing hangovers and ordering greasy food from diners you'd otherwise never step foot in.

Regardless, I took his "next available appointment" and showed up at the meeting spot: a Chipotle in Lincoln Park.

Yes, our second date was at the McDonald's of Mexican food. Trust me, I was aware of the downgrade that date-number-two was starting off with.

Moments after a homeless man had asked the cashier for the key to the bathroom, in walked a man with a five o'clock shadow. With him, he carried the faint smell of stale beer in the threads of his plain, black cable-knit sweater. I couldn't believe it was Patrick. Did his stylist get laid off? Was he out of razors? Call me superficial, but was I baited and switched?

"So, where do you want to go?" asked Patrick.

No plan this time? Was he punishing me for not forfeiting my membership? Don't read into this, Emily. Not here, not now.

"Um, I don't care." I was clearly being that passive-aggressive, borderline disinterested girl most guys can't stand, but couldn't help it. In an effort to salvage our encounter, I changed my attitude around and sweetly suggested, "Somewhere quiet where we can catch up."

Patrick hailed a cab and directed the driver to an intersection unknown to me. Next thing I knew, we were in the beer garden of one of the busiest bars in Wrigleyville, watching a Cubs game on a flat-screen with the lingering scent of fried tortilla chips stalking us. So much for a romantic setting.

As I settled in, I immediately resented this Sunday afternoon hang slot and missed my beloved Tuesday nights. But before I could sob into a napkin and have a total basic-bitch meltdown, our beers came and his phone rang. He took the call. Which wasn't rude at all.

Kill me now.

"Holy crap. You're kidding me. Right now? I mean, I could. But I just sat down at the bar with Emily."

There are very few instances in life that I'd rather be referred to as "a chick" or "some girl," but this was one of them. I didn't know who was on the other line, but I couldn't think of a reason for them to know who "Emily" was so soon.

Patrick rushed through the conversation and hung up the phone.

"Who was that?" I asked.

"It was my brother-in-law. He's in the hospital with my older sister. She's in labor!"

"Wow! That's crazy. You better go. Don't worry, I'll pay for our drinks," I offered.

"No way," he retorted.

"No, really it's no big deal. Bud Light is on special, it's going to be like eight bucks or something..."

"No, I meant, there's no way I'm leaving without you. All my family will be there, you'll get to see the baby. This is an incredible opportunity to meet my folks, and lord knows they will love putting a name to the face finally."

Wait what.

Finally?

It had been less than a week.

I didn't quite know how to respond to this. I just knew that a front-row seat to a stranger giving birth wasn't par for the course for a second date. Did he really think I was ready to see his sister crown, let alone meet his parents? What was I supposed to do? Hold one leg back while his mother held the other as we told his sister to breathe through the pain? Hell, I needed to breathe through the pain of this proposition. I'm all about spontaneity, and I have been known to watch an episode or two of A Baby Story, but the impromptu role of "birthing coach" didn't seem like something I was quite ready for. I had gone on approximately 1.25 dates with this guy and didn't even know his last name. Clearly, the only miracle of life here was me finding a way to end this thing. Immediately.

"I really think you should just go. I'll take care of the bill. You call an Uber. Then...text me to let me know how it goes later. Okay?"

He just stared at me like I was explaining to a fourth grader how to get on a bus and go to school. I didn't mean to speak to him like he was an idiot, but I feared that if I didn't spell out the exact next steps, I'd somehow wind up squashed in the backseat of a stranger's Honda Civic with an "It's a Girl!" balloon blocking the rearview mirror.

"Okay. I'll call you later," he said.

I said text me, but whatever.

Patrick then got up from his chair to leave, but not without planting a see-you-later-honey kiss on my lips.

I immediately wondered two things: when did I become his girlfriend, and what did we do for our six-month anniversary? It was our second date, which had lasted about twenty-five minutes mind you. I've made out with strangers on the dancefloor longer than that.

As I watched him drive off in the Uber, I found peace in the fact that I was left alone with my beer and his: a consolation prize for enduring all this unforeseen weirdness. I know women are supposed to be the ones rushing to the altar, but Patrick was certainly the one doodling my name in his notebook with little hearts all around it. At that, I downed both of the shitty brews and paid the tab, which was symbolic of what I needed to do with Patrick.

It was time to close out.

CHAPTER EIGHT/LESSON EIGHT

• Really good-looking people usually have really bad habits

Let me tell you a little something about guys on dating websites: there's a whole lot of average going on. Average looks. Average personalities. Average profiles. Average abilities to use emoticons in an appropriate way. You get the point.

Also, spoiler alert: most every guy is going to be a "laid back," "easy-going," "simple guy" who "hates drama" and is "uncomfortable talking about himself." You're welcome. I just saved you sixty bucks and the nausea.

But when Logan announced himself in his dating headline as "The Hottest Guy on Match.com" and had the profile pic to back it up, my interest was immediately piqued.

For those wondering, yes, I—like you—have learned valuable lessons from Max and Nev of MTV's Catfish and absolutely made sure to run Logan's shit through a reverse Google-image search just to be sure he was who he said he was...at least in the pictures he uploaded. And lo and behold, the hottie checked out.

Now back to his egotistical headline. Was it kind of douchey? Yes, totally. Did it mean he'd probably send me a dick-pic within two weeks? Sure. But he was making a compelling statement and coupling it with bonafide, shoulders-up photographic evidence which was enough for me to write him an e-mail.

As I began typing, I was interrupted by my own thoughts: what was this guy doing advertising himself on the Internet? Logan was the type of guy you could throw in a bar on a Friday night and every single girl would go straight into vulture mode. Did he not realize he literally could put an end to his Match.com stint, save himself the membership fee (plus the cost of food), and have his pick of the litter simply by tossing on slim-fit shirt and, I don't know, going outside?

So, naturally, I figured there must be something wrong with him. What could it be? Used to be a woman? Heroin addict? Super fan of Jesus Christ? The curiosity ate away at me until it dawned on me that he could be thinking the same thing about me, to which my answer would have of course been, "nothing, I'm literally totally normal and fine."

Recommitted to the cause, I continued to work on my e-mail to the hottest guy on Match.com. Carefully coining each sentence, I was essentially pulling together an RFP for a date with Logan. If I ended up hearing back from him, at least I knew it was hard earned.

Sure enough, I did hear back. And the response was favorable, minus the part where he told me he was twenty eight years old and working full time as a cashier at The Home Depot (the upside there obviously being the discount on potted plants for my back porch). Regardless, all was forgotten and forgiven when he extended an invite to grab food and drink at a super swank sushi restaurant downtown. I couldn't wait to order a deep-fried imitation crab and avocado roll with this guy.

I have to admit, I was a little nervous for this one, and not because I had been known to eat sushi with a fork in public. But, rather, because I was wondering how my physical appearance would compare to that of the hottest man on Match in real life. As I made my way to the restaurant, I found myself collecting last-minute feedback from as many reflective surfaces as possible: the windows at a 7-Eleven, a mirror on a parked Vespa, the front-facing camera on my phone, etc. All appeared to look good, but then again, appeared is only as good as the last makeup tutorial you watched on YouTube. And for me, that was "Kylie Jenner full-face drug-store knock-off routine."

Just steps from the restaurant, I managed to lock eyes with a man who I certainly hoped was Logan. Or if not, the next Bachelor on ABC. He had captivating brown eyes and a dimply smile and was sitting at a table in the outdoor eating section all alone. With a slight wave, he confirmed his identity and I shouted Yassss in my head.

"You found me," he said.

Yes, I most certainly did. And not only did I find him, I found myself smitten upon first sight. It was as if I had died and gone to Match.com heaven. I only wish our initial greeting could have been filmed for one of their commercials, because this was the shit that would make people into instant believers.

We had a fabulous table close to the bar where an expert mixologist was creating some of the most beautiful things I've ever seen poured into martini glasses. The chef, also just a few feet away, was rolling sushi in an open kitchen, making it easy for him to check on us and send off-the-menu items over to our table on a whim. From the excellent food, to the crafty drinks, to the bathroom attendants who looked like supermodels, this date was baller on all fronts.

We talked about your run of the mill first date stuff. He made me laugh and I genuinely felt comfortable with him. When he asked if I wanted to check out his condo after we finished our meals, I was a little surprised. Not that I found his request forward for a first date, but that I really had no hesitations about leaving the restaurant and heading home with him. Next thing I knew, we were walking arm-in-arm toward his high rise in the West Loop. It was all very Emma Stone-Ryan Gosling-La-La-Land.

"Do you see that little place at the corner?" he asked in reference to a small shop resembling a hole-in-the-wall mini-mart.

"Which one? The one with the light-up 'massage' sign? Yeah, I see it. Why?" I replied.

"I get Happy Ending massages there."

He's funny. A little brash. Unexpected. Always keeping an eye out for innuendos. He's just like me, I thought, as I waited for the punch line.

He kept silent and we kept walking. And then it hit me: there wasn't even so much as a "just kidding" in sight.

So, wait. Come again (no pun intended), Logan?

In our silence, I began to tear this apart. That was a joke, right? Should I laugh? If I laugh, will it perpetuate more bad humor? Oh god, he was serious. Does this make him a deviant? What other weird/sort-of-illegal stuff is he into? I can't bring this guy home to my family.

None of this was congruent with my plan to become his girlfriend and use his discount on paint for my bedroom. Why, Logan, WHY.

He sensed the gears in my brain turning and finally intercepted my silence.

"Does that bother you?" he asked.

Still shell shocked, I said nothing back.

"Look, some people smoke a cigarette when they leave the office, others pour themselves a stiff drink. I sometimes pop in for a Happy Ending. It's really not a big deal, we all have needs."

Masturbate, Logan. Save your money and your dignity and masturbate.

In fact, I would have judged him far less if he had announced that he liked to beat it every now and again when he felt stressed. I mean, who doesn't, right? Regardless, any conversation surrounding who should touch his penis, and when, why, and for how much and how long, was not at all appropriate at this point in our meeting. The iceberg had been hit, now it was only a matter of time before this ship would sink.

Yes, he was pretty. But his bold claim to fame on Match.com should have come with some fine print indicating that his cute came with a little crazy. I, under no circumstances, could seriously consider dating (read: spending the next five minutes with) with someone who may or may not have had a punch card for an XXX massage parlor in his wallet. I had to get away from this borderline-stranger who was campaigning to bring back hand jobs, a form of intimacy that dies after you graduate high school.

That's when he sensed he was losing me. As such, he threw this out there: "Don't act like you wouldn't get a Happy Ending massage if they had them for girls." Cue ship cracking in half and going down, fast.

Despite his failed attempt to normalize his bizarre hobby, the answer was still no. The only people who I pay to be in proximity to my privates are my waxer and my gynie. No "masseuses" allowed, no matter how happy the ending may be. And that was my final answer.

At that point, I looked at the time on my phone, pretended to be more shocked about it being 10:30 on a Tuesday than about his hand-job fetish, and doubled-back to the subway station alone. Upon returning home, I promptly deleted his phone number, blocked him online, and showered off.

Ladies and gentlemen, how about a hand for Logan.

CHAPTER NINE/LESSON NINE

- Embrace the theme of your twenties: "Welcome to the shit-show"

One Friday night, Katie invited me to attend a seemingly classy event at the Museum of Contemporary Art. The event, dubbed "First Fridays," was a once-a-month, after-work get-together that showcased a particular artist's work alongside delicious Wolfgang Puck appetizers. This particular Friday was Calder and banana-themed food: nothing like abstract art and phallic delicacies to kick off the weekend, amiright?

    The night started off innocently enough with a ten-dollar admission fee and a couple glasses of warm, cheap wine served out of a plastic cup like the kind you get on a Southwest flight. After my buzz set in, I accidentally deep-throated a chocolate covered banana that was part of a tray of passed apps (hey, how would you have eaten it?). My ability to take it down without so much as needing a napkin from the server afterward acted like a magnet, drawing two middle-aged Jewish men from Manhattan over to where Katie and I were standing. Pretentious conversation with our new best friends, the ambiguously gay duo, ensued.

    As the sun set, the discussion moved towards our respective summer homes in the Hamptons. While talking about the best lobster roll in Montauk, it occurred to me that I was slightly intoxicated. And for the first time in a while, this particular buzz was not due to someone doing me wrong. I was a happy drunk, for once, surrounded by good friends, new friends, art, and finger food. The sum of its parts felt great.

Around 9 PM, the event started to thin out. Katie and I had to make a game-time decision regarding our next steps. Hanging with the Jews was out of the question. The more we drank, the more this Friday night would inevitably feel like Thanksgiving dinner with my extended family and that wasn't my idea of a good time.

"You want to go to Ralph?" asked Katie.

She was talking about the bar at the Ralph Lauren restaurant on Michigan Avenue. This place was a beacon for wealthy, WASP-y people. I was neither, but clearly this was her night and that was her watering hole of choice, which left me no choice but to dial back my Jew and head for the land of French martinis and madras-print everything.

At Ralph Lauren, the servers slick back their hair, speak with fake accents, and wear pressed linen from head-to-toe. There's no PC way to say this, but the interior looks like a slave owner's library. Most every man dining there has white hair and a nicely groomed mustache and the women who accompany them have likely never consumed a bottle of Barefoot wine.

So when Katie and I rolled in and our combined ages were still less than the median of whomever was in the dining room, it was apparent we were a breath of fresh air for the bartenders, Danny and Russell. And by the way, that's what you get at Ralph: a bartender for each of you. The gents promptly presented Katie and I with drink menus and their business cards. Yes, their business cards. Katie, taking charge yet again, politely declined the menus (those are for amateurs) and ordered confidently for the both of us. Right away, this was starting off better than most of my recent first dates.

"Russell, I'll have a Ketel One martini, up with a twist, and extra cold, please. And Danny, meet Emily."

"How do you do?" Danny said, extending a royal hand.

"Emily will have a French martini, chilled just the same."

"Extra cold?" he mirrored.

"Like my soul," she said with a wink.

With their marching orders, the soldiers got to work on Operation Intoxication. Waiting for my mammoth martini to make its way over, I took a moment to soak in the scenery, observing that I was very clearly not in

Omaha anymore. No one was wearing a Husker's jersey, there weren't stale pretzels on my table, and I doubt anyone had protested abortion outside a Walmart earlier in the day. It was nice.

Our drinks arrived and there was no other option for toasting: "To us and our fabulous lives in the big city," said Katie with big grin. I wasn't sure how much truth there was about the fabulous part. After all, our apartment didn't even have central air. But I clinked my glass against hers nonetheless.

Danny and Russell must have found our excitement amusing, because throughout the next hour of our patronage, they more than once "made too much" of another customer's drinks, sending the excess to our table.

By the time we got our bill, it had occurred to me that the chocolate covered banana was definitely not enough to soak up all the alcohol I had consumed thus far. I was inebriated and very much in need of excusing myself to break the seal.

"Do you know where the ladies' room is?" Like it was her own house, Katie gave me spot-on direction to the restroom, which happened to be through the back of the restaurant, down an elevator, and to the left. I could only hope my motor skills would be up for the navigational challenge.

For some reason, as I waited for the lift, it seemed like a brilliant idea to text Trent (remember him?). I don't know why, but liquid courage was taunting me to pull out my phone and type something.

"I know you're dating my ex-friend now, which is utterly disgusting on every level, but next time I'm in Omaha, let's get a drink. We can put it behind us and celebrate your downfall."

I had no idea where that came from, but I did know where it was going. Directly to his text inbox. Before the elevator doors could even shut, I had punched in every number of his cell by heart and hit "send".

Arriving one level down in a quiet vacant ladies' room, I stared myself down in the mirror before going pee. My eyeliner had sunk into the creases below my eyes and my hair had fallen flat. My bra strap was showing and my deodorant had stopped working about three hours ago. As I corrected one shortcoming at a time, I knew right then I had made a huge mistake with the text I had just sent. I aired my crazy like I was drying a t-shirt outside my window on a sunny, windy day. What's worse was that I did this in a time when my better judgment was clearly MIA (as was my brand-new MAC lipgloss. Seriously, where the fuck did I leave it?). I didn't even give myself a chance to think it through—what did I really want to say to Trent? And why? Where was this coming from? And what answer did I really expect could come from a back-handed jab?

As I sat down to take a marathon piss, all I could do was hope my cell service serendipitously cut out during the ride down to the loo.

Surfacing back to bar-level, Katie had cashed us out and was ready to head to the next bar: this one, the polar opposite of Hugh Hefner's lounge.

Bull & Bear was the name of this River North hot-spot and there were guidos of all ages on the prowl to take advantage of any twenty-somethings they could attract with the shine of their chain necklaces. Normally, I'm above a place like this. However, in relation to my level of sobriety, it was the perfect venue for late night shenanigans with my roomie.

My drunken haze didn't prevent me from taking the occasional peek at my phone. My text to Trent, sent more than sixty minutes earlier, had officially been ignored which felt like hell.

As such, I proceeded to briefly make out with a black guy in exchange for a free round of SoCo Limes to take a bit of the sting off. Simultaneously, Katie canoodled with a few freshly divorced middle-aged men in exchange for an invite to an after-hours bar called Crescendo, where these men had thousands of dollars' worth of bottle service roped off and waiting for their arrival.

"Get in the car," Katie shouted at me as she filed into the back of a black SUV with a man twice her age and his friend.

Oh, what the hell, why not. I hopped in.

Once inside the club, about twenty-five people, including myself and Katie, proceeded to dance to house music in a roped off area the size of Harry Potter's bedroom. For the rest of the night, Katie and I did our parts to contribute to a $2,600 bottle service tab, toward which we chipped in nothing but a fake phone number scribbled on a cocktail napkin. However, if letting a forty-five-year-old divorcee pull my hair to the beat of an Enrique Iglesias "Hero" remix could be considered currency, I'd say that actually I overpaid that night for sure.

"Hey, this club is going to close soon," said one of the divorcees (I never did get his name). "Why don't you and your sister (My sister? You wish.) come back to our hotel room. We have a hot tub," he sloppily pitched to me.

At that point, I exercised my ability to say "no" for the first time in twelve hours and downgraded our "baller status" by grabbing Katie and throwing her in a cab back to Lincoln Park.

"That was fun," Katie said as she rolled down the window and let the summer breeze air out some of the Axe body spray that had inadvertently got into the fibers of our clothing.

"That was fun," I concurred; knowing in the back of my head what wasn't fun: that god damn text I let slip earlier on. The regret was haunting me, big time.

Alas, we arrived home and bid each other goodnight. Both of us passed out in our dresses until 4PM the next day.

Ten missed calls, four text messages, and two frantic "Are you alive?" voicemails from my mom later, I finally came to. Stumbling into the living room, I saw my accomplice, bloated with the mixing bowl next to her, barely contributing to society. I felt similarly sinful and dehydrated, and only two things could remedy the situation: a substantial charitable donation, or a Turkey Tom with cheese from Jimmy John's.

After our freaky-fast delivery, we took turns rehashing the night, selectively choosing which events we'd immortalize, and which would remain unspoken. The drunken text to my ex would go under the latter.

By definition, I fell off the break-up wagon. In fact, not only did I fall off it, I tumbled down a dirt road, too. What I sent him was vastly inappropriate and a huge step backwards in the recovery process. Not to mention, it went unanswered, which meant I had ceased to be relevant to him anymore. All I could do was clear out my sent messages folder and forget it ever happened. Just like the ten or so other things I regrettably did that night.

CHAPTER TEN/LESSON TEN

- The thing you never thought would happen will

This particular "fail" was timed perfectly with a couple of other things going on in my life. First, the expiration of my first three months on Match.com. What can I say? Time flies when you are having no fun at all going on one atrocious date after the next. And while I had no plans to renew my membership, I did manage to find an inner peace knowing I had reached my financial goals of being wined and dined on someone else's dime. That part, however heinous it was, was a success. Plus, it rhymed.

The other thing this timed-up with was a work-sanctioned trip to Las Vegas. (How about that for an oxymoron? A work trip to Sin City.) Regardless, I was heading there to check out the marketing at one of our hotels, and for whatever reason, I decided to turn my trip into a long weekend and really relax by holing up in my hotel room with the black-out curtains drawn 24/7.

In theory, it was a good attempt to remain clean and sober, but being part of the hotel industry meant that more than just my room cost was covered. It was unprofessional of me to ignore the free drink coupons and complimentary nightclub admission passes my counterparts had left for me in an envelope upon check-in. After all, this was Las Vegas not Cleveland for crying out loud. Therefore, I proceeded to get wrecked: this time alone and in a different time zone, for forty-eight hours straight. I was one "whose-fucking-baby-is-this?" away from starring in my very own version of The Hangover, but, hey, when in Rome. Right?

~ ~ ~

Returning to work the following Monday, I needed some serious detox, and my appearance proved it. My face was colorless, my skin puffy, and my hair ratted. Worst of all my go-to loose-fitting clothes weren't feeling so loose anymore—a sure sign of the point of no return. With a can of coconut water in one hand, and a greasy breakfast sandwich in the other, I took comfort in knowing I had no scheduled meetings that day. Although, that didn't stop me from having one totally unscheduled one on my way home from work that very same day.

Once my hangover subsided and I closed out of Facebook, it became apparent just how behind I was on my actual job tasks come 4PM. Let it be known, however, that if I could have made a living by being paid to like photos of engagement rings and babies, I would have most certainly qualified for associate of the month.

Leaving the office about an hour later than usual, I was able to mark a few things off my task list, before heading out and beginning my post-work routine. As follows:

- Step one: take out my phone and text my mom
- Step two: pay attention to the streetlights and make smart decisions regarding the quickest way to walk the block-and-a-half to my bus stop
- Step three: get on the bus, put headphones on, and make it home to microwave a Lean Cuisine and set the DVR for Dance Moms

That was it. Simple enough. Just three easy steps were what separated me from point A and point B, Monday through Friday. But on this particular day, an x-factor—or more like an ex-factor—was thrown into the mix.

"Emily!" I thought I heard.

"Hey, EMILY!!" I definitely heard.

Turning back, I saw two people. One was shouting my name. I wasn't even one hundred yards from of my office, and I was already being called back for something I evidently didn't do right. Story of my life.

Circling back, it no longer was what these people wanted, but rather who these people were. It was Trent. And his father. In Chicago. Outside my office. Calling my name in the middle the sidewalk. I assure you, this was not the residual effect of anything I ingested while in Vegas. This was real.

First, I don't even know how they recognized me. Fresh off a two-day bender, I looked nothing like my usual self, which in and of itself was intensely mortifying. Second, what were the mother-fucking chances? I was working later than I was supposed to. The finicky traffic light sent me right then left instead of left then right to my bus stop. My head was down—deep, down—texting on my phone during the exact moment they recognized me, in the middle of rush hour, in a city of three million people. This couldn't be happening.

Oh, but it was. It most certainly was.

I didn't know what to do as their bodies actualized before my eyes. Trent's father threw his arms around me before I had a chance to figure it all out, leaving my bloodshot and weary eyes to stare into Trent's from over his dad's left shoulder. I hadn't made eye contact, or any contact, with this person in a very long time, and I wasn't prepared for the impromptu relapse.

Trent's dad, oblivious to absolutely everything that had transpired with our relationship (less the fact we had broken up and I had moved home to Chicago), wasted no time explaining that they were in town for a conference and heading to dinner in a little bit, to which he emphatically insisted I come.

"I believe it's at, oh, what's the name of the restaurant, Trent?"

"Rosebud, dad. Rosebud." His voice. Wow. Hadn't heard that one in a while, and now here it is, saying the name of an Italian restaurant not too far from my house but way too close for comfort.

"Oh, yes. That's it. Rosebud. Will you join us, Emily? Will you? It'd be great to catch up," his dad proposed.

Would it really be great to catch up? Would it? I mean, I can't imagine "catching up" about your son's new girlfriend (a.k.a. my former intern and good friend), and the reason your son stood me up in the beginning of the summer could be any sort of great. Entertaining? Excruciating? Potentially deadly? Sure, those sound a little more like it. But "great?" That's really only reserved for how I felt when I saw a bus coming out of the corner of my eye.

While throwing myself in front of it sounded like the more appropriate thing to do at the time, I really just wanted to get on it, or at least claim that I had to get on it. Really anything to increase the three-foot radius that currently existed between my ex-boyfriend and myself, all while I was looking my personal worst.

"You know what? I have to go. That's my bus coming," I said.

"Dinner?" his dad asked again.

I swallowed hard and said, "I can't do dinner, I'm sorry. I've got to get home. How about you call me when you're done? It was so good running into you..."

Lies. Lies. Lies. It was so NOT good running into them; in fact, it was bad. Very bad. So bad that once I turned the corner to fake like I was boarding a bus that had already drove off, I fell back against a brick wall and let my body melt like a stick of butter to the ground. As I slowly collapsed, I began crying.

I jimmied my cell out of my pocket and proceeded to call my parents' home phone. I barely remembered the number, but was even more impressed when it started ringing. The sound confirmed they were, in fact, still paying for a landline. Why did I do this? Because there was no caller ID on their home phone, so no risk of being sent to voicemail. I was in despair and needed one of them to answer my SOS. This time, and after just two rings, it was my dad. Lucky him.

My steady tears turned into all-out sobbing the moment I heard him answer. It must have been something about hearing the voice of the only man who had never done me wrong on the other side of the line. Regardless, this early evening hysteria was weirding out every innocent bystander and my poor father was scared and confused, trying to get me to just calm down, breathe, and "tell him what hospital I was at."

Oy vey.

"I just ran into Trent and his dad outside my office."

"Did they see you?"

Oh, did they ever.

"What? How? I don't understand..."

"They are here for a conference, I don't know—they were just there. Randomly. On the street!" The sobbing ensued.

"Well I'll be damned," he said.

Yeah, me too.

It was clear my father didn't know how to solve this. The best he could do was pretend to listen as he Googled all the therapists in the area that were accepting new patients and took BlueCross BlueShield of Illinois.

"Em, I totally understand it," he began.

"Chicago is supposed to be your turf—your safe haven—and he violated that. He blindsided you by being here without the heads up."

He was right. It's not like I owned the city or anything, but it was where I bravely decided to seek refuge when the shit hit the fan in Omaha for the final time. Because of the choice I made, it was as if I had put a four hundred-mile restraining order on the hurt and heartache Trent had caused. And if anything were to change in regards to the distance that I purposefully put between he and I, then a text, call, or an e-mail was in order on his part. I deserved the right to brace for the invasion: if only for the sole reason of getting a minute to put on some damn makeup just in case.

Even though courtesy was never really his thing, I couldn't exactly blame him this time for not reaching out to me beforehand. I wanted to, but I couldn't. Enough time had gone by to assume we had simply amounted to what most people become: bitter exes. And besides, what were the odds that he would have parked his car in the garage that just so happened to be connected to my building? He hadn't the slightest idea where I worked, or what time I left the office. Just like I was unaware that there was an industry convention going on in the city. And on top of all that, he still had a girlfriend—oh hey, Layla—which, ultimately, was reason enough for him to not contact me…for any reason at all.

I got off the phone with my dad and stopped into a drugstore for a bottle of water and a Snickers. I may or may not have grabbed a box of tissues and a wine cooler while I was at it. With my basic-white-girl survival kit in hand, I began the trek home with a heavy heart, and grocery bag that the city taxed me 10 cents for.

Ironically, I had visualized that moment in my head repeatedly: you know, the one where I saw Trent again for the first time since our breakup, and I've got to tell you, it never looked anything like that. For one thing, I was at least five to ten pounds thinner, my outfit was adorable, and my makeup perfectly done. For another, I pictured it planned. This whole "chance encounter" thing was bullshit. It wasn't fair. And, I cringed at the thought of what might have been running through his head in the moments after we met.

"She really let herself go."

"I'm not missing out on anything."

"I really upgraded with Layla."

Shoot me. Seriously. Shoot me.

Even though I had invited him to "call me when he was done with dinner," I knew my phone wasn't going to ring. I suppose it probably was for the best if we both just pretended like randomly running into each other out of nowhere had never happened.

When I finally made it home, I changed into sweatpants and continued to break out in tears over the next hour like a hormonal hot mess. For about the eighth time that year, emotional stability was simply not in my forecast. However, a hot shower to wash the remaining Vegas remnants off my body was. I considered that progress.

When I got out of the shower, I went back to my room to blow-dry my hair and turn in for the night. That's when I noticed a blinking light on my phone: I had a missed call. And when I checked who it was, I proceeded to let out the phrase-of-the-day, as coined by my father: "I'll be damned."

It was Trent. He had called after all.

I instinctively called him back, and from the moment I heard the first ring, I panicked, sending my inner dialogue into another tailspin. Why am I doing this? Why am I calling TRENT? Why was Trent calling ME? I thought we were going to pretend that this whole episode never happened?

It was one unanswered ring away from going straight to voicemail. And as I took the phone away from my ear to hang up, I heard him say, "Hello."

There was a slight echo to his side of the line, which made me believe he had excused himself to the lobby or bathroom to field my call in private. Rosebud was by no means a quiet restaurant. In fact, it was two stories tall and booked full every night by locals and tourists alike.

"Hi," I paused a moment to gather my bearings, shocked that the sound of his voice was still doing something to me. "You called?"

"I did. My dad and I want to know if you'd like to come to the restaurant and have dessert with us. We're almost through with dinner and I know you've got a sweet tooth. They have tiramisu."

My head was spinning. Was this a curveball—or a bullet? Should I try to catch it or dodge it?

"Yeah, you know me. I'm not one to turn down a surplus of free calories."

Trent laughed and said, "So, we'll see you in . . .?"

"I'll hop in a cab in five minutes. I can be there in twenty, I guess."

"Text me when you're here. See you soon."

Click.

An invite. Some banter. And follow-through. I was three-for-three with Trent, which was a complete surprise to me. For as short as it was, I can honestly say that brief exchange was one of the more peaceful encounters I'd had with that man in quite some time.

As I stepped into my walk-in closet and selected the top and bottom I'd wear out that night, I realized that no matter what would happen at the restaurant, I owed it to myself to take the second chance at our first encounter. I wanted my moment—the one I had pictured in my head time again. The one I had actual control over. The one that would yield me a free slice of tiramisu in the end. I hate to say it, but I simply wanted to reclaim my opportunity to unearth the regret that I ultimately knew was at the core of Trent even after all this time.

Moments later, I found myself in the back of an Uber heading to the Gold Coast and about to take part in my very own Scene from an Italian Restaurant at Rosebud. On the way there, I felt jitters, excitement, uncertainty. As strange as it sounds, it felt a little like I was going on a blind date. Except this was just dessert with someone I actually had a relationship with for nearly two years.

Pulling up outside the front entrance, my trembling hands set out to text Trent that I had arrived. But before I could queue up a new message, to my surprise and delight, Trent was right there waiting for me and helped me out of the car. This was already much closer to how I wanted things to happen and I immediately felt at ease with my do-over.

At the restaurant, I found myself in a familiar situation. It was Trent, his father, and I, sitting around a dining table going to town on a piece of cake the size of a German Shepherd puppy. His overly talkative dad and I were feeding off the energy of the conversation, just like the old times. We caught each other up on our life happenings, bantering back and forth about everything from Nebraska weather to Chicago traffic. The time flew by and Trent stayed quiet on the sidelines. The few times I looked over at him, he had a comfortable smirk on his face. It was a look that said, "Yes. This." Before long, the bill came and I knew the night was wrapping up. I knew that the boys would be leaving just as quickly as they had come.

"It was great seeing you, Emily. But we've got a long day of travel ahead of us tomorrow, I think it's best we get back to our hotel," said Trent's dad as he signed the check and collected his leftovers.

"Totally understandable," I responded. "Thanks for inviting me. This was...fun."

And it was. It actually, really was.

Before I could scoot back from my seat and put on my jacket, Trent rested a hand on my shoulder and leaned into my ear.

"Can you wait a minute?" he asked.

"What's up?" I said.

"I mean, we didn't even really get to talk at all."

I took the last sip of my wine and wiped the corners of my mouth.

"I'm sorry about that. You know how me and your dad can get with a little wine in us," I smugly said.

"I know, but I was hoping we could catch up, too. Is there a bar or something around here we could go to and grab one more drink?"

This wasn't Nebraska. Of course there was a bar nearby—ten of them, in fact. But the question was really whether or not I'd accept an invitation to a one-on-one with him. I don't know why, but I said yes to him for the second time that night.

"Dad, you can go ahead without me," Trent said. "Emily and I are going to grab a drink. I'll take a cab to the hotel after."

"All right, you kids have fun. Don't stay out too late," he said. Inside, I had to chuckle a bit because I couldn't think of any parent who would condone his in-a-relationship son going out and having an alcoholic beverage with his ex-girlfriend on a business trip the night before they were supposed to hit the road and drive eight hours across the Midwest. But, oh well. For once, this was not my problem.

Leaving the restaurant, the closest bar happened to be none other than my old stomping grounds: Ralph.

Even though that was the scene of my last major crime (texting Trent drunk while en route to the bathroom), I knew the place would be abandoned at 10 PM on a Monday. And above all, I knew where the bathroom was just in case I needed to make a break for it. Chicago may have been invaded, but thanks to Katie, Ralph was most definitely my turf.

It was as if the dimly lit corner table in the bar had been reserved especially for us. Everything about the bar was eerily perfect for reuniting with an old flame, however unavailable he was. However unsavory our ending may have been.

"Hello, Danny. Is Russell off this evening?" I asked.

"Russell left around 8pm. I'll give him your regards."

From there, both knew the drill.

"French Martini for me. Kettle, up, for him."

"Extra cold, coming right up," said Danny.

The first sip was pure heaven, but unfortunately Trent and I spent the next two hours neglecting the rest. He and I picked up right where we had left off: like no time had passed, no damage done, no hearts broken. It was surreal—as was the moment Trent put his hand atop of mine after sharing a laugh about an old inside joke.

"Whoa," I asserted with big eyes and a tensed-up posture. It literally took his physical touch to remind me who I was with, and what had happened between us in the months up until now. All of a sudden, electricity flowed through my bones I became angry.

"Can I just say one thing?" I said. "Just one thing." I could feel the volcano getting ready to explode. I didn't know what words would be next. Even I was terrified of what was coming. And before he could grant any sort of permission to continue, I had already starting speaking.

"You are dating my friend Layla. You are dating…my friend…Layla! That's the most disgusting, hurtful, thing that I've ever had to accept; let alone had to find out from the social media grapevine."

"I know," he squeaked in.

"No, you don't know," I corrected. "And you know what? I never called you out for it—or her for that matter. I never posted a passive-aggressive status to my Facebook, never showed up at your door, never said a bad thing about you. Do you understand what kind of self-control that takes? Do you understand what bottling that up has done to me? All so you two could hold hands and skip around without any outside interference? Do you know how bad that sucks, Trent? Do you realize that not even 400 miles of distance makes that sting any less?"

He had nothing to say. That, or he knew better than to try.

"Trent, I'm not trying to hurt your feelings. Hell, I'm not even trying to cut you down now that you're sitting right next to me and it's finally easy because I'm not some text you can ignore, some call you can send to voicemail. No, now you have to listen. Because now that I have the opportunity to tell you face-to-face what I once tried to mask in drunken text message, I'm going to fucking take it. You hurt me—more than dating my friend, you led me on. You led me to believe that what we had was worth waiting for. You were supposed to do the fighting, and I was supposed to do the waiting. I did my part—and for what? So you could take the easy way out and date my friend? Some chick who kinda looks me, worked at the same place I did, and would never have the backbone to say you can't actually treat me like garbage or I'll walk?"

"It was a fluke," he said beginning his defense. "I don't know how it happened with her."

"Oh, I don't want to hear that," I said. "You know how these happens, Trent."

An explanation. An apology. I was looking for anything but an excuse. He didn't seem to understand that.

"Well, what did you want me to do, Emily?" He finally was starting to dig deeper, and as harsh as the shift in his tone was, I welcomed it. Perhaps now the fighting part was commencing.

"You left me, remember?" he reiterated. "You moved."

I couldn't believe that he actually thought I had abandoned him: that one day I just decided to leave him there like a baby girl in a dumpster in China. Did he forget that things weren't going great, like, at all? Did he forget that he refused to change? That he didn't want the commitment? That he could care less what the fuck I was up to Friday through Sunday. I told him exactly what the repercussions would be if he didn't straighten out and he did nothing to fix things. Nothing. This was so unfair, like fighting with a child.

"Trent, I went away, yes. But don't you pretend for one second that you don't know why. And let's just clear the air right now: the ship never sailed for me. Can you believe that? Even after all this bullshit, the ship still hasn't sailed. Call it delusional or call it true love—I'm sure they are probably the same anyways—but what I felt with you, I don't feel with any other person. And I still fucking feel it. That says something."

"What does it say?"

"That we should be together, God dammit!"

I polished off the rest of my now-warm martini, paused, then calmly reiterated, "It says that we should be together, Trent."

A smile came across his face.

"Seriously? That makes me so happy you don't even know."

"No, I guess I don't." He appeared shocked by my response. "You were supposed to come here. We were supposed to figure this out months ago, remember? Why is it news to you that I am more than willing to give up my life, once again, to be with you?"

I tried to locate Danny and order another round, but before I could raise my empty glass in the air and flag him down, Trent put his arm around me and pulled me in for a kiss.

I didn't know what the fuck was going on—and I sure as hell didn't know why I couldn't pull myself away. This was wrong. All wrong.

"Wow," he said after our minute-long make out. "I really need to think about things."

"Yeah, you do," I concurred in regards to the understatement of the century.

Moments later, the bartender approached our table and quietly let us know it was last-call. How symbolic.

We closed out and found ourselves standing on Michigan Avenue at 12:30 in the morning.

A taxi approached, and like a gentleman, Trent let me take it.

"You take this one. I'll call an Uber," he said.

He kissed me again once more and whispered that he loved me. I returned the sentiment and stepped in the cab. Just as we were about to drive-off, the Say Anything moment that I had coveted all along was about to take place. Trent ran after the cab and knocked on the window, seconds before the driver was about to gun it through a yellow light.

"Stop!" I said to the cabbie, as I rolled down my window to hear what Trent had to say.

Anti-climatically, it was nothing.

"Say it!" I demanded from the backseat. "Trent, SAY IT!"

And even though I did my part to lead the witness, he still refused to take the stand. Instead, he looked down at the ground and muttered quietly, "Get back safely."

Once again, Trent talked a big game but didn't say shit. Maybe not much had changed after all, I thought as I directed the cab driver to take me back home.

CHAPTER ELEVEN/LESSON ELEVEN

- Therapy: more expensive but less fattening than ice cream

The following few days were brutal wondering how this cliffhanger would play out. I mean, correct me if I'm wrong, but he did just cheat on his girlfriend with me, right? While it wasn't my job to police his morals, I assumed he chalked up the bad behavior to the fact that deep down he knew what he had to do: dump her and get back together with me. The business trip kiss was a necessary evil on his part in order to see the light. Plus, let's face it; I never intended to be the other woman. I just wanted to be the woman. Still.

But apparently, things didn't register with him like they did for me. He treated Chicago like Las Vegas and left what happened there to stay there. I didn't hear from him. Not an apology. Not an epiphany. Not a word.

Beyond the fact that we shared dessert, drinks, and a kiss, the real unsettling part to me was that all of it indicated I had absolutely no control over anything—nothing at all. The law of cause and effect failed to have any such meaning with that boy, which made me realize that everything I could do to move us forward would be futile. Then it clicked: Trent was my

"Groundhog's Day." No matter what I would do, the same nightmare involving him was going to replay itself day after day. With him, it was always going to be six more weeks of a cold, harsh winter.

It was time to warm up.

Though I had joked about it before, I needed to actively seek out a professional therapist. My friends and family were maxed out with all the Trent issues I had dumped on them over the last year, and I didn't blame them for wanting me to pay someone to euthanize them once and for all.

Like any other relationship I try to start with a man, I found Tom (a licensed social worker) on the Internet and e-mailed him to set up our first meeting. He returned my message with a phone call and we arranged an appointment. No bikini wax was needed, but I was undoubtedly nervous for alone time with this new man.

Tom had an atrocious website and an inconveniently located office. I suppose that's what you get when you are trying to score a discounted psych visit on your parents' health insurance plan. He obviously was also a male, which made me wonder why on Earth I'd go to him with boy-related issues that he would probably say were just a symptom of PMS. But the truth was, I didn't want to run the risk of paying for advice from anyone who may have been half as hormonal as me in her hay-day. I needed a male doctor, and that was final.

I had never seen a therapist before. But the good thing was this wouldn't have been the first time I vented to a perfect stranger. Only this time, I hoped he wouldn't offer me two cigarettes in exchange for some train fare under an awning in the rain.

Even though I was confident that this was the right choice, I still couldn't bring myself to tell anyone I was going to see a shrink. It was sad how desperate I was to hear someone tell me I wasn't as bat-shit crazy as I thought and apparently I was willing to spend $120 an hour to get the validation.

As I sat in my car, with five minutes before the start of the appointment, the anxiety I felt, in regards to potentially being written off the moment I began the story with "Well, you see, I was dating this guy…," crept in. Regardless, it was time to head into the dilapidated building that Tom's practice was in, pre-appointment jitters and all, and whine about how my ex-boyfriend doesn't love me anymore.

I hooved it up five flights of stairs and wondered things like: What are we going to talk about? How am I going to segue into certain topics? Do

I lie on the couch or just sit? Will there be snacks? Am I expected to make eye contact? Can I cry? The only thing I was sure of was that I'd be doing most of the talking, and then picking up the tab. This really was starting to look more and more like a Match.com date.

Before I knew it, I was standing in front of Dr. Tom's door. I looked down at my phone just in case a Hail Mary text from Trent came through at the last second. Something along the lines of, "I'm on a plane headed your way. I love you."

No new messages.

The fairytale was officially over; and things were about to get real. Finally.

When I opened the door, the only word to describe what I saw was "abandoned." There was no real waiting room, no front desk, nothing hung up on the walls, and no real sign of any human life. I didn't hear any voices, tears, or telephones—just the sound of a box fan humming along trying to combat a freak, late-fall heat wave. I looked for a bell to ring, a light switch to flick on, something to let him know I was in the building. No such things. So I took a seat and sent brain waves to Tom instead.

I waited for about ten minutes before an older gentleman, the prototypical new-grandfather, emerged from another room. It was Tom. He welcomed me and gestured toward the Hinckley Springs water dispenser before saying he'd be right back.

It was my last chance to bail, and boy did I contemplate doing just that.

He soon returned and invited me to follow him into the therapy room.

Of course, he had a couch, after all, that's a staple when it comes to therapy. But his couch was more like something you'd find on the side of the road with a sign that read "FREE, TAKE ME!" attached to it. This thing had seen some life, let's just say that.

Aside from the as-seen-in-my-grandma's-basement sofa, there was a collection of Superman figurines strewn about the room. I just prayed that whatever came out of Tom's mouth would be more put together than his attempt at creating a feng shui environment. Regardless, I tried my best to accept this as my new "safe zone" and began the appointment.

The first ten minutes with Tom felt like what I imagine a horse feels moments before it is about to take off at the Kentucky Derby. It's not that I was about to piss myself, nor was it that I was poised and ready to have a guy riding me with a whip in hand; it was merely the fact that I was anxiously awaiting the gate to open so I could take off running with what I had come to so eloquently discuss—boy problems.

"So, Emily, you briefly mentioned prior to our meeting that you wanted to discuss your previous relationship. Why don't you tell me a little bit about that."

And we're off.

Poor Tom. If words were vomit, I would have been projectiling in his face right then and there. I was literally going a mile a minute like a twelve year old hopped up on a Pixy Stix at a slumber party. Though it definitely didn't sound like it, I swear I was making a solid attempt to explain things in well thought out, chronological order. But as I went along, I'd think of things I wanted to spit out before they disappeared into the oblivion of my racing mind. I know this must have equated to an incoherent mess, but at least I was trying. And wasn't that the key all along? Trying to move passed this?

Therapy is hard, it really is. Tom had a yellow, lined notepad (think college professor circa 1984) on which he was feverishly jotting things down in pencil, probably a grocery list in hindsight. But after about forty-five minutes of my anecdotes, tangents, and one-off comments about it being hot in there, Tom finally was able to get a word in edgewise.

"Well, you know, I don't know this person, and until I properly assess him, I can't really make an official diagnosis on what may have or may not have been going on with him. But from what you tell me, two things come to my mind," said Tom.

"The first thing is that he sounds like an asshole."

Wow, he was good.

"The second is that it appears like he may have something called Narcissistic Personality Disorder. Do you know what that is, Emily?"

I admitted that I wasn't proficient with the term and invited him to continue. We were making progress, I could tell.

"Well, at its core, it refers to a very selfish person."

Again, Tom was spot on, but I wasn't paying him to tell me that my ex was a selfish asshole. I already knew that. Thankfully, he continued.

"Narcissistic Personality Disorder is when someone is so overly in love with themselves, they don't need love from another, but they want it. They want it because when completely controlled by the narcissist himself, it adds to his self-love."

Interesting.

"There is no concept of give-and-take, no concept of compromise or sacrifice, and most importantly, no concept of longevity with a narcissist. A narcissist doesn't engage in a relationship for true love and commitment. In fact, narcissists fear those things, because they indicate that they'll have to stop loving themselves in exchange for loving another. Yet being with someone gives them validation. Do you see what I'm saying? It's a vicious cycle for the other lover—and most significant others don't ever leave it because the constant push and pull from the narcissist keeps them entangled and unsure if something is actually wrong with the dynamic or not. You are a lucky one. You were aware of it—and you left it behind."

Tom nailed it on the head. Cumulatively, Trent and I spent 104 weeks intertwined in this push-pull madness until he finally let on to the fact that he was incapable of giving me more during our argument about long-term relationships. Looking back, as painful as this was to hear from him, it was probably one of the only times throughout our entire relationship that he was the real him: sincere with his feelings, capabilities, and desires. Had I stayed with him, I could expect nothing more, and sometimes maybe less, than the break-even emotion I got from him at the end of the day.

For a long time after we broke up, I felt like I was the selfish one because I wanted more than what he could give me. Though he hadn't cheated on me, called me a bad name, or slapped me in the face, I sometimes wish he had, because then I'd have a solid reason for pulling the plug and packing up.

I struggled with this a lot, and I let Tom know that. Perhaps he just wanted to empower me not to go home and eat my feelings straight after this session, but he confirmed that my post-breakup emotions were certainly symptomatic of dating someone with this disorder. Tom told me I had to let go of my guilt and realize that it wasn't like I was "snobby bitch" and Trent was "Mr. above-and-beyond boyfriend" in whom I always managed to find faults. It was that Trent had a personality disorder, one of which I was the victim. And, when it finally dawned on me the part I was playing in this sick set up, I wanted out.

Tom said that was fair.

I'm not sure if he had a crystal ball, but Tom let me in on a little secret just before our session was about to expire, and that was that if I had stayed with Trent, absolutely nothing about the dynamic of our relationship would have changed in a year, five years, or even a lifetime together.

You can't change people. I have heard that time and time again from a variety of sources, some of whom I was paying an hourly rate to, and some to whom I wasn't. But whether it was free advice that came out over a cup of coffee with a friend, or that was up-sold to me in a poorly decorated office somewhere just outside Chicago, I knew that those four words comprise a universal truth that just needed to be accepted.

No matter how special I thought I was, I wasn't tech support. I couldn't re-hardwire someone's brain—not through cleavage, not through conversation.

My maiden session with Tom was coming to an end, and I couldn't have felt like I got more for my money than if he'd thrown in free pizza before I left. I had a fresh perspective on things, one that even allowed me to accuse my ex of having a personality disorder, which was liberating in its special own way.

Prior to this day, I imagined my relationship with Tom would be long and fulfilling. However, it was more of a one-night stand—quick, totally uninhibited, and very satisfying. Plus, I wasn't going to think about him at all the next day, and I really didn't see a reason to call him again in the near future. He had simply served his purpose for me, and that was that.

Regardless of whether I'd see him again, Tom concluded by assigning me two tasks: one that had to do with Trent, and one that had to do with Trent's successor. First, he told me to go home and sift through some memorabilia from our relationship. This didn't sound exciting to me, as I wanted to revel in my progress for at least an hour before having to totally immerse myself in it again.

"Put aside any emotion and treat it like a fact-finding mission," he said, explaining that the challenge was to locate one written letter from him, or one photo of the two of us, in which an honest love was detectable. It could be in the way he phrased a sentence or signed his name on a note; or it could be the look in his eyes, or the smile across his face in a picture. In two years, you'd expect I'd have at least a couple of Valentine's Day cards and some photos from the vacations we took together. But even in just doing a quick mental inventory of things, I knew that I would not be able to produce the evidence Tom was asking for.

Instead of cards or letters, Trent did expensive jewelry and clothes—items, nice items. And, even though we had photos together, some of which were in frames throughout my old apartment, they all maxed out at half smiles and side hugs. Tom's point? Narcissists are total commitment phobs; so much so that they don't issue written words or put any detectable emotion on their faces in photos, so as not to have any documentation that something could be real and forever. This was equal parts fascinating, eye opening, and heartbreaking. I wasn't even worth a genuine smile?

And as far as the second task went, Tom's challenge for me was to have an open mind, and an open heart, and really pursue the next great guy who came along: don't go looking for him online, but rather "come across him" and then give him a shot. And not in the warm tequila kind of a way (sorry, Katie), but simply insofar as an honest chance. Little did I know, this wasn't going to be hard. But it also wasn't going to be easy.

It was just going to be.

CHAPTER TWELVE/LESSON TWELVE

- Bad boys: just get them out of your system

Just when I resolved to stop meeting guys on the Internet, I stumbled down a rabbit hole on a hidden gem known as Twitter. Primarily using it as a tool to stay abreast of all the happening people and places around Chicago, I soon became semi-addicted to what was going on in 140 characters or less at any given moment. Not to mention, any forum that promotes people pumping out their crazy in a digital public setting was definitely something I wanted to be a part of.

There was no strategy with it. For a while, I just chose to follow those who kept me entertained. If they appeared good-looking in their tiny profile photos, that helped, too. But vanity aside, I soon realized the true beauty of this tool: keeping tabs on total strangers. Let's face it; few things are more fascinating than sitting behind a computer screen and getting your stalk on.

Nevertheless, someway, somehow, I found myself in a mutual "followship" with an up-and-coming musician in the city. According to my Twitter feed, and a quick Google search, he was a twenty-something, tatted up drummer from New York City, with whom I had nothing in common.

His tweets contained profanity and links to extinct 90s metal music. Mine discussed cupcakes and a tumultuous relationship with leggings as pants. However, one Saturday morning I woke up to a direct message from the dude: "Want to throw down some time?" Translation: he was asking me out. I think.

Perhaps he had a Jewish-girl fetish, because I truthfully couldn't imagine any other reason he would want to spend any sort of prolonged time with me in a confined space. I mean, the second he figured out I've been known to listen to Justin Bieber (pre-puberty), I was sure he'd try to strangle me with the cord of my headphones. And yet, I excitedly replied in the affirmative and hoped he'd make good on this unexpected invitation to connect in real life.

"Yeah, I'm in," I coolly said.

Later that week, he messaged me again to solicit an after-work drink at a bar in River North. Same-day meet-ups were a little impromptu for my liking, but my hair was cooperative enough that day for me to say yes. So when the clock struck five, I headed to the bathroom to apply eyeliner for the first time in three weeks. Shortly thereafter, I was hailing a cab and heading over to a blind date brought to me in part by Twitter.

On the ride over, I shot him a courtesy text. "Hey, I'm ten minutes out. Can you save me a seat?" I requested. If I knew anything about Chicagoans, it's that they single-handedly keep Maker's Mark in business on weekdays between 5 PM and 7 PM while they drink away their complacency. Getting to know "Travis Barker 2.0" would be hard enough; I didn't want to wind up standing at a crowded bar behind a douche bag with an untucked tie looking like he was sitting one out at a family wedding, on top of it all.

"Don't worry, it's just us," he replied—part romantic, part opening narration of a murder- mystery episode of Dateline.

Moments later, I arrived at the meeting spot. It was a bar I'd never been to (let alone heard of) before. With no time to Yelp the joint, I was heading into murky waters indeed.

As if I wasn't uncomfortable enough, no one who could possibly have been Jacob was in this bar. When I walked in, it was just the bartender, an elderly couple, and me. Is this the part I get taken? I wondered.

Just when I was about to deem the entire affair a total waste of mascara, a well-dressed guy came out of the bathroom sporting just the neck tattoo I needed to see in order to identify the body. I was in the right place.

Jacob hugged me right away, which was an awfully affectionate move from a man with a tattoo of a dagger on the middle of his jugular. However, I gladly accepted his embrace and secretly enjoyed the scent of cigarette smoke and cologne. To me, there is something hypnotic about a vice masked in musk. Regardless, it was evident he was a total fucking badass, and I was turned on by the fact we looked like Jesse James and Sandra Bullock during their hay-day. Somewhere in my mind I knew I had a fantasy about this, and I had Jacob to thank for bringing that to light.

For someone who does relatively okay in new situations, I didn't know what to expect from this guy. I've really only ever been attracted to pretty boys or borderline bible thumpers (usually, these are one and the same). This guy had a nose piercing that reminded me of a weird phase I went through in college, along with a beard that looked like it could benefit from a quick once-over with a Popsicle stick. Nonetheless, I was completely and inexplicably starry-eyed to the point I needed a drink. Or three.

Everything down to my glass of white wine and his tumbler of whiskey was an utter paradox. Just as I had suspected, we couldn't be more different if it were Opposite Day, every day. There wasn't a single thing we had in common: from eye color to smoking habits, to family dynamic, to education levels, to our respective city accents—we were on two ends of the spectrum.

I sucked down my white wine faster than a real housewife of Atlanta, and naturally became more infatuated with this person. Suddenly the fact he needed braces, his obvious smoking habit, the defacement of his body…none of it mattered. In fact, things kept getting hot and heavy with each unsettling thing I learned about him. As such, you can only imagine the flutter of butterflies that flew through my stomach when he told me he had a girlfriend. Look, I had seen Cheaters once or twice, and shockingly, this didn't resonate on any level it should have. In fact, I reacted the same way to this as I did when he told me he had a cat: momentarily put off, but generally still interested.

His relationship status appeared to me as more of a fun-fact than a roadblock. Absolutely no part of me felt discouraged by the news that he was "taken". He must have felt the same way, because he kissed me. Right there at the bar, in between sips he leaned into me and planted one on my lips. There was no lead-in, there was no romanticism, and there certainly was no regret.

He better not kiss and tweet, I thought.

Several hours had gone by and we remained the only two patrons in the place. With the bar as our stage and Jacob as my one-man audience, I took it upon myself to deliver a monologue. It went something like this:

"It's weird. I kind of like you."

Then, he stepped onto the scene and took the spotlight.

"You don't want to. Trust me."

Not quite the line I expected he'd deliver before chasing his words with a swig of whiskey and a painful wince. I could tell in his crystal blue eyes there was something to this. But furthermore, I could tell he was still somewhat smitten, and I hadn't yet been completely rejected. Trust me, I know exactly what that looks like.

I thought for a moment it may have been the whole girlfriend-guilt thing creeping up like some kind of a delayed acid reflux, but the fact that we'd already been to first base and back several times in a public bar without anyone calling us "out" meant that she was not a valid concern this evening. So, what was it then?

He laid his cards on the table: "I'm self-destructive, Emily. I'm a fucking addict. Trust me, you want to stay away."

"An addict, like . . ."

A pause just big enough to park a large SUV came between us before he outed the cold, hard truth.

"Like, I do fucking lines of coke off a stripper's tits and tend to disappear for a few days." He swallowed hard and then looked me directly in the eye. "I lock myself up and go off the radar. I stay up all night and sleep all day. I'm up and down; I'm left and right. I'll be happy, and I'll get angry. Really, fucking, angry. You don't want to be involved with this, all right? Trust me."

This was the third time in three minutes he had urged me to "trust him." But with each layer of crazy he added to the cake, I couldn't help but want a bigger slice. Despite everything he told me, I still felt it made more sense to keep a bigger distance between horsemeat IKEA meatballs than between him and me. I assure you that countless things about him disgusted me, but he still unexplainably remained one of the most attractive people I had met. Perhaps it was his honesty that I found incredibly appealing. You know, so many guys are assholes in disguise. They come off one way for the first couple dates, but reveal themselves as secret jerks shortly thereafter. To Jacob's credit, at least he was coming right out and admitting his faults, however severe they were.

I know what you're thinking: I'm the crazy one, the unstable, self-destructive, broken one. And in hindsight, I probably was. After all, here is this guy who was not only waving his freak flag in my face, but also literally choking me out with it and I wasn't even bothering to gasp for air.

But this wasn't a matter of impaired judgment, or needing an easy hook-up after a solid dry spell. Even though I knew nothing about addiction, I at least knew I should have been running—no, sprinting—for the hills after he put a bullet through our otherwise routine date. But I couldn't resist the temptation to peel back another layer. I had front row seats to a show, I just didn't know which one I'd be seeing. Regardless, I figured my willingness to participate could only lead to one of two things: an unexpected love affair, or an even better story to tell.

"Now would be the time to back out," he said.

It was as if he was a recruiting agent and I was a freshman ROTC student about to sign up for mortal combat. He was trying to smack some sense into me; warning me fair and square that I was entering a world of pain, and to be clear, none of it would have anything to do with Christian Grey's red room. No, this was the type of pain that could only be summed as: all sorts of fucked up. It was The Jerry Springer Show circa 1998, but worse, because this was real. There was no script, and there were no cameras, and certainly no live studio audience to witness—or object to—what was going on here.

"Last call, guys," said the appropriately timed bartender, as he wiped down the counter in front of us.

Jacob chugged the last sip of his fifth whiskey neat. I left a sip of my white wine behind and waited for the words that were next off his tongue.

"Can we go back to your place? Can we watch a movie? Can we just sit and talk some more?" he begged. "I honestly don't care. I just don't want to be done hanging out with you yet."

For the record, I answered: "Yes, absolutely."

Frankly, I had no valid explanation as to why I wanted to be with this man in private, especially slightly uninhibited and after midnight on a school-night. I guess deep down maybe I knew this wasn't going to work—like, at all. I mean, I cut coupons, he cut coke—big difference! But all things considered, he'd have a higher chance of being found dead in a gutter than ever meeting my parents, so what was the harm in cabbing it back to my place for a nightcap?

Before long, Jacob and I engaged in some steamy "everything but" while my roommates were asleep in the apartment. Little did they know, I had brought home, and was near nude in bed, with a man who had a tattoo of Satan on his stomach, which—mind you—I only discovered after an attempt to get to third-base with him. From every direction, this was a complete and utter farce. I didn't know if I wanted to laugh, cringe, or cry. So instead, I carried on, and I just enjoyed myself. Hedonism for the win.

Later that night, or early that morning, however you want to look at it, Jacob packed up his things and got ready to leave my apartment. I suppose it wouldn't have made a moral difference if he slept over or not, the damage was already done, but in an effort to maintain any sort of ethical bearings, I urged him to head home for the night. To sleep in his own bed. Upon walking out the door, he looked me up and down and said, "This. This needs to happen. How do we make this happen?"

This clearly meant us. But what us meant was a mystery. And how to make it happen? How to make a relationship with a drug addict, whiskey-dependent musician who was dating SOMEBODY ELSE happen? That should be a question on a standardized test, because I certainly had no fucking clue.

All things considered, this unlikely "courtship" had all the makings to be one of the most romantic love stories ever told, however every fundamental aspect for it to actually get off the ground was completely jacked. Did I or did I not want this to work?

I left him hanging as I let him out the back door quietly, and when he left, I felt equal parts guilty and giddy. It wasn't that he had a girlfriend who was asleep in her bed while we were wide-awake in mine; it was more the fact that I had just done something dirty with someone dirty. Even smoking pot rubbed me the wrong way, but here was a man who was probably leaving enough remnants behind in my bed to send a drug dog up my stoop. Regardless, the lingering scent of cigarettes on my pillow indicated he was still a breath of fresh air for me, someone completely comfortable with who he was, despite how entirely fucked up that was. Though I hadn't yet seen the brunt of his self-described ugly, at least through our boozy night together, I still could detect his talent as an artist and his compassion as a human, which proved well for consolation prizes.

I thought about him the entire next day. Every chance I got, his face floated to the forefront of my mind, dagger neck tattoo and all. I knew

I had legitimate feelings forming for him when breakfast time turned to lunchtime, lunchtime turned to dinnertime, and I had absolutely no desire to eat anything. Thinking of him was an appetite suppressant in the best possible way. It was that feeling you get when you're too consumed with chemistry to consume a single calorie, and I hadn't felt that in quite a while.

I could tell the feeling was somewhat mutual as per a text message I received from him later that day. "Can I see you Sunday? I need to."

He needed to.

If strongly desiring to see me was part of his addiction, I was becoming increasingly okay with it. An addict? So he says. But adorable and endearing? One hundred percent, confirmed. So, in response to his invitation to hang, I steamrolled any trace of existing weekend plans and did my part to make this secret meet-up possible.

Sunday arrived and so did he—at my doorstep, just in time for a late lunch. The two of us posted up in our true form right at the bar and proceeded to have just the time we'd expect sitting at a counter throwing back a few drinks. At that moment, I was exactly where I wanted to be, sitting next to exactly whom I wanted to be near, and it felt wonderful. Try not to be repulsed or think I'm kidding, but everything from his could-use-a-washing skinny jeans to his slight beer belly was so wonderfully not-my-type that I wanted to prematurely tell the world, or even just our waitress, that this was my man.

After we closed out our tab, we did what any normal "couple" in Lincoln Park would do. We held hands and ran errands. He smoked cigarettes and dropped rogue f-bombs, while I commented on the unseasonably warm weather and rolled up the sleeves of my J.Crew parka.

When we finally made it back to my place, we cuddled up and started to watch a movie. A few moments later, the phone in his jean pocket rattled our closeness. Jumping to retrieve it, he stared at the number and his eyes lit up.

"Who is it?" I shuttered at the thought that it might be his girlfriend.

"Someone in the industry," he responded. "Sorry, I need to take this," he said, picking up and moving into another room.

Phew. Crisis averted. Duty was calling and I thought nothing of it, while I continued to sip a glass of wine and watch the flick as he respectfully took the conversation into another room.

"Babe," he returned to the sofa. "I need to run a quick errand, but

I'm going to come right back, okay?"

Babe? Swoon.

"Really? Okay. Where are you going?"

"I've got to go pick up some coke real fast. It's really good shit, and I'm just going to snag it now and come straight back. I'd invite you to come, but, yeah. Thirty minutes, that's all I need—tops." For as, how do I say it, highly illegal as this all was, he was remarkably cheerful. His excitement gave the situation some much-needed innocence.

Before I could process the who, what, and where of it all, Jacob adhered a kiss on my cheek and headed out my door with an uncanny pep in his step.

Indeed, it was courteous of him to invite me on his little field trip, if you will, but I was glad to have stayed behind at the sober house and await his return instead.

Ironically, I didn't find his errand odd, nor was I put off by the fact he was embarking on an impromptu drug run. I momentarily equated it to what I would do if I had just found out a secret sale was announced at Nordstrom, and I just let it go. After all, it was Jacob being bad-ass Jacob, and I knew that on-the-fly weirdness was part of his M.O., as were the occasional fling with drugs and alcohol.

Twenty minutes later, and he was on his way back. And right at the thirty-minute mark, he walked through the door, just like he said he would, and kissed me hello. Back in my arms, I was convinced that he was simply just one gigantic case of the good out-weighing the bad, which is why I said it was okay for him to do a line of coke off my dining room table just a few moments later. I mean, if I'd just come home with a pair of Christian Louboutins, I would have wanted to put them on and prance around my apartment, too.

Up until that Sunday afternoon, I had only ever seen one other person do cocaine and it was under entirely different circumstances. It was Mindy and it was in the ladies' room at an upscale restaurant in the city. She did a single bump off of a car key in between freshening up before dessert. I watched her do it—curiously and judgmentally. And if you recall, it didn't lead to good things.

Well this time, I didn't watch Jacob do it. I felt the picture I had in my head of his bad habits didn't need a real-life visual to go along with it. Again, I really wanted to like him, and for this to work itself out in the end, so I kept my eyes fixed on the television as I listened to him take a big sniff, followed by a couple coughs, and a sigh of relief.

Seconds later, he rejoined me back on the couch as if he had returned from fetching a glass of water or something. That wasn't so bad, I thought to myself.

Finishing up the flick, we took things back to my room. And by "things," I don't just mean the chemistry between us. I mean the drug paraphernalia that was now living in my house: a debit card, a rolled up 20-dollar bill, and a button bag filled with white clumps of cocaine to be specific.

Heading back to familiar territory, we soon found ourselves in a similar situation to our initial meeting: we were nearly naked and making out in my room. No one was complaining.

"Hold on," he said, gently pushing me off him. I was almost positive he was searching for a condom. Fiddling over the nightstand, I liked the direction this was going. I laid back, inhaled, and prepared for the moment I had been waiting for.

But something was off. The entire segue into sex was taking much too long. I propped myself up on one shoulder and glanced over to see how things were coming. Jacob was preparing another line on top of one of my favorite books that only moments ago was resting innocently on my bedside table.

I was somewhat frustrated he stopped the flow of our encounter to snort cocaine.

"This stuff makes you last for hours, it makes stuff really wild," Jacob said off-handedly, while hunched over his ingredients.

Oh. Well then…

I stayed quiet as I waited for the hedonistic side effect to kick in. But, as the minutes rolled by, the only real symptom I saw that Jacob became more talkative than usual. Brazen, energetic, engaging, are all adjectives I would use to describe how the mood went from sultry to spunky. Needless to say, the heat of the moment had suddenly cooled off and given way to a good talk about anything and everything.

For the next four hours, we laid in bed and totally opened up about our lives, dreams, goals, likes, dislikes, families, friends, favorite foods, and middle names. It had been a while since I had conversation that went so deep with anyone, romantic lead or not. Drugs aside, it felt good to have reciprocal banter with a new and interesting person. True, it wasn't the steamy sex I had set myself up for, but it was workable: perfect for a Sunday afternoon.

In all this time, we discovered a few things we had in common, such as our mutual like for cheeseburgers. But for the most part, the chat was yet another reminder of just how different our blueprints really were. Regardless, our open discussion showed one thing: that we were getting good at learning each other's flaws and accepting them. He might have had a thing for coke, but I had a thing for being emotionally lost and slightly obnoxious. He didn't care. He thought I was funny. Special. Sexy. Perhaps this could work after all.

I don't know if it was that I got so wrapped up in our conversation, or if I simply chose to ignore what was going on next to me, but during this entire time, Jacob had taken nearly twenty lines of coke, spaced about twenty minutes apart, and dwindling closer and closer as time went on. He polished off an entire eight ball from the top of a paperback best seller that I had planned on reading later that night. While that seemed excessive, I reminded myself I had no frame of reference as to what "normal" was when it came to using hard drugs. That was Jacob's area of expertise, and I wasn't going to challenge him. I wasn't going to suggest "Haven't you had enough?" or ask, "Are you almost done, there?" even if I thought and wondered both.

The concern amplified when my head, which was lying atop his untrimmed chest, started to feel the vibrations of his thumping heart. Not to mention, he was emitting heat like a nuclear reactor and I could no longer comfortably sit so close to him anymore without overheating and feeling clammy myself. When I flipped over to look into his beautiful eyes instead, they were completely taken over by the darkness of his gigantic pupils. I was positive that all these things were a side effect of the drugs, but I was even more confident that Jacob knew what he was doing when it came to dabbling and dosing. Again, I said nothing and muted my worry by reminding myself to be grateful for the time we were spending together, alone in the comfort of my bed.

After a few peaceful moments, Jacob broke the silence.

"Emily," he said. "I don't feel well."

It was like I could hear the record scratch and the brakes squeal. I shot up straight in the bed, fueled by the panic I had been idling this whole time.

Fuck. Fuck. Fuck. Fuck. FUCK.

I knew what to do when someone had too much to drink. I knew what to do when someone had been dumped. Hell, I knew what to do when someone falls and cracks their head open. But I had not seen nearly enough Celebrity Rehab to have the slightest idea what to do for someone who has seemingly overdosed on a highly illegal substance, in the comfort of my double-sized bed, smack-dab in the middle of my yuppie Lincoln Park apartment.

My first reaction was to get him out of my place before he suffered a life-threatening stroke or seizure, as Lord knows a domestic "Amanda Knox" trial would have surely ensued if that were the case. Given who he was in the musical community, I could already see the headlines erupting throughout the city. My ass was going to continuously get reamed in 140 characters or less, in 24 hours or less, if I didn't get this man out alive.

How could I let this happen? I should have stopped him or at least expressed some detectable amount of disdain during all of this, even if for no other reason than he chose to use the cover of my favorite book as a surface to mash up his cocaine. I was going on a business trip that week, it would have been nice to have some literature in my carry-on that wouldn't attract the attention of every drug-sniffing animal in O'Hare International Airport.

But even beyond that, I had gone through D.A.R.E., and I knew right from wrong. I didn't hang out with people who did this. People go to funerals for people who did this. Why all the sudden was this as acceptable as peeling an orange and eating it in front of me? I was mad at myself. I was mad at him. I was mad at, and stuck in, this awful situation.

So, I let him lay in the dark for about 15 minutes, similar to what you'd do in a high school nurse's office. With him in a trance, I began to Lysol every ounce of my dining room table and nightstand. Even though by this time, it was after midnight and every sane person was asleep, I even resorted to pulling out a vacuum and sucking up any coke crumbs that may have landed on the floor. With our romantic connection now officially dead and gone, it felt necessary and appropriate to immediately clean up the murder scene from our deflated time together.

After destroying the initial evidence, I managed to get him up, dressed, and on his way. I helped zip up his jacket and pull the hood up over his head. That's when I grabbed his cheeks and demanded an answer, "Are you okay?"

His big black pupils resembled an oil spill across his eyes, but he looked me straight in mine as best as he could. "Yeah, I'm feeling better. I'll call you when I'm home, okay?"

From a lover to a worried mother, what gives? As far as I was concerned, I'd had more than a few shit-show nights myself, and I always seemed to make it back to my place and pass out in my heels. That said; I had confidence that the kid could manage the five-minute walk, despite the rather aggressive recreational Sunday night activities in which he had just partaken. Nevertheless, at least the fresh air couldn't hurt his attempt to sober up.

Just a few moments before shutting the door on him, he did something unexpected. He very lovingly and sweetly kissed me on the lips and said goodbye to me in the doorway, much like the way he greeted me after completing his drug run several hours before. Where did that come from? More so, how was it making everything okay? This display of affection in the eleventh hour gave me some sort of sick hope that things between us were salvageable, despite the genuinely fucked up way things came to a screeching halt. I hate to admit it, but I reasoned that if he was still able recognize what we had while he was clearly on another planet, I could potentially let this go.

"Go home," I said, as I watched him head down the stairs from my doorway. For a minute, I stayed to look out the window and watch the streetlamps reflect off him as he faded out into the distance. With that, I retreated to my bedroom—the scene of the crime—and rested easy after all.

~ ~ ~

I woke up to my alarm blaring just a few hours later and stared at the ceiling before moving a muscle. Tiredly, I recounted the night. I couldn't tell if it was a dream or actual reality, but I had to get to work, so I chose to ignore the fact that anything out of the ordinary had happened. I put it all in the past.

When I finally shushed the alarm, I noticed that I had not received any communication from Jacob confirming that he had in fact made it back to his place. I found it a bit odd, as he seemed to be relatively good with phone etiquette so far. However, if being high was anything like being drunk, I was more than positive he'd made it back to his place and simply passed out in his bed before getting the chance to shoot me a text or call. To be sure, I did a quick check of my Twitter feed to see if had posted anything. His silence on that front as well confirmed that he likely was sound asleep, and would be for at least the next few hours.

I, on the other hand, headed into work with the façade that I was fresh off a lazy Sunday just like the rest of my coworkers. It was days like this that I really wondered if anyone else at my work lived a double life even remotely like mine: hospitality industry pro during the day, drugs, sex (well, not yet but hopefully soon!), and rock-n'-roll by night. Regardless, I started chipping away at my to-do list, occasionally checking my phone for a message from Jacob.

By 1 PM, I found his silence disconcerting. From what I knew about coke, I thought it kept you awake. However, not confident in the "contrabands" Jeopardy category, I let it go. Besides, I recalled him recounting a recent coke binge and saying that he didn't tend to surface from these things until the afternoon of the following day. Remembering that piece of valuable intel, I let it go a little longer before finally deciding to call him.

I'm not going to lie; the thought of texting him scared me. I didn't want the "R u ok?" paper trail linked to my cell phone number in the off chance that something bad actually did happen to him. Terrible, I know, but I had seen enough CSI to know not to dig myself into that hole just yet.

His phone rang and rang, hinting to me that it wasn't dead. That, however, did not mean that he wasn't. I started to feel a deeper level of panic when shortly thereafter I noticed a user on Twitter had mentioned Jacob's unusual silence for the day in a public tweet. It wasn't just me. The world was starting to take notice of the lack of inappropriate posts coming from him, and thus, I instantly became paranoid. My heart sunk as it dawned on me that I was partially responsible for this weird, potentially grim, reality.

Nearing the end of my workday, I decided to turn off my phone, e-mail, and Twitter altogether. I couldn't take the silence from him and the noise from everyone else. I had to get my mind off things and decided to eliminate the social distractions by working late a few extra hours at the office. I refused to go home because that would mean too much time had come and gone without me hearing from him. I refused to step foot back at my place without knowing if he was dead or alive, quite the problem to have let me tell you. Regardless, I figured I'd enjoy planned silence for a few hours, and then, turn everything all back on in the hopes of being pleasantly surprised. Like powering back on after a flight lands, I was sure to expect the ding of a few texts, voicemails, e-mails, or instant messages—any or all would have been fine. I was just looking for something to confirm that he was in fact still among the living and just emerging from the deepest sleep of his young, talented, ultra fucked up life.

With not a soul left in my office, it was time make a move. I powered up and waited to get back on the grid. There was nothing from Jacob. Not a single vibration, blinking light, or little envelope icon was from him. There was, however, a tweet that I could only imagine was about him.

It came from the same user that called him out on his unusual silence earlier in the day, a music blogger from Chicago who followed his up-and-coming career closely, and who took a liking to Jacob. This man's post read: "I need everyone's prayers for a good buddy of mine, even though prayers may not be enough to save him."

I ran to the bathroom, shut the stall door, dropped my head into my hands, and sobbed for the first time in months. I felt the dead-end despair I could only imagine a girl who was sixteen and pregnant would feel after finding out she'd made the biggest mistake of her life. I was ninety-nine percent sure that the worst possible situation had just now become reality, and I blamed myself for being responsible for this outcome.

I knew better, I should have done better. So why didn't I? No part of this—from the first message he sent me on Twitter, to the last message I should have received from him when he got home the night before—felt right; and apparently, this was the only way the universe could get through to tell me. Though not a religious person, I had a very frank conversation with God right then and there. I told him I understood his point, and then I prayed. For the first time of my life, I prayed to God asking him to please let Jacob be okay. Please.

I spent ten minutes alone in the stall sitting on the cold hard floor, propped up against the wall, eye-level with the toilet seat. As the cleaning crew came in for the night, I knew it was time I pulled myself together as best as I could. I ripped off a foot of toilet paper and blotted the remaining tears from under my eyes, obliterating the last bit of eye makeup I had left for the day. It was in this moment that I began to understand a fraction of the truth he told me the first night we met: "You do not want to get involved with this."

Returning to my desk, I took a deep breath and toggled back over to my Twitter feed. I decided to direct message the music writer, even though I didn't know him personally, even though I knew it was invasive and inappropriate, even though it would link me to this mess. And, even though it was a long shot to think that this stranger would name names (preferably in five minutes or less). I had to get some clarity on the issue. One way or another, good news or the absolute worst, I needed to confirm whether this tweet was in fact about Jacob.

"If you don't mind me asking, who is your tweet about?" I hit the send button and waited for a response: a behavior I had become eerily familiar with for the day.

Moments later, this man wrote back: finally, someone on the edge as much as I was. My hand was trembling as I navigated the mouse to the message. I could barely click to open.

"One of my friends from high school," it said.

Half of me was relieved, half of me was not. I still had no concept of Jacob's whereabouts and no clue if he was alive. However, now that I knew that this guy was responsive, I decided to throw my discretion to the wolves and flat out ask him if he'd heard from our friend.

"I'm sorry. I thought it was about Jacob. I haven't heard from him today. Have you?"

Suddenly, I found myself in the psychological thriller version of You've Got Mail as I played Meg Ryan glued to a computer screen waiting for a stranger's reply to come through. It was making me physically ill, playing Russian roulette with my Twitter inbox. I couldn't believe how I had gone from having butterflies in my stomach to a complete and total knot, all from the same guy, all within twenty-four hours.

A moment later, a message came through from my source. This time, I wasted not a second opening it, thinking I might as well not take my time in finding out whether I'd be scarred—or incarcerated—for years to come.

"Yes, a couple hours ago. He's practicing for a show tomorrow."

I'm not saying that this tweet made me think I needed to consider going to church regularly, but at that moment, I closed my eyes and thanked God like the savior everyone said he was.

Back to real life: preparing for a show? Whatever. I truly didn't even care that Jacob had fallen off the map and for whatever reason didn't feel it necessary to communicate with me after his bender. All I could be was glad that he was alive, and that I would be able to see my friends and family without a sheet of Plexiglas between us in the foreseeable future. Plus, I really don't look good in jumpsuits.

Another thing I was glad about was just how fucked up things had gotten over the last twenty-four hours. From drug overdoses, to nervous breakdowns in the bathroom at work, to the violation of my favorite paperback book, there was now officially no way I could see passed the problems he so clearly admitted he had from day one. Despite its short yet dramatic run, the curtain had to close on my fairytale romance with this problem child. It just had to. And at 8 PM, I finally packed up my belongings and headed back to my house.

"It takes a special girl to date me," I recalled him saying the day before.

I wanted to pride myself on being able to deal with his problems, perhaps even eradicate them from his repertoire altogether. I wanted to be the "cool" girlfriend and the "special girl" he needed. So, what did I do? I turned the blinders on, and came to believe that being okay with letting your significant other self-destruct by snorting drugs off the back of a bestseller you were two-thirds the way into was acceptable. Well, it's not.

I may not have known much about addiction then, but I do now. And I'm confident that Jacob didn't need a "special" girl. Jacob needed months and months of in-patient rehabilitation followed by a twelve-step program, and a sponsor to keep him on-track every day for the rest of his life. He needed a new cell phone with zero contacts in it, a new city, and a new lease on life. At the very least, he needed to step out of the limelight and step into a Narcotics Anonymous meeting—immediately.

Admittedly, I was so obsessed with letting him be who he was that I forgot who I was: a caring, compassionate person who worries about people, and who genuinely prefers that the company she keeps gives a flying fuck about living to see the next day. And I tell you, there is only so much crazy you can sit back and take before you start to miss the guys whose wild weekends cap at cosmic bowling and cold-pressed coffee.

You know, I probably could have found an eloquent way of explaining to my parents that I fell head over heels for a tatted up atheist with serious addiction issues and bad teeth. In fact, I would go so far as to say, I would have welcomed the challenge. But no matter how well versed I can be, I sincerely doubted my ability to ever explain my role in the death, disappearance, or destruction of Chicago's latest and greatest loose cannon. I love a scandal, but I'm no Olivia Pope.

Sometime around 10:30 PM that night, after I had settled in with a hard-earned glass of wine, my phone buzzed. It was Jacob. He had apparently come down ever so slightly from his mega-high, just enough to hit the call button in between preparing for his show. But this time when my phone lit up, and I saw that it was him, my face and my smile did not. I tried to run with a bull and got speared through the heart. I learned my lesson, and sending him straight to voice-mail was my practical exam. I owed that, and a glass of Pinot Noir, to myself.

PART THREE

CHAPTER THIRTEEN/LESSON THIRTEEN

- Never underestimate a nightcap

As you already know, at the time I was working in hospitality: an industry comprised entirely of women over the age of forty-five who drink a bottle of chardonnay alone at night and gay people. Aside from a freak exception or two (like myself), that's literally the entire demographic. As such, it didn't take Dr. Ruth to diagnose why exactly working 50 hours a week was leaving me in a serious dry spell.

Another exception to the middle-aged drunks and the gays (and the basically-celibate me) was James, the company's twenty-eight-year-old auditor. James was a one-man department. His workspace was located just on the other side of mine in the sterile cubicle farm. Believe it or not, for almost an entire year I came to this office, tucked myself into my nine-to-five silo, and never even realized that a semi-attractive man, who might have been single and willing, was within an arm's reach this whole time. Shame on me for having the blinders on.

Eventually he broke the silence by sending me an instant message saying he was selling cold cans of Diet Coke from under his desk for 50 cents less than the vending machine if I wanted one (spoiler alert: I did).

From then on, the lines of communication were opened, and we became pals.

For some reason, James and I never hit it off as more than work friends, but that was all right with me. Instead, we platonically fulfilled a mutual need to have someone, anyone, we could talk to about things other than gay bars and wine clubs.

Over time, James and I got very comfortable with each other in a platonic way (imagine that). In many ways, I felt closer to him than my brother and we shared everything. I'd complain about irregular periods and sex woes, and he'd ask me what the real deal about penis size was. No topic was off limits as we both capitalized being each other's portal into the opposite sex: something we used to strengthen everything from our relationships to our orgasms.

One thing I always appreciated about James was his ability to talk me off the ledge. He was gentle, calm, and cool. I was (am) neurotic, sometimes bat-shit crazy, and a major worrier, as most basic bitches tend to be. As such, more often than not, and especially on Mondays, I'd start our conversations off with my guns blazing. I'd divulge all the details, relevant or not, about some situation that ended up badly. But for everything that I would deem a crisis, he somehow artfully would turn them into no-big-deals.

My advice for anyone with a vagina who thinks they're destined to wind up alone? Put down the vibrator and find yourself a James.

Speaking of winding up alone, one day my point of contention was the need to date again. For anyone who is unaware, Chicago is cold and lonely for the majority of the year and it's much worse in the wintertime. So before shaving my legs would inevitably become a distant pastime of mine for about the fourth time in my adult life, it's no wonder I wanted to set my sights on someone to keep me warm until the time of year when the sun sets later than 4:30pm.

So I confided in James. I admitted that I saw a therapist, started a blog, ate pints and pints of ice cream, watched the Grey's re-runs, and leaned on my friends for advice. By all accounts, my break-up routine was quite normal and my post-ops were successful. The case of the cancerous ex and the all-wrong rebounds were cured. But when was the rehabilitation process going to really begin?

Clearly the big problem was how to meet a guy—a good one, a normal one—without the help of the Internet per Tom's orders. Old habits don't die easy and as I had conditioned myself, my preferred method of testing fate was logging onto the World Wide Web like it was some sort of water well to get my fix. I was no worse than Jacob running off to Lincoln Park to score some questionable blow. Okay, maybe I was a little better than that, tbh.

"All right, Em," James began in a private message to me from across the cubicles. "I see what you are saying and you definitely deserve to be mixing in some solid dates on top of everything else you've got going on."

Everything else I had going on? Well at least I was doing a good job fooling people that my life was somewhat productive because at this point, the in-and-out of everyday had sufficiently boiled down to going to work, microwaving a Lean Cuisine, not feeling satiated, blogging about men trying to pick me up for dates wearing cargo shorts, continuing to binge on a box of clearance chocolate from TJ Maxx, and—of course—the constant pursuit of trying to pass off leggings as pants in the workplace.

I digress.

"So let me ask you this," typed James, as I sipped my morning Starbucks.

Oh, God. Here it goes, I thought.

"Would you like me to see about setting you up with someone that I know?"

Oh.

You know, I never thought to ask James who he may have had in his Rolodex that may be looking for a super basic white girl with moderate baggage from her ex, a super clingy mother, and a job that pays as close to minimum wage as you can get. But lo and behold, he apparently had someone (possibly more than one?) looking for just the right amount of wrong.

Not to mention, I knew the type of person James was, the things he was into, and the crowds he ran with. He was an amateur chef and heavily into the music scene in Chicago. That said; James's fleet of available guys was bound to be able to play an instrument or cook a steak. Both were solid starts in my opinion.

"Well, who'd you have in mind?" I responded coyly, cracking my knuckles as I tickled the keyboard.

"Ricky Cardullo."

Ironically, I knew the name. Ricky was a hipster DJ who spun mash-ups every Monday night at a bar in Wicker Park. His jeans would likely be tighter than mine and his haircut trendier, but that describes about 50 percent of the credible dating pool these days.

"I don't know," I typed back. "A DJ?"

His guarantee was this: "You'll have a chill time with someone you wouldn't have met otherwise."

I thought about the simplicity there was in that statement and realized, what's the harm? Add the potential round of free drinks and the chance for first base action, and I was in.

~ ~ ~

The following Saturday night, I received a text from a number that I didn't recognize. Considering all good things must come to a beginning, I figured the anonymity could lead somewhere promising. It turned out to be Ricky. He was asking me out for a drink that night at a place called "The Map Room." How trendy and worldly sounding, I thought as I texted back my acceptance letter.

Now keep in mind this was my first date since the crash-and-burn known as Jacob. Though his brush with death was forever burned into my memory, I decided the best strategy with moving on from that was to boil it all down to a learning experience. In hindsight, this actually, has become one of my favorite pastimes. No matter how big the fuck-up, chalk it up to a learning experience and there's no reason that you can't be getting your nails done and sipping rose by the end of the day without a care in the world.

So, with my last crazy hurrah out of the way, I deemed myself free and clear to meet Ricky and let the universe guide us however it would. As such, I took a little more pride in getting ready than usual, just in case the universe decided this was going to be my future husband.

"I'm seeing Ricky tonight BTW," I texted James. "And I did my hair."

"Good for you, Em! Throw a little eyeliner on, k? And have fun," he replied.

As I applied a thick layer of liquid liner on the tops of my eyelids, it dawned on me how borderline unnecessary that would be. After all, Ricky and I were meeting at a bar in Wicker Park, a section of the city I didn't often venture to for the pure and simple fact that I didn't own enough second-hand flannel shirts to fit in properly. Even though it was a hub for hipsters, I had already dressed myself that night like I was on my way to an

Ariana Grande concert.

Fuck it, I thought. Maybe he'll actually enjoy seeing someone who only unintentionally doesn't shave their pits for once.

15 minutes later, I arrived at The Map Room. It was unmarked from the outside and resembled a dilapidated bungalow. To put things into perspective, my Uber driver passed it twice and when the driver asked, "Is this it?" I responded, "God, I hope not."

As I walked in, the place was exactly the opposite of what I was prepared for. It was as if there was some ban against high heels and freshly curled hair. I know it was the dead of winter, but how could I be the only one in a bar on a Saturday night wearing a little bit of bronzer and attempting to show some collarbone? There was a fine line between standing out and sticking out, and based on the looks I was getting, I couldn't tell which side of it I was riding.

After doing a mini lap of the bar, it was clear I had arrived a little earlier than Ricky. While I generally am of the belief that on-time is late, something told me punctuality wasn't exactly a huge priority for a man whose livelihood revolved around impromptu dance parties. Regardless, I curtailed my tendency to judge by getting myself an alcoholic beverage. Immediately. It went like this: I asked to see the wine list. They only had beer. I asked for a Miller Lite. They only served craft. I asked to start a tab. They only took cash.

Awesome.

Getting over those several hurdles, I finally made my way to a table in the back of the bar with a pale ale destined to give me massive heartburn and bloat and waited for my date. I kept my eyes peeled for some guy in too-tight pants and a leather jacket smelling faintly of weed to make his way toward me. A short time later, someone who fit just the bill rolled up to the high-top table, threw down his slouchy knit hat, and gave me the quickest hug I had ever experienced. Was it that hard to tell it was self-tanner and not chlamydia on my cheek?

"How's it going, Emma?" Ricky asked with minimal eye contact as he pulled a wad of sweaty singles out from his pocket and ordered and IPA from the server.

"It's Emily," I said.

"Huh?"

"Never mind."

"So what up?" he asked.

What up? Were we old friends catching up at a Starbucks? I mean, if he really wanted me to go into it, I was asking for a raise at work, was currently on a diet that involved tricking my body into thinking it was pregnant, and had already deemed this night a total waste of lip gloss.

Sparing him the dissertation, I pulled a generic response from off the shelf and fired back just as blasé as he.

"Not too much, yourself?"

"Same."

As the minutes rolled by, it became evident Ricky was a regular at The Map Room and had his order—and his dollar bills—read to fire off. He also came prepared with a business pitch as to why I should hire him and his DJ partner for my next family reunion. It was like, okay, I get it. You know how to layer 80s music with anything by Jay-Z, cool. I could tell he wanted me to be infatuated with his career, but instead I was enthralled with how he could fit into size zero jeans and I did not.

I didn't need to ask to know that Ricky had never stepped foot onto Michigan Avenue in his life and probably preferred that the girls he date know how to roll cigarettes and restore vintage pianos than how to prevent ingrown hairs after a bikini wax. Not saying that a guy has to be exactly like me or into the things I am, but I could just tell that some of the very things that made me me were going to be of little interest to a guy like Ricky.

But aside from the date's going-nowhere nature, I owed it to myself, to Tom, and to James to stick it out. After all, James promised me a "chill" time and I wasn't going home until I got it.

"James said a lot of nice things about you," Ricky said.

"Oh, really?" I asked, setting a mental reminder to write him a thank-you card.

"Yeah, painted a real nice picture. I was actually going to ask you out last night," he declared as out-of-nowhere as it gets. "But I ended up eating an ecstasy pill and things got pretty, pretty, pretty weird."

First off, does everyone do drugs now? And secondly, you eat an ecstasy pill? Like, do you put it inside of a sandwich or something? Bake it into a cookie? Straight shoot it and chase it with a shot of Malort? Clearly, my relationship with casual drugs was far less intelligent than my relationship with casual men, but I was learning. Fast.

To that, I nodded and smiled and choked down more of my flavorless, flat beer. Ricky's Friday night date with the other "E" in his life immediately exposed him for the man—or rather, manchild—he really was and I was over it.

You know, I pride myself on being able to pass an indefinite amount time with a definite stranger. This is why I'm good with taking the middle seat on an airplane. But my short time with Ricky was becoming rather painful, even after a good college try. (I mean, I was drinking a gross beer that came from a dirty tap, how much more thematic can you get?) But the truth was, I never had to be a more unauthentic version of myself in all my years of dating as I sat there and pretended like I cared about his Hall & Oates mash-ups and party drug preferences.

Do you have any idea how exhausting and difficult it is to pretend to like bands you've never even heard of while simultaneously acting like DJ-ing is a legitimate career for a man who was pushing thirty? Trust me, it takes a lot out of you, and I honestly couldn't remember a time that I needed to get a drink by myself just to take the edge off of getting a drink with someone else (if that makes any sense at all). But that was exactly what I intended to do, just as soon as I could catch a break.

I secretly hoped Ricky's high would wear off and he'd just crash out right at the table so I could leave with ease. But no such luck was mine to be had. Two hours into our meeting, Rick was still dropping the beat with me. Glancing at the time, I cringed at the thought of how far away last call was and knew I had no choice but to pull the plug on this irreversible coma of dates. So in an effort to get a little life support, I made up lie.

"I'm kind of drunk," I said to Ricky, hoping that faking sudden inebriation would suffice as the reason for my early, yet inevitable, departure.

"Yeah, me too."

Thank God.

"And I have a big day tomorrow, so I should probably head home and sober up," I added to seal up the story.

"Yeah, I know how that is."

Call me crazy, but Ricky knowing what it was like to have a big day ahead of him seemed less probable than him owning anything from J.Crew. Thankfully, he didn't seem to have any objection to my cue to leave as he was jonesing to zip up his doll-sized leather jacket and light up a Natural Spirit cigarette anyways.

At that point, we awkwardly hugged for the second time in the evening and said goodbye as we parted ways. Sadly, me getting into a cab and leaving was the first thing that felt right since arriving.

"Ricky's a no-go," I texted James before throwing my phone deep into my purse as a sign of my utter frustration.

And that's the point at which I should have gone home.

Even though the date was a beyond a bust, for some reason the wind didn't feel quite out of my sails just yet. After all, it had been months since I attempted to pull myself together and I had already blown my diet for the night with six-hundred-calories worth of beer. Why not see what else this Saturday had in store for Stella, who was only just starting to get her groove back?

So, instead of telling the driver to take the fastest way back to Lincoln Park, I took my time in replying to his query, "Where to, Miss?"

"How about Milwaukee and North Avenue, please."

At that corner was a tapas restaurant I had gone to during the summer with one of my best girlfriends. I instantly got nostalgic thinking of the warmer weather and remembered they had amazing cocktails. Good memories and delicious sangria were more than enough reason to lure me in for my "after-drinks" drink with myself. So, with an extra wad of fresh singles in my wallet from the preceding cash-only bar, I quickly paid the cabbie and headed in as a solo drinker to a lounge that was ironically called "People."

The first person I saw was the bartender, who was noticeably attractive and had kind eyes. That's a fancy way of saying he was hot. As I sat down, he greeted me with a cocktail napkin and a handshake. His name was Colin and he appeared to not be under the influence of any illegal club drugs, which was already an excellent re-start to the night.

"What brings you in tonight?" Colin asked, giving me a chance to settle in on my barstool and take off my jacket before taking my order.

I know it was just a routine question for a bartender to ask an incoming patron, but for some reason when he posed the question, I gave more thought to it than I normally would. And while I didn't need to go into detail about the exact "choose-your-own-adventure" path that found me a seat at his bar, thinking for a split second how and why you wind up anywhere was a tiny little momentary mind-fuck.

"I've just got some extra cash to blow," I coyly replied.

"Fair enough. What are we drinking?"

"I'll start with a white sangria. No, red," I said.

"Sounds good, Rachel."

"Emily. My name is Emily," I clarified to a stranger for the second time that night.

"You'll never believe me, but I was going to go with that. Oh well, I'll be right one of these days," Colin said, as he went off to mix my drink.

I knew right away I wanted to interact with him far more than your average bartender whose duties usually cap at making change for a ten. Colin was different. And, while I suppose it could have been part of the whole charming-server bit, it seemed like we were after the same thing in the end: just the tip.

I soon asked to see a food menu. This was a strategic move to prolong our interactions. I assumed noshing on something would lead to ordering more drinks which would lead to more conversation which would lead to exchanging phone numbers. While it was never my goal to blow a diet I'd spent half a month committing to, I figured it was all worth it if the end-game was a sext or two.

"So what's good here?" I asked.

"Besides me?" Colin continued to play along. "Kidding—go for the house-made mac n' cheese. Sinful, but so worth it."

Sinful, but so worth it? Like the fact that I was now on my second date of the night after lying by omission to get out of the first one?

"Sounds delicious," I said, closing my menu with affirmation. "I'll have that."

What started with a recommendation for the house-made mac n' cheese quickly turned into a storytelling session between the two of us, complete with an impromptu sangria taste test. Before I knew it, I was a little (lot) drunk on Spanish wine and Colin had now shifted from my bartender, to my neighbor, as he posted up on the stool next to me. Maybe this was the guy who James meant to set me up with all along?

Colin and I talked all night about everything from our families to our favorite sushi bars and everything in between. I was shocked that I went from solo-diner to semi-dater all in a matter of hours, but took it for the win it was and didn't overthink it much.

"Besides a really good bartender and a flight of sangria, what's the one thing you can't live without?" Colin asked playfully. I liked the random Q&A. I really did.

"Cheesecake," I responded without hesitation.

"Solid choice. Sorry, but will you excuse me? I have to close my bar-back out for the night." He disappeared behind the bar and into the back of the restaurant.

Close out for the night? What time was it? I shuttered at the thought that it could be close to two in the morning. As he drifted to the back, for the first time in a couple of hours I was alone, giving me a chance to dig through my purse and find the phone I so purposefully chucked to the bottom of my bag much earlier in the evening. I clicked to power it on: 1:30 AM

God, help me.

Moments later, Colin returned.

"Will you do me a favor and share this with me?" he asked, presenting a plate with a slice of cheesecake drizzled in chocolate syrup along with two forks.

Will you do me a favor and marry me?

Clearly, the universe was rewarding me for being the trooper that I was on my last date (which, mind you, was earlier that same night) by delivering me a good-looking boy who was delivering me a good-looking dessert. Though my diet was shot straight to hell, I was in my own personal heaven.

While most people hit-it and quit-it, I split-it and quit-it, and asked for my tab as soon as I shoveled in my portion of the cheesecake. Needless to say, I had lost track of time in a big way and overstayed my welcome in a part of town I had no real business being in, seeing that I didn't listen to indie rock and couldn't seem to find a fashionable way to wear a scarf.

"Colin, can you close me out?"

"I sure can. Sign here," he said, slipping me a string of receipt tape. To my shock, it was blank.

"With your phone number, please."

I stared at him in awe.

"Unless that's too forward? I just thought it'd be nice to go out with you again, maybe try that sushi place I was telling you about?"

Perhaps my shocked eyes didn't properly communicate it, but I was most definitely interested in consuming another 2,000 calories with him. I hadn't had such easy-going chatter with a guy since my therapist, Tom. At that, I left him my phone number, correct area code and all, and hugged him goodbye.

"Get home safe, sweetheart," he said, as I put my jacket on and double-checked that my phone was in my purse.

"You, too."

All in all, a break-even kind of a night.

~ ~ ~

But as fate would have it, there was one more serendipitous moment left to get in before the buzzer. One that would push the night well into the green. And to this day, it gives me chills to think what my life would be like if it had never happened. Like, what if I had gone straight home after my date with DJ Disaster, or had decided to loiter a little longer with my new favorite bartender, perhaps back at his place? The answer to those questions is easy: I would not have been where I needed to be for the defining moment of my life thus far.

In other words, I would not have met the one person whose path I know I was meant to cross—right then and right there.

CHAPTER FOURTEEN/LESSON FOURTEEN

- Step 1: Lock eyes with a stranger. Step 2: See what happens

I think we can all agree at this point, Colin is great. If you're not team Colin, then you never wanted Rachael McAdams to pick Ryan Gosling in The Notebook and I don't know what kind of a monster you are.

But—Spoiler Alert—Colin's role in the story ends right here, right now.

Look, I'll start by saying that Colin had taken care of me in a way that no bartender had before. No, he didn't take me to the back and give it to me while pressed up against the beer cooler. But he did something else that was incredibly thoughtful, and without even realizing it. That's the funny part.

Colin was my timekeeper. There's no other way to describe it. He fed me lines and he fed me drinks, and through both he was able to keep me at People and kick me out just in time for me to have my moment. To meet him.

There's no way that Colin knows the role he played in the alignment of the stars that night, because I never actually spoke to him again. No, he didn't fuck up and send me a dick pic that made me block his number right away. He just became pleasantly irrelevant in the whole scheme of things. You'll see what I mean shortly.

Anyhow, the orchestration of the rest of my evening fell entirely on his shoulders. Sounds like a lot of pressure, I know. But he performed flawlessly and I'm silently indebted to this man, as blissfully unaware of that as he is. All I can say is that someday, I hope to be someone else's "Colin"—in fact, I pray that I already have been.

Leaving the tapas lounge, I was shivering cold and slightly disoriented from all the boys and calories that had unexpectedly fallen onto my plate that night. On top of that, impracticality overruled rationality that evening, as I had chosen to leave home without a real winter jacket, figuring that the time spent outside of Ubers and bars would be minimal. Problem is, a moment of cold in the Windy City can feel like you're going down in the Titanic's icy waters especially when everyone and their brother is trying to order an Uber to get home and it's surging 5.6 times the normal rate with an average pick-up time of 22 minutes.

That was precisely the case as I stood on Milwaukee Avenue wondering if I'd make it home without hypothermia with only 12 percent battery left to my name.

Another logistical nightmare of Wicker Park was that half the bars in it were calling last call at 2, and the other half were staying open until 4 for after-hours. So people in the area were either trying to go big or go home. Regardless of each other's preferences (for me, home), we were all in search of the same thing—a vacant, warm ride to get us where we wanted to go.

As such, I gave up on Uber and decided to tempt fate the old-fashioned way—by hailing a taxi. I swam my way through the crowd of smokers toward to the curb and looked both ways. It was evident there wasn't a cab on the road that didn't already have someone just as semi-drunk as I was texting the old "Wyd?" from the backseat of a toasty cab. Sad as these booty-call-seekers were, I envied every one of them for the simple fact they were going from a warm cab to a warm bed because at that moment, I had neither of those things anywhere near the horizon.

Frustrated, I started walking down the block, having no concept of direction—and that had nothing to do with my blood-alcohol level, actually. This part of town was famous for six-cornered intersections everywhere you looked, which made it appear like I was trapped in some sick urban maze where men walked around with mustaches and JanSport backpacks.

Disillusioned, I picked up the pace ever-so-slightly, making a conscious effort to gaze over my left shoulder in three-second intervals hoping to catch sight of a cab with its service light on.

The colder I got, the less rational I became and I legitimately started to fear it would be forty-five minutes to an hour before I found a ride home—if I found one at all. I have to admit; a very small part of me thought about shooting DJ Ricky a text. I'm sure his pad wasn't too far from where I had wound up, and if anything, he struck me as the type who would have a decrepit futon and a worn-out "Alf" t-shirt from 1987 with my name on it for the night.

Alas, I couldn't let thrift-store-finds or questionable futon stains become part of my destiny after a night that had made a serious comeback. So, I kept focused and visualized that a car would soon come for me.

Moments later, I spotted an occupied taxi that appeared to be slowing down about halfway up the block. And despite what the drunk hipster girl in her embroidered satin bomber jacket ten feet away from me was thinking, I knew that ride was mine for the taking. As such, I stalked the cab like a lion hunting its prey as it began to slow down even more.

Lucky for me, I then heard the click of the power locks and knew it'd only be mere moments before I'd feel warmth again.

Though it could have easily been misconstrued as me needing to take a gigantic piss, I was standing just a foot away from the door, rapidly bouncing up and down as I tried to stay warm and keep myself from prematurely ripping away at the door handle like it was the last pair of size seven and a half UGGs on clearance. During this time, the man occupying the backseat was taking his sweet time paying for his fare. Oddly enough, he too was forking it over in singles. What the hell was going on with this all-cash revolution?

The man in the backseat—stylish, attractive, in his thirties—looked up at me from inside and sympathized with my chill. He opened the door and waved me in to warm up as he finished collecting his change. I heard him thank the cab driver before exiting into traffic through the other door. He had an accent—a beautiful, unidentifiable accent. It immediately haunted me in the best possible way.

"Wait just one moment if you could, sir" I asked of the taxi driver as I quickly stepped out of his cab and back into the numbing cold.

"Excuse me," I said, teeth chattering. It was directed at the man who had just rode in the taxi before me. He turned around.

"Your accent is gorgeous. Where is it from?"

I knew he spoke English: I had just heard him. I knew he understood me: he smiled.

But he didn't answer me.

He just looked at me—half in that do-I-know-you-from-somewhere way and half like he was just kind of admiring a painting in a museum or something. Since he was most certainly a stranger, and I was of course no work of art, especially not after collecting bartenders and DJs for the last six hours, I didn't quite understand the purpose of the staring contest. But I wasn't complaining. His eyes were a beautiful blue that pierced through the dark of the night and I was staring deeply at them, through them, awaiting my reply.

He broke the quiet shortly thereafter, "Holland."

"Holland," I repeated.

Holland, I thought.

I had my answer, and still did not move.

"Would you like to come get a drink with me?" asked the man.

No. I wouldn't like to get a drink with you.

I didn't say that, but I certainly thought it. For one thing, it was late—really late. We all know nothing good happens after midnight, so that meant no one makes it out alive after 2am. For another, I was drunk, hence the reason I had the balls to badger this poor man about his accent in the first place. And not to stereotype or anything, but I had absolutely no business saying yes to anything propositioned by a foreigner, even a really attractive one.

Not to mention, I had actually just read an article in Marie Claire earlier that day by a journalist who had met a charming European man (much like our nameless Dutch friend), had a few drinks with him, and ended up a rape victim because of it. Granted, she lived to tell about it in an award-winning piece, I wasn't after the same journalistic notoriety. Furthermore, I had clearly put myself in the presence of enough strange men for one night that I needed to just go home. If anything, I knew my mother would have approved of this choice and I owed her one.

So, while I vowed to prevent my night from becoming inspiration for an episode of Law & Order: Special Victim's Unit, there was undeniably something about this man that didn't make him a total creepazoid. In fact, I truly wanted to say yes to his invitation, if only to hear him order a drink or ask the bartender where the bathroom was—seriously, anything to catch another wave of his accent. But despite his voice oozing an angelic charm not typically heard in this devilish city, I couldn't bring myself to do it. I just couldn't say yes to getting an after-hours drink with him.

Positive that the cab driver was either wildly annoyed or wildly entertained by this whole potential courtship-in-the-making, there I stood, one leg in the car and one on the street, continuing to run the meter. I couldn't stop admiring this beautiful man standing three feet away from me in the cold who was waiting for my final answer. It was now my turn to break the silence, even though I could have happily stayed in it a little while longer.

"Look, I can't tonight—it's late and I've got to get home. But, please, will you take my number? Take it and call me—or don't—or something." Like a bumbling idiot, I rattled off my digits giving him no choice but to punch them into his phone. His flip phone. It had been years since I'd seen one of those. I hoped to god that ancient artifact would save my number properly. And that it didn't mean he was involved in human trafficking.

"Oh, and I'm Emily," I thought I should add in. The third time I made my name known that night to another man.

"I am Floris," he said.

I smiled at Floris and committed to getting into the cab once and for all.

"Where to—miss?" the driver said, mocking the entire song and dance.

"Lincoln Park."

Finally.

CHAPTER FIFTEEN/LESSON FIFTEEN

- Yelp everything, Google everyone

While I'm sure my cab driver that night had seen quite a few things go on in the backseat of his Prius, I can bet that none were as innocent and serendipitous as that. Again, like Colin, I can also bet that this cab driver had no idea the role he'd just played in fate, for he was the courier.

He had brought me Floris.

Yes, that was his name. At least that's how he signed a text message that arrived in my inbox around four o'clock in the morning. I'm sure he was completely lit when he sent it, but he said—in cute, but broken English—that it was "fancy" meeting me, "Emele," and he hoped that my cab ride home was quick, safe, and warm. Perhaps he wasn't a European rapist-killer after all?

I replied back to him sometime after waking up the following morning, thanking him for getting out of the cab when and where he did, and said that I looked forward to meeting up. I wanted to gently lead him to do the right thing: to call me, to ask me out, to read me the motherfucking phone book in that sexy, stylish way he spoke.

Unfortunately, the drunken haze we found each other in was simply too good to be true, or perhaps he had not yet emerged from his hangover, as I did not receive a reply to the text I sent. But with me being sort of a shade-ball who liked to meet-and-greet as many boys as she could on a Saturday night, I suppose it wasn't at all ironic that I had given my number to someone who probably ended up moving on to the next great thing in Wicker Park that night. Something told me Floris wasn't the type who had trouble meeting ready-and-willing girls.

~ ~ ~

The weekend had come and gone with nothing major to write home about. I hadn't heard anything from DJ Ricky, who was probably sleeping for the first time in seventy-two hours. I had also yet to feel inspired to set something up with Colin, despite the fact that he had successfully navigated to my heart by way of cheesecake and had texted me to see how the rest of my weekend was going. And Floris was still a complete no-show on my screen. Zero for three's not bad, right?

So I contacted someone I knew would be happy to have dialogue with me: my mother. Middle-aged and menopausal, there was no doubt this woman enjoyed any and every opportunity to live vicariously through me. So I gave her a small window into my big-city life and mentioned just briefly that I had a new hobby, which was seeing how many back-to-back dates I could have in one night.

"And then I met this guy from Holland," I segued.

"Holland?" I could hear the Jew in her disbelief.

"Yes, Holland. He was getting out of a taxi when I was getting in. I don't know anything about him, but he was really good looking and I gave him my number."

"Emily . . ." my mom said, unsure as to whether she was condoning or condemning.

"Yup, he texted me at four in the morning, but I'm sure he was a waste-case at that point. So, yeah."

"Did you write him back?" she asked. Who did she think I was? I had been off the horse for a while, but I still knew how to ride.

"Of course I did," I said. "Haven't heard back yet, though."

"Well keep me posted, he sounds like the most promising of them all if I'm keeping all my notes straight," she said. I also found it interesting she was treating my love life like a day at the races, placing bets on who she thought would be the frontrunner.

I got off the phone with her shortly thereafter, pledging to keep her posted on the boy-front. From there, I let most of the details from my uneventful weekend fade into a graveyard with all the other lackluster moments I had been compiling since living in the city. At that moment, I realized the irony of it all. It was so funny that I had spent all my life up until this point thinking my Chicago life would be the answer to it all. And upon surveying the seen, it had done more harm than good in the short time it had been my home.

With that observation, I pulled myself out of bed to ride out the rest of my Sunday.

And there I was: vertical for the first time in twelve hours. Go me.

~ ~ ~

Monday came and went like any other. There was nothing extraordinary about my day; in fact, it was rather quiet. From what I could tell, DJ Ricky was still in a coma, Colin was on hold, and Floris had forgotten I ever existed. So, with no distractions, I tinkered away at my to-do list until it was finally time to catch a train and head home. And that's what single in the city was like. Riveting.

The ride from downtown to Lincoln Park was about thirty minutes by way of the Red Line, which was my preferred method of transportation compared to the bus in the winter months. There were fewer stops and it stayed warmer when the doors opened between them. As I rode home that day, my cell service cut out like it normally did when zooming at 75 miles per hour a hundred feet below ground. But when I finally came up from the underground, my it was my life that suddenly switched to another track.

My phone buzzed with a voicemail. Knowing that it was more than likely my mother, who routinely called between 5:15 PM and 5:20 PM every weeknight after I left work, I decided checking on it could wait. I was numb and hungry from the day, and I just wanted to get home where I could strategically ignore my roommates and retreat to the fate of the DVR.

Once home, I continued to play keep-away with my cell phone and proceeded to fix myself a sandwich. After that, I put away laundry, read a magazine, and Googled the diet plan I was on to see if it had any links to cervical cancer. I pretty much did anything and everything to occupy the evening and avoid unwanted small talk with my closest female relative, my mother. What can I say? I know my day was uneventful, but I just wasn't in the mood to hear about rousing hot flashes and mood swings.

Just before bed, which was around 9 PM that night, I went to set my alarm and realized that the voicemail icon was still stuck on my screen. Something about it lingering there annoyed me to the core. So, in a last-ditch effort to clean up my user interface before turning out the light on my nightstand, I called my voicemail, fully expecting to hear my mom announce she clipped a Kohl's coupon and would save it for the next time I came home in case I needed a pack of Jockey underwear. But instead of her sharp, nasally New York accent, I heard that unforgettable Dutch one inviting me to dinner the following night.

"Emele," he began. It was as if I could hear him misspelling my name. I didn't care, though. The European flare was nice and made me feel fancy. Alas, I sprung up from under the covers and listened intently to what was coming through the line.

"Hello, it's Floris. I texted you the other night and did not hear back from you. However, I have two days off and would like to have dinner with you tomorrow if you are interested. Please call me when you can, so I can see about making the reservation. Okay, dear? Thank you."

Shit, shit, SHIT.

My complacency with checking my phone had put me almost four hours behind on his offer. Did I miss out on the limited time only offer?

My mind raced over this voicemail. He wanted to do dinner. I wanted to do dinner. Wait. Could I even do dinner on my diet? So many questions in my head, so many butterflies in my stomach. Also, can you believe it? My mother called it! The "promising" one had made contact.

Back to that dinner, huh? I immediately envisioned it with him at some placeless location, listening to him ask questions about the menu such as, "What is double-down fried chicken sandwich?" I pictured him asking me to translate things, asking me why I picked this restaurant—whatever one it would be, asking me about my life. I thought about me getting lost in his rare, anti-Midwestern genetic make-up. I saw it, clear as day, me; a dark-hair-and-eyed half-Jew on a date with a man of the Aryan race. How twenty-first century of us. How taboo. How were we going to make this happen?

It wasn't long before my fantasy was interrupted. The butterflies in my stomach were replaced by a gut-wrenching fear that I'd be unable to reach him so far after-the-fact. I immediately hit redial, only to hear his line ring and ring. The excitement through my blood came and went, as my effort to reach him was null and void.

I went to compose a new text message, but remembered what he said in his message—that he never heard back from me. What did he mean, he never got my text message? I wrote him back, that I knew for sure as confirmed by my sent message folder. I wondered if it had anything to do with him having an international number and global phone plan. Perhaps he could reach me while in the States, but I couldn't reach him? I had a sick feeling that was it, and that we weren't going to connect. Ships passing. I called back one more time and left a message anyway, hoping that he'd be more inclined than I was to check his inbox sooner rather than later.

What also was nauseating was my preconceived notion that every foreign man who steps foot on this side of the sea gets instant third-base action from anyone with whom he exchanges numbers. Girls on this side of the pond are just sluts like that—not me, of course. But a part of me was sure that because I didn't respond right away, he had already moved down on the phone tree and dialed the next cute American girl he added to his contacts this week. It was that accent, I tell you. He could have had whomever he wanted.

In my silence, I decided to build a case against him so as to not feel hurt when, two weeks later, I would inevitably be still dwelling on the fact that we never got together.

First off, I didn't have to acknowledge his broken English text message with the gross misspelling of one of the country's most common names. And I could have penalized him for the misused emoticons, but I didn't. I wrote him back regardless of whether he got the message and I still was fully open to sitting next to someone who probably would never understand what I meant when describing this situation as a total "White Girl Problem."

Secondly: two days off? From what exactly? That didn't make any sense. And where could he work without being a U.S. citizen? Something was fuzzy with this one; and I was confident I could get the story—if I could just get the call back. And moments later, that's exactly what I got.

I instantly picked up the phone. Thankfully, my neurosis didn't block my manners, and I was able to greet him in true American fashion. By saying, "Hello."

"Emily (Emele)," he famously began.

Admittedly, I was a little drunk when I met him. And like most things when you're a little drunk, details can get a little fuzzy. What wasn't fuzzy at all, though, was that voice. It was so poignant that it took me right back to Milwaukee Avenue, in the freezing cold, last Saturday night, where I stood one foot in the cab, one out, staring at the most interesting man I had seen outside of the Gay Pride Parade last year.

"Listen. I'm so glad you called. I can't talk long now, I'm at the Belden Stratford, at L2O, but if you are able to do it, I will make a reservation for two at Schwa tomorrow evening. I'm not sure of the time yet, but I'll speak to them tomorrow and let you know. Okay, darling?"

Yes. Okay. Absolutely. Where do I sign up? My inner dialogue was loving this. Especially that whole darling thing.

"That sounds wonderful, Floris. Call me when you have the time settled and I will for sure answer my phone," I said, having learned my lesson.

"Of course, Emele. Goodnight, miss."

All right, crisis averted. But what the fuck was Schwa? Moreover, how the hell did you spell it (so I could google it, of course). And how did he know about it and I didn't? And what was L2O? I knew the Belden-Stratford was an iconic Lincoln Park hotel, not far from my apartment, but L2O wasn't ringing a bell at all. Nonetheless, it was all irrelevant, because I had a date on the horizon with Floris, and I could finally fall asleep and rest easy knowing that ninety-five percent of the girls in my neighborhood weren't as close as I was to living out a fantasy with a sexy European man.

And on that note, I went to bed dreaming of the grammatically incorrect sweet nothings he'd whisper in my ear as he struggled to unhook my American-made bra. Because, let's face it, that's where this was going.

Or was it?

~ ~ ~

The next day at work, for once, I felt somewhat equipped with decent water cooler material. It had been weeks since I reported anything juicy, and as my luck would have it, I had been replenished. Also, as my luck would have it, I ran into James in the break room early in the day. He was just the man, outside of Floris, that I wanted to see.

"So what happened with Ricky?" he asked, stirring his coffee.

"Irrelevant," I answered.

"What? Why?"

"Because I have a date tonight with someone new."

"Good lord. Which bar did you meet him at?" he asked.

"I actually met him outside the bar," I corrected. "Yeah, we met randomly on the street in Wicker Park on Saturday night."

"After your date with Ricky?"

"No, after my second date with Colin."

"Who's Colin?" asked James.

"Irrelevant again," I insisted.

"I may need a Venn diagram for all this, but who's the guy?" James asked as we made our way back to our desks. It was time for the conversation to segue from verbal to chat room.

"He's foreign and has a really cute accent," I typed.

"Oh, Em. Only you," he responded in that condescending way a person with an unfulfilled European fantasy does.

"So where are you guys going?"

"Umm—some place called 'Shuwa' I think? Or 'Shwan' maybe? I don't know, I couldn't really hear him and I have no clue how to spell it."

I knew I was way off, but seeing that James was an aspiring recreational cook, he quickly decoded my attempt at pronouncing the name of this could-be restaurant in Chicago.

"Wait. SCHWA?!" Finally, I elicited a response from him other than disapproval of my tanking love life.

"Yeah, sure, that sounds about right."

"Oh my god," he said.

"What? Does it suck? Is it Inidan? You know my stomach can't do Indian on a first date."

"Emily," he typed as he looked over the cubicle to make sure I was still paying attention to the chat window on my desktop. "That place...takes MONTHS to get into. Okay? MONTHS. Who is this guy? Who does he know?"

"That's a good question, actually. I really don't know all that much about him. Just his name and his number at this point. And that he can't spell my name right, but whatever."

"Okay, well, do you want my advice?"

"Always."

"Dress up and be polite. You want him to leave him no excuse not to pay."

"Why? What happens if he doesn't pay?" I asked.

"You won't be able to afford your heating bill this month."

Frightened, I closed out of the chat and immediately did my overdue due diligence on this Schwa place.

I started with Yelp and didn't even need to do a search. There it was, smack dab on the homepage. Schwa was listed as number four on the list of the top five restaurants—in the nation. By no means was I a foodie, but it didn't take culinary fandom to realize they were good. So I clicked into the reviews to confirm just how good.

The menu appeared to be eight to ten courses and chock full of things I'd never even heard of. Portillo's hot dogs? Yes, of course. I'm fluent. Deconstructed apple pie soup? Say what?!

I then turned to Zagat, the bible on restaurant reviews.

"Willing 'guinea pigs' devour the 'mind-bendingly creative' New American 'experiments' of 'punk rock cooking genius' Michael Carlson at his 'cutting-edge' Wicker Park BYO hot-spot," was the beginning of the summary. And from the sound of it, I was going to a rave, not a nice dinner. Really, what the hell was I stumbling into? Would I need a wristband to get in? I read on.

"Bring an 'open mind, some booze, and some big bucks' and strap in for an 'exhilarating' night out."

We all know bringing booze would be no problem. In fact, I'd require it if I was going to make it out of my house and actually do this date. But the open mind part scared me. What restaurant suggests you show up ready for anything? What was this, a swinger's party?

After Zagat, I finally made it to their actual website. Because the menu changed so often (a reflection of what I could only assume was their cooking team's undiagnosed bipolar disorders), there was only a "sample" of what you might expect to eat posted up online. The menu—which really was just a list of ten items followed by a price—began with something called, an "amuse."

Amuse? Will they be going a magic trick or an opening number? I figured with the $110 price tag staring at me from the bottom of the menu page, that had to be the case. $110 for shoes, yes. $110 for dinner? No. There was no way that could have just been the price of food.

Could it?

The second item said, "crab" in bold font. Crab? Crab what? Rangoon, I hoped.

Below that, "pine, mushroom, plantain:" a list of random ingredients that don't go with each other? Well that's helpful, I thought.

The rest of the menu went on just like that. It was a cat-and-mouse game with ingredients, some bolded, some not. Some I had heard of, some I had not. Where was the lobster macaroni and cheese? The breaded chicken sandwich? The value menu? The kid's meal?

Aside from the missing staples, the other confusing part was what to order. Was each of these mysterious items $110? Was it a packaged deal and you get them all for one lump sum? Could I sub out the scary ones such as "tiger fish—carrot, marshmallow, cardamom" for the one I actually understood: "dessert" (no further description). I prided myself on my ability to scout a menu prior to any date and know precisely what to order before even leaving for the restaurant. But this was different. I was at a loss and took comfort in only one thing: that this place was BYOB. At least the bottle of booze would be the one part of this date that would be somewhat familiar to me.

By this point, I had stopped trying to decipher anymore of the menu, which was about as foreign as Floris. It finally dawned on me that this meal was set up as prix fixe. Meaning these bat-shit crazy chefs were going to force me to eat whatever concoctions their lunatic minds came up with for the night, up to ten times. And then afterwards, if I lived to tell about it, I would owe them half my life savings. Remind me again, how badly did I want to have dinner with Floris?

The final item listed on the menu page was not edible, nor was it very palatable in any other capacity: "No cell phones."

Wait, so no lifeline at the expensive restaurant with the off-kilter culinary team? What does this guy want from me, I questioned.

Look, I understand the concept of taking someone out to dinner for a first date. But this was a really nice dinner. There had to be a trick. Was I going to have to perform a sex act for each course that was served? Would each have to be more perverse than the last as each plate that was dropped? And on another note, he couldn't possibly be expecting me to pick up even half of the bill, right? After all, he invited me to a place that was charging $110 a head. All I required to be happy was a hot dog with ketchup on it. If he had his heart set on Schwa, I felt like it would have been courteous of Floris to let me know if he was expecting to—no pun intended—go Dutch on this one. Because let's face it, if I were on my own for it, I was going to have to pawn some jewelry or blow someone on my way to the restaurant if I even wanted to so much as nibble on the botarga/polenta/chocolate...whatever the fuck that was. And with that ominous "no cell phones" policy listed clear as day on the menu, how convenient would this all be when I couldn't call for help or text my mom a final goodbye.

Just as my anxiety was spiking, Floris interrupted the research I was conducting in my cubicle with a timely phone call.

"Hello, Emele."

"Floris, hi. How are you?" I wondered if he could hear the fear in my voice.

"I'm just about to start at Alinea, but wanted to let you know I had gone over to Schwa this morning. I requested a table."

As per the conversation I had with James, I was prepared for Floris to tell me they couldn't seat us until the summer of 2019. But he informed me otherwise.

"Michael Carlson is holding a table for two at 9:15 tonight for us. Can you make it?"

A table for two for us? He had to be in Holland's mafia. Had to be.

"Yes, I can make it," I said, scribbling Michael Carlson's name on a Post-it.

"Okay, wonderful. Anything else, Emele, before I let you go?"

I don't know what possessed me, but there was something else. So, I asked it.

"Do you even remember what I look like?"

Whoops!

For someone who was hoping not to pay for her dinner, it was completely ballsy and inappropriate of me to suggest his senses were as impaired as mine on the night we crossed paths. Definitely not the taste you want to leave in someone's mouth prior to having the nicest dinner of your life, but I couldn't help it. It was word vomit at its finest and I was genuinely curious to hear his answer.

Thankfully, he responded quickly and cheerfully. "Of course I do! You look like a little deer."

"A deer?" I said, slightly flabbergasted that I was compared to a forest-dwelling animal.

"Yes, a deer," he was resilient in locking in his final answer. "You have little brown deer-eyes and you have a very captivating stare about you. Just like a compact deer in the woods."

I assumed "compact" meant "skinny," which was enough to put a smile on my face.

"See you at Schwa, Floris."

I googled Michael Carlson's name immediately after hanging up. The first hit: "Schwa's Michael Carlson Arrested for Setting Off Fireworks" was a post from the well-known foodie blog, Eater.

The next? An article in GQ Magazine. The journalist, Alan Richman, said that in 2007, Carlson, 33, and with a new baby, cooked him a legendary meal in his 26-seat restaurant and then disappeared on a three-day cocaine, alcohol, and ecstasy binge. Hmmm, I wondered if he knew Ricky?

But aside from all the omens, the writer made special note that Schwa's food was right up there with the top restaurants in the nation and that even Michelle Obama had eaten there. To the best of my knowledge, she survived. Right?

CHAPTER SIXTEEN/LESSON SIXTEEN

- Never underestimate Plan B

Just prior to the date, I somewhat agonized over what to wear to this dining occasion. I had nothing with Armani Exchange written clear across the breast, which I believe is the attire-of-choice for European men. I wanted to look nice, but I wanted to feel comfortable. I wanted to come off sexy enough for him to pay, but conservative enough to not have to throw down for a threesome with the waiter after dessert. I settled on a blue mini-dress with winter-approved black leggings, tall black boots, and my hair pulled back to show off some dangly black earring. I looked drastically different from when we met on the street, but still enough like a "little deer" for him to know it was me. Hard to believe that was the look I was going for.

Per usual, I wanted to get to the restaurant early so that he could find me inside. For one thing, I wasn't wearing my glasses and things were a little out of focus, which is generally fine with me on a first date. I don't need to see anyone's gigantic pores or unsightly imperfections. But let's not forget, I was slightly intoxicated when I met him. And like I said, the only thing that was clear in my memory was his voice. While I could probably pick him out of a line-up, I wasn't positive I'd be able to readily identify him in a crowded restaurant full of people roughly the same age and gender. Regardless, I hopped in a cab and directed it to the restaurant, which was in an area of Wicker Park that I had never ventured to before.

This was quickly adding up to be more a of a murder mystery than a romantic evening, but I was hungry, so I foraged on for what could very well have been my last supper.

Even the cab driver had difficulty placing this restaurant, as according to the building numbers, we had passed it twice. Circling around the block, we deduced that the restaurant had to be this tiny shop sandwiched between a porn store and pawnshop. It was unmarked, but I was definitely there. So, I got out and my driver zoomed off. I didn't blame him for wanting to get the fuck out of this neighborhood, since the only people on the streets were "working" and would have no need for a ride unless he'd be willing to loan out his back seat for 15 minutes so some Average Joe could get their D S'd.

Regardless, I was alone, I was early, and I was locked out. That's right, Schwa was closed. And not "Will Return in Ten Minutes" closed: I'm talking lights out, chained up, and gated shut. Could it have gone out of business between this morning and now? Could Michael Carlson have gone on another one of his infamous benders? Will I get caught in a drug-deal gone bad if I hang here long enough?

This couldn't be right and I was immediately out of my comfort zone. My heart started pounding, as I must have gone into fight-or-flight mode. Embarrassed to call Floris out of fear that I went to the wrong place, I started power walking to the nearest public place, a gas station up the block, and phoned a friend—James.

"The door is locked?" he asked.

"No, it's CHAINED SHUT," I corrected.

"Em, that's not a good neighborhood to just be hanging around in while I google this . . ."

Oh, for fuck's sake, I thought. I was supposed to be seated by now. Someone was supposed to be taking my jacket off for me as I awkwardly scooted in my chair in tandem with an unnecessary push. Instead, it was me and a few hookers loitering in the parking lot of a Shell gas station at 9pm on a Monday night. If my mother had a snapshot of my life at that moment, she would have probably called the funeral director right then and there and made plans for my burial.

"Yeah, Em, I can't find anything that says it's closed for good.

You're just going to have to call Floris and find out what the deal is. I'll stay by my phone if you need anything."

Little did James know, I actually needed quite a few things. I needed mace, a tactical knife, brass knuckles, and a ride home for starters. But I had no time for any of that, because, lo and behold Floris was calling. This was officially a shit-show.

I said goodbye to James and clicked over trying my best to spurt out a not-so-panicked "Hello?"

"Hello, dear (deer?). I'm just arriving now, I will see you in a moment, okay darling?"

Evidently, from his enthusiasm, Floris was not at all concerned about the closure, so I fought the urge to pick up a bag of Funyuns and a Gatorade and walked quickly back to what would most certainly become "the scene of the crime."

I saw him get out of his cab with two bottles of booze, one in each hand. My date, along with our third (a rose) and fourth (some champagne) wheel, had arrived. I just prayed that the bubbly was not reserved to be opened and sprayed across my chest during some point in the night.

Dirty thoughts aside, Floris looked exactly as I remembered, which was nice because it confirmed I was a high-functioning alcoholic after all. He was tall, remarkably handsome, with piercing blue eyes. He had a boyish innocence about him, but he most definitely was a grown-ass man, much older than guys I had dated before. He wore jeans with a few stylish rips in them and a tan, zip-up jacket. He had just a little bit of gel in his short blonde hair. All in all, he looked glowing. He looked good.

"Emele!" he exclaimed as he kissed my right cheek, my left cheek, and then my right again. What a shocking shake-up from the "What up" DJ Ricky had to offer just a few nights prior. I tell you, the kissing, coupled with his boot cut jeans, transported me to another continent and I was okay with that.

"Emele, you look wonderful," he said, releasing whatever lingering what-am-I-going-to-wear agony I had left from earlier in the night. "Are you ready to eat and tell me all about yourself?"

Clearly, he had not glanced over at the door yet, because there was no mistaking what I was seeing. Strewn about the front door were the types of chains used to affix tree trunks onto the back of a semi-truck that's speeding down the highway. Since I already had his eye contact on lock, I shifted my gaze to the right. I could tell he was excited about our meal and it was the gentlest way I could think to break the news that it simply wasn't happening.

"No, no, no! What is this?" Floris said with surprise and disgust. He was genuinely shocked, which was a sign that either he was a really good actor in addition to being a hit man, or that this was a completely unexpected event to him as well. My guess was the latter; at least that's what the version of me who wanted to live another day was going with.

Floris jiggled the chains, as if some miracle was going to open them. I found this ironic, considering that even if we were to get in, it wasn't like there was a soul within a three-block radius that had any sort of God-given talent besides fellating. Who would cook for us?

Upon closer inspection, he noticed a handwritten note taped to the front door. I had most certainly missed this glorified Post-it. All it said was, "Decided not to open tonight. Sorry for the inconvenience."

And then, there were two.

There, Floris and I stood on a cold January night, smack dab on Ashland Avenue amidst some snow that probably wouldn't melt until sometime in mid-June and a few prostitutes who were looking to keep someone warm. A used-car dealership was across the street and their metallic, plastic flags were whipping around in the wind. Nothing about this scene screamed "first date" the way we both thought it would, that was for sure.

"Where should we go?" he said.

"Fuck if I know," I mumbled under my breath as I kicked a clump of dirty snow into the street.

"Come again?" he said, unfolding a piece of paper he pulled out his back pocket.

"Oh, I said I'm sorry, I don't really know."

With nothing but a streetlamp to illuminate the flawed moment, I tried to make out what was written on the note. It was a list of what I could only assume were restaurants, though I had never heard of any of them. Blackbird. Avec. Sepia. The list went on with a few other pretty-sounding names.

"Oh, Emele, this is nothing to worry about," he said unfolding the piece of paper. "Thankfully, my team at Alinea had many recommendations. We can pick another. Let me study this list for a moment."

As Floris's eyes returned to the paper, I tried to remember where I had seen Alinea before. Was it a hotel? A jewelry store in the Gold Coast? A salon/spa in Wicker Park?

Then it hit me. Earlier that same day, when I was on Yelp's homepage, I saw the top-five-in-the-nation. Schwa was four, but Alinea—Alinea was number one. The number-one restaurant in America.

As if it wasn't already apparent, we had much to discuss at dinner, whenever and wherever that would take place.

"The restaurant MK, the Publican . . ." he mumbled to himself. "A-ha. Bonsoiree. Have you been to Bonsoiree?" he asked.

I tried to think of a polished way to say, "I eat fifty-five cent packages of lunchmeat and fight my roommates for the microwave for most of my meals," but I simply decided to play it cool and go with: "No, I don't believe I've been there yet. Let's try it."

Seeing that Floris was equipped with the same flip phone from a few nights before, I took it upon myself to call an Uber. Moments later, we were on our way to a new dining destination that I'd never know how to spell without the help of an Internet search bar: Bonsoiree.

Now I don't know if we were huddling for warmth or if I was just violating spatial cues once again, but our knees were touching during the trip over to Logan Square. I only know this because there was a hole in his jeans right above his kneecap, through which I noticed a dark tattoo—of what, I couldn't tell—at least not yet.

Soon, Floris began asking me questions.

"What is the name of the town you were born?"

"Hinsdale."

"And the town you grew up in?"

"Elmhurst."

"Hinsdale and Elmhurst, so pretty. I am from Rotterdam. Doesn't quite have the same allure, does it?"

"I'm sure it's beautiful," I generically responded.

"It is. You must go there some time. And your parents, what are their names?"

Was he gathering information to steal my identity?

"Alice and Jimmy."

"Are they still together?" he inquired.

"Yes. They are."

"I could tell," he said sweetly before retreating to silence for the rest of the short ride over.

I could tell he was trying to create context. He was being polite, getting to know me by asking real questions. I appreciated this and assumed it was not a quality typically associated with axe murderers. So, I went along with it, and felt for the first time since the morning that I just might make it out alive after all.

CHAPTER SEVENTEEN/LESSON SEVENTEEN

- Count memories instead of calories

We pulled up to a place that looked like an albino Rubik's cube. It was perfectly square and white. It was tiny and I could see the heads of plenty of middle-aged patrons eating food far too fancy for me. Didn't these people have to be home in time for the ten o'clock news? Where were the other girls in mini-dresses and dangly earrings? It didn't take any sort of a genius to tell me that nothing I was wearing—down to the bright orange Victoria's Secret thong I had on that night—belonged in this pristine institution.

I saw a funny-looking star on a plaque on the wall with the world "Michelin" on it. Why is there a plaque about tires here? I wondered.

Bonsoiree was a 42-seat restaurant that also slung eight-course meals for a pretty penny. While I hadn't had the chance to study what foreign things their particular menu featured, I realized it wouldn't make a difference anyway as I noticed servers whizzing by me with meals that were plated inside wooden boxes with fragrant steam emitting from them upon opening. I was bound to have absolutely no idea how to eat whatever it was they had to offer. I was just going to have to jump in.

"Did you have reservation with us this evening?" the host asked as he consulted his computer screen and gestured toward the packed restaurant.

I secretly hoped the fact we didn't would ultimately land us at one of those late-night gyro shops in Albany Park, as that was more my speed than having heaps of silverware on the table coupled with linen napkins that got swapped out—black or white—depending on what the guests were wearing.

"No, we did not," Floris began. "You see, we were trying to eat at Schwa but Michael Carlson closed the restaurant down tonight so now we have nowhere to go. My team at Alinea had recommended we come here instead. Can you accommodate us?"

Apparently "Alinea" is a panty dropper word in the culinary world, as the host immediately responded that if we could just give him a brief moment, he would be glad to pull a small table from storage, dress it with a tablecloth and dinnerware, and put us in a quiet area towards the back of the restaurant so we can enjoy an intimate dinner.

As he went to fetch the furniture, another man swooped in offering to chill one bottle of champagne, as he opened the other and poured us two glasses.

"Welcome, and cheers. Enjoy your evening, you two," he said.

I said thank you and clanked my glass against Floris's, all the while attempting to gain my bearings.

What the fuck was going on? From a shutdown at Schwa to first-class service from a host working the stand in a glorified shoebox with high ceilings?

A few moments later, Floris and I were finally seated, and even though we had spent the last hour or so together traveling to a dining destination, it was the first time I really looked at him. He was far more beautiful than the light from any streetlamp on Milwaukee or Ashland Avenue could indicate. Regardless, I could actually process with whom I was about to enjoy dinnertime, and story time. And guess what? I liked what I saw.

I obviously knew he was older than me. It was evident in the way he carried himself, especially in comparison to the other males one would typically encounter in Chicago after midnight. Not to mention, he had small, inoffensive crow's feet that accented his crispy blue eyes. I guessed he was around thirty or so, but wanted to confirm.

"Floris, how old are you?"

"I'm 34, Miss Emele."

Wow, a full decade older than me.

"Will you excuse me?" he said. "I'm going to get my Moleskine from my jacket before we start our meal. I'll be right back."

"One away on twelve," I heard a server whisper to a cook as Floris got up. I wondered if they were talking in code about our CIA-style meet-up. Later, I found out this meant, in layman's terms: someone's up taking a piss. Don't approach the table with food until he's back.

I went back to his age for a moment. Thirty-four. I was twenty-four. He was the oldest man I had gone on a date with, and I wasn't sure what to make of it until it dawned on me: nothing. Make nothing of it, because just like any semblance of the Schwa snafu, age was but a fleeting issue. So was the fact that he was retrieving a notebook before dinner. That's not to say I didn't secretly ponder the thought: was I being interviewed? Even though I felt more at ease, the desire to piece this night together remained strong.

~ ~ ~

The menu set-up was different than anything I'd seen before. Eight prix-fixe courses awaited the two of us, 16 dishes in all, no menu. Floris returned and a server approached the table.

"Good evening, I'm Andrew," he looked at both of us individually and nodded. "If no one has any food allergies, then I will go ahead and start preparing the first course."

Floris looked at me for the green light, and I granted it to the man. For someone who was used to combing through a menu with a keen eye before deciding on the fish n' chips, I was yet again relinquishing control and letting fate fill my stomach. In hindsight, I wouldn't have had this perfectly paced meal any other way.

"Great, I'll be right back out with tonight's amuse bouche and get you two started."

Amuse. There was that tricky word again. I had no idea what to expect, but I was excited to see the show.

Moments later, he returned. "Here we have a braised rabbit with a truffle gnocchi. Enjoy."

Here we have a what?

In one bite, Floris closed his eyes and ate his "amuse" out of the white porcelain spoon it was served on and jotted a note in his small leather-bound book. I followed, sans the note taking, of course, and ingested.

God damn, that was good.

Just then, Andrew swooped through to pick up the serving pieces again, clearing the way for Floris and I to begin the process of becoming entrenched in one another's stories.

Going against the whole "ladies first" thing, I let Floris lead. I needed to get a feel for whom he was with before I could prepare an appropriate statement about my life in response. Besides, he owed me context—a lot of it. At least that sounded like a fair trade after thinking this date could have been a death wish the whole time.

"So tell me about yourself," I invited as I took a sip of my champagne, which was good—remarkably good. The best I had ever had, to be precise.

"Well, like I said, I am 34 years old."

That accent. And it was only the beginning.

"I was born and raised in the Netherlands, I'm fluent in Dutch, English, and German. Do you speak any other languages?"

"Parli Italiano?" I asked.

"Si," he said with a wink.

"So, how did you get here? Like, what's your story?" I coerced.

All the while, the serving team buzzed around in the background. They were like tour guides accompanying each plate with a thirty-second spiel about what it was we were about to eat, but even their abridged-edition needed a CliffsNotes version in my mind. But it didn't really matter because I really only had the capacity to give my attention to one man that evening. So I concentrated on making sense of all the flavors and textures that made up Mr. Floris.

"Well, I live in Rotterdam, Holland. I am the chef de cuisine at my own restaurant, In de Keuken van Floris—meaning, In the Kitchen of Floris."

So, he's a chef. Now this is starting to make sense.

"Oh, really? What's your restaurant like?" I asked right as the server came by to top off my champagne.

He told me his station and his stoves were in the center of his tiny restaurant so that every patron dining in his intimate space could have a "chef's table" seat.

His food was modern, he said. I had no clue what that meant.

He went on to say he had dedicated his everything to cooking, so much so that he didn't have much of a social or family life. From what I knew of the way our country glamorized chefs, I found it odd for someone of his culinary stature to just simply cook and then go home, returning the next day to humbly do the same. Where were the drugs, sex, and rock n' roll? The fancy photo shoots? The stable of women?

"So, what about your family? Do you have a wife?"

"No, no wife."

Well that was good.

"But there is Marlies."

Well, that was bad.

Marlies was a girl he had spent a year or two with, but they had recently ended things. She was a lawyer and had been laid off from her job several months ago. As a result, she fell into a deep depression, taking him through her downward spiral while she was at it.

"I had to get out, Emele. I had to get away, you know? It was bad, really bad, for a while."

"So you decided to take a vacation to Chicago?" I assumed.

"Not quite. I emailed Grant Achatz. He is the chef at Alinea, the number-one restaurant in the United States." Thanks to Yelp, I was actually fully-aware of that one.

"What did you say to him?"

"I asked if I could spend two weeks in his kitchen externing. The extra hands on the line would cost Achatz nothing, I just wanted the experience at a three-Michelin Star restaurant and would take responsibility for my own expenses."

Considering I personally wouldn't book an Airbnb for more than $35 at a max of two nights, I couldn't imagine what it must have cost him to fly to America, put himself up in a hotel room, and experience the city for two-plus weeks.

"So he said yes to you then, yeah?"

"He said yes. He said he'd been following my work as intently as I was following his, taking cues mostly from the way I plated things. Can you believe that?"

I widened my eyes to express awe even though I had no way of knowing if this was in fact a big deal at the time.

"Anyways, it turned out we were using a lot of the same techniques and had the same underlying principles when it came to cooking and running a kitchen. He is like my American counterpart in a way, you know?"

I didn't know, so invited him to tell me more. This, of course, exposed me as a complete foodie fledgling but it was worth it. I was highly intrigued.

From the way Floris described him, Achatz was like a modern-day Willy Wonka: a genius when it came to working wonders with food. Achatz accepted his offer on the accord that Floris would work a seventeen-day term, fourteen hours a day, with just two days off—the second of which being the very Monday we were eating with each other at Bonsoiree. His other day off was the day before, and he spent it at L2O, the place from where he had called me to ask me out for dinner at Schwa.

Context. Finally.

It was all starting to make sense.

It had now dawned on me that contrary to what I had previously believed, Floris was most definitely not "on something" the night I ran into him in Wicker Park. He was actually "off something"—that being a grueling fourteen-hour shift at the number-one restaurant in the nation—Alinea. And here I thought he was just a creeper on the prowl. My bad.

"So what were you up to the night we met?" I very curiously asked.

"I was trying to go to Violet Hour, actually."

If bars could have Michelin stars, Violet Hour would have earned a few. It's an upscale cocktail lounge in precisely the part of town where we met. There was no standing at the Violet Hour. In fact, their host team kept a keen eye on the in-out ratio of patrons at all times. They politely demand that everyone sit in velvet, high-winged chairs to keep things classy. All in all, just cool people sitting down in cool chairs drinking even cooler drinks. That said, the lounge had apparently made its way onto the short-list of recommendations from the Alinea folks due to its crafty cocktails and strict seating policy and Floris was headed to try it before they closed for the weekend.

I knew my memory was foggy that night, but from my best sense of direction it hit me that where the cab driver dropped him off was not in front of Violet Hour. In fact, he was about two blocks short from his target destination. Floris explained to me that the cab driver didn't quite know the exact location and neither did he, so he had the driver pull over somewhere in the vicinity. I, too, was somewhere in the vicinity and just so happened to be awaiting a vacant cab. Funny how that worked out.

"What were you doing that night?" Floris asked.

I decided to be honest.

"I was out of my element, Floris. I was having a really bad date at a really bad bar and just when I thought I was going to go home, I went one more place."

"You went to Rodan?" he asked. That was the name of the place his cab pulled up to just before I hopped in.

"No, not actually. I had to walk about a block or two in search of a cab since it was so crowded after last-call. In front of Rodan is just where I was when you pulled up. Kind of funny that you were getting out precisely where I gave up on the search, right?"

"Well, I'm glad I was there," he said, raising a glass. "To being there," he toasted.

Speaking of toasting, we were now on our second bottle of champagne, about which I commented, "This is great!". I'm sure to him he thought it was a nod to his BYO pick, but internally, I meant it about this evening, which had been flawed to perfection from the start.

"I'm glad you like it. I'm a champagne sommelier, so I have complex tastes. It's been hard to find exactly what I like in America. But this is quite good, isn't it?"

I wondered right then if internally, he was referring to our date.

~ ~ ~

Sometime around the fourth course, I learned more about Floris' personal life.

"Tell me about your family," I gently begged.

"I have a sister and a sweet little niece. Any free time I have goes to her. And, let's see, I bought a house and live in it alone. I drive an Audi back home and I've become an expert on fitting cases of champagne into its tiny trunk," he smirked.

"Does anything bother you?" I asked, wondering if this man has ever had a down day in his life.

"When people let me down."

He told me that he hated the feeling of being disappointed. To him, it was the worst in the world and why he valued taste so much. His sense of taste was always loyal to him. It was something that he could always count on, something personal to him, not eligible to be argued with by anyone else. I supposed I felt that way about my writing. After all, I started a blog so that I could post an entire thought without being interrupted, protested, or told to put real pants on. Once I hit the publish button on my laptop, my observations were set free and I felt better.

Eventually, he turned the tables on me. I had anxiously been awaiting the floor the entire time he was talking wondering how I would manage to tone down my usual antics and communicate slowly and clearly to a man who didn't share my first language. I wanted to come off less like a teenage wasteland and more like a poised young lady. This was not going to be easy for me.

"What do you do for work, Emele? Do you cook?"

I nearly spat out my champagne. Do I cook? Does microwaving meals that start as powder count as cooking?

"No, I don't. I actually work in hotels. I put 'heads in beds,' you could say."

"Heads in beds? That's funny, I like that!" Floris scribbled that down in his black book, which I now understood as the place he kept notes on flavor, presentation, cute little sayings that rhyme, etc.

So to be clear: he was a top chef, a homeowner, a family guy, and a gorgeous European man. Meanwhile, I sold hotel rooms, tried to keep my cystic acne at bay, and wrote menial blogs for fun. Well, at least I was keeping up with the theme of the night: having absolutely nothing in common besides being in the right place at the right time last Saturday night with a perfect stranger.

The other thing we had in common was dish number five. I had no idea what we were eating, but it was warm, rich, and delicious. Floris told me it was a crustacean of some sort, but I tasted cheese (go figure). All the while, it was served inside of a beautiful, large shell. To eat it, you gobbled up the contents in one bite with a tiny spoon, custom made for the restaurant.

"Oh my god. That was delicious," I exclaimed.

"You like it?"

I confirmed with a nod.

"Me too. Should we have another?"

Just as soon as I had a chance to process the question and answer it with "yes, we should order twelve more," the server came to scoop the empty shells away.

"Andrew, excuse me," Floris said to the waiter.

"May we have another one of those?"

"You want another of course five?"

"Yes, Emele really liked that one. I did, too. We'd love to have it again."

Was that even possible? Don't they portion out their food ordering so that no jackasses like us ask for seconds?

The server looked at us inquisitively.

"Let me check with the chef," he said with a certain skepticism.

Shin Thompson was his name. He was a petite man, attractive, and in his thirties if I had to guess. Ironically, even though he was the executive chef and clearly owned the place, he was not found on the line dripping with sweat hunched over delicately assembled dishes like the rest of his chef minions. In fact, he was posted up on the other side of the kitchen window with his back to the guests. In his right hand, he was clutching a black Bic pen, a yellow highlighter, and a red marker—all with their caps off. His eyes were affixed to a yellow legal pad as he directed orders to his workers.

"Four at eleven. One no dairy, one no gluten. All in," Shin calmly said, as he made all sorts of markings on his sheet to reflect the given orders.

"Heard, chef," his team replied in unison.

I watched Shin from my vantage point. He was a maestro conducting an orchestra of some of the most highly skilled chefs in the nation. Their determination to execute a flawless service was noticeable, even though I could not fully decipher the code in which Shin was speaking to them. I later learned what he was doing was called "expo'ing," and arguably it is the most important aspect of any fine dining institution. Apparently, he had climbed up so far in his career that it was now his turn to step out of the heat and steer the ship.

His concentration never broke except for when our server approached him. Andrew was inquiring about a repeat of course five, the life-changing scallop and crab motoyaki we had just devoured. The server did his best to be discreet about putting a table number to the request so Shin could see just who was asking for such an outlandish request. We made brief eye contact before I could feel my cheeks flush with embarrassment.

Let it be known, this was the first request of its nature in the restaurant, ever. Even today, it is still talked about among their tenured staff.

Our waiter wrapped up the pow-wow with Chef Shin and returned to our table.

"I spoke with Chef. How about I stop by after the savory courses are through and see if you are still hungry for another of course five. If so, we'll gladly make it again for you. If not, we will move to the dessert courses."

"That sounds great. Thank you." Floris was pleased with the compromise and I was pleased that the awkwardness was, for the moment, over.

~ ~ ~

After moving away from the savory courses, it was time we segued into something a bit sweeter: talking about my family, friends, likes, dislikes, talents, and tastes.

"I'm a writer," I told Floris. "People call me 'the Carrie Bradshaw of Chicago.' Do you know who that is?"

"If they compare her to you, she must not be a chef," he said, pointing with his knife at the way I was eating our cheese course with my fingers like they were chicken nuggets. We both shared a laugh about the faux pas. He knew I didn't know better and I knew he had a sense of humor about it. It worked.

"Well, she's—I don't know how to explain it. She's like the sassy little sister we all wished we had."

"How did you get started writing like that?" he asked.

I took a moment to think about that. How did I get started writing like that?

"Well, I wrote in a diary when I was five years old. I would make up outlandish stories about the people in my class and refer to all the boys as 'my boyfriends.' I guess it would only make sense that twenty years later I would have a blog about relationship woes and the perils of being in your mid-twenties."

"Oh, Emele. Have you had some troubles?" he sweetly asked, in between properly consuming the food on his plate.

"I've been let down, you could say. But I have my blog, where I basically volunteer to be the worst-case scenario of my generation on a weekly basis and help others get through the same things. It makes me feel less alone when at the end of the day, the guys interested in talking to me only want to get two things by the end of night one: ass and wasted."

My wild, say-anything antics were coming through as the burn of my previous relationships flared up. Realizing this wasn't the time or place, I quickly reined them in, cooling off with a sip of my champagne. In the quiet, it hit me that besides the crew cleaning the kitchen, Floris and I were the only two people, left in the restaurant.

"Emele, you know what is funny?" Floris asked, repositioning our banter back to familiar, upbeat territory.

"Before I called you today, I was riding the elevator in the Hancock building. You know, that very tall building downtown?"

Yes, I knew of that one.

"It was such a magical moment because I was the only one in there, so I kept riding it up and down, jumping to make myself float. I was having such a good time. I was carefree! Do you know what I thought about every time I had to wait sixty seconds for it to get to the top?"

"Gravity?" I asked.

Floris almost spat out his drink. He was starting to understand my wit, and I was starting to loosen back up.

"No, silly. You. Actually, us."

"Us?"

"Yes. I thought, what if there is a greater meaning behind meeting this girl from the taxi? What if she is supposed to play a bigger part in my life?"

I couldn't believe it. Was I really having this conversation with this man in this city? Normally my dinner conversations with men included topics like how stoned one or the other got last Saturday, or why there are no decent bars in the Loop. It's never about fate, serendipity, star-crossed lovers, or whatever was going on here. The way he referenced "us" was just so overtly romantic.

And I wasn't prepared for it, but I was so pleasantly surprised by it.

Just when I got swept up in the poem that was this conversation, Floris brought us both back down to the ground floor of the Hancock; back down to Earth.

"Alas, you can't be that person for me, and I cannot be that person for you. I have a restaurant, a home, a life, and a livelihood in Rotterdam. In Holland."

He was right. He was a rock-star European chef, wise beyond his years, making a name for himself a continent away. I was a little lost millennial, feeding her shopping addiction through a run-of-the-mill job out of a cubicle in downtown Chicago. And aside from all the logistical challenges, there was the obvious: Floris had less than a week left in the city, all of which was going to be spent at Alinea, the number-one restaurant in the nation, the number-three in the world, the whole entire reason for his westward expansion, blah, blah, blah.

I got it. "Us" was going nowhere.

"So, this is it?" I asked, as we were about to wrap up and cash out for the evening, three hours after we had initially met up. I wasn't upset, just confirming the conclusion at which we had arrived.

"Not yet," Floris replied. "Waiter?"

"Yes, what can I get for you?"

"I'm terribly sorry, but we forgot to ask for that repeat of course five. Is it too late?"

Oh, god.

"I'm sorry, sir. The motoyaki is eightysixed."

"Ah-hah. Well, fair enough. Thank you anyways, everything was lovely," said Floris as our waiter continued closing down the restaurant.

"Eightysixed?" I asked.

"Eighty-six is a term restaurants use when something runs out. They are out of the motoyaki."

"So—eighty-six this date?" I said with a smile.

"I'm afraid so, Miss Emele, eightysixed it is. But I had a lovely time with you and I really, really enjoyed your company," he said as he signed the check, picking up the entire tab for the two of us.

"Likewise, Floris."

I didn't know what the protocol was here. Was I supposed to suggest we be pen-pals? Was I supposed to hug him and say, "See ya around"? I had no clue how to wrap up this perfectly unplanned evening, so I kept things casual and asked for his e-mail address while I dug around in my purse for a rogue business card. I know, what a horribly awkward way to truncate an evening that otherwise flowed perfectly.

"Miss Belden?" he said reading my name off the business card.

"That would be me."

"Any relation to the Belden-Stratford hotel? Are you the heiress?" he asked.

"Unfortunately not. I'm just a regular girl."

"You are far from that, Miss Belden."

I said goodbye and thank you to Floris with a hug and another trio of cheek kisses before we both got into our respective cabs and headed home from a most exquisite evening.

When I came through my door, I had a text from my co-worker asking if I had survived the night.

As it just so had it, I did survive. More than that, I had lived. For the first time in months, I had lived.

So, very clearly, the night was not about the delicious food, it was about the satiating three-hour conversation that two people who never should have met had just had. That night, I went to bed feeling full in a way that had nothing to do with the food we ate.

CHAPTER EIGHTEEN/LESSON EIGHTEEN

- Allow yourself to be pleasantly surprised

The next day started like any other, except that that morning I awoke slightly more unkempt and groggy. Perhaps due to the bottle of champagne and eight courses of rich, delicious food that invaded my body after being used to eating only iterations of bars and shakes for the last three weeks.

But unlike any other morning, I was definitely more intellectually stimulated than usual. My batteries were recharged. And while I wouldn't call them butterflies in my stomach, there was warmth in my heart that was nice. I had a good night, and it didn't involve having to get to second base with anyone. Talk about a win for the home team.

Treading through my e-mails at work, I tried not to think about Floris much at all and was secretly hoping that James would not ask for more details about my evening.

Truth was, I couldn't have imagined a date going better. But my time with him was like sipping on a $120 pour of fine, aged scotch. It was incredibly awakening. I was able to enjoy it at my leisure with each swig being better than the last. But once I reached the bottom of the glass—that was it, and I knew it—there'd be no seconds. It would be as eighty-sixed as course number five.

Floris was a treat that I did not have the privilege of experiencing more than once. And although that was an unfortunate reality, at least he was upfront and honest with me about it from the get-go, which is more than I can say about the rest of the shady Chicagoans who I had found myself casually dating before him.

But sometime in the middle of my day, right around when my hunger returned, my cell phone rang. It was Floris. Even though I picked up before I had a chance to evaluate whether it was a mirage or not, the remarkable voice on the other line confirmed it was, in fact, the exact man on my mind.

"Emele, hi, it's Floris. How are you, darling?"

For some reason, when he called me darling, I didn't get a creepy or gay vibe. Instead, I got goose bumps, which to me, meant that I had struck hot-guy-gold.

"I'm good, how are you? Aren't you working?" I asked, considering he was supposed to be riding out the rest of his days with his head down in the kitchen at Alinea, forgetting the mere fact he ever treated a cute, little American girl ten years his junior to an expensive dinner the night before.

"Yes, I am about to start at my station. But, listen; I have to see you again. I didn't sleep at all last night thinking about our three-star night. So, this morning I talked to Chef Grant and asked if I can have more time off."

"Floris, you shouldn't ha . . ."

"He is letting me work just in the mornings until Friday and Saturday, I'll have to work both of those nights because those are the busiest. But I'll have Sunday completely off."

So, let me get this straight. Floris asked the best chef in the world (Grant Achatz) for extra time off from his (transcontinental, temporary) gig, so that he could see about a (very basic) girl (me)?

Ballsy.

"Wow, that's great," I said, stunned.

"So if you are able, and if you want to, I would like to try Schwa again tomorrow night. Will you join me?"

Little did he know, there was absolutely no need to pose that as a question, since the answer was undoubtedly going to be a capital Y-E-S. I was being given a second chance to further a once-in-a-lifetime connection. A second pour of that top-shelf scotch, if you will.

"I am able. And I do want to," I replied. I was smiling ear-to-ear.

"Fantastic, 7:15 tomorrow. I confirmed with Michael Carlson myself. I will see you there. Again."

7:15 it was.

~ ~ ~

Floris putting me on the books for another couple of dates rendered me two things: excited and broke. I soon realized that the reason we could not mutually text each other was that I did not have an international phone plan attached to my account. I imagined that was an extra cost to tack on, so if his calls were somehow managing to funnel through, I was sure I must have been paying a fortune.

I was right.

That day after work, I walked myself into a T-Mobile store and began a choppy explanation of what I could only describe as my so-called life.

"Hi there," I began. "I met someone from Holland who has been calling me a lot. He has texted me a bit, as well, but I cannot seem to get my return messages to go through. Today we spoke for about eleven minutes total. Do you know about how much that costs?"

"Yes, ma'am. That's a dollar a minute. And it's a dollar per text message as well."

I had accrued at least fifty dollars in overages since knowing Floris.

"Yikes. Well then, I suppose it's good he'll be leaving soon. Thank you."

I turned to head out of the store. I already knew what was coming: an angry call from my mother, whose phone plan I was still on, whenever the current billing cycle ended. I imagined the conversation going something like this: "Why the hell do I owe an extra $200 this month? Who the hell were you calling in butt-fuck Europe?"

To which I would respond: "Well, mom, remember when I told you I met that strange Dutch man on the street last weekend? Well, I thought I was falling in love with him, so I texted him routinely at three o'clock in the morning, which just so happened to be when he was getting off work for the night, and then I shipped him back to where he came from six days later because, just like everything else in my life, this had to be difficult, expensive, and unbelievable."

And just as she was about to scold me, I would remind her: "You told me this was the one that sounded promising, remember?"

This whole situation was a farce. The thought of having to actually justify this chance encounter was daunting. Even though she half-supported the idea when it was so distant from reality, my mom undoubtedly would be a non-believer in this whole European love affair thing. My best bet was to start cutting my grocery budget for the following month and getting my story together.

"Ma'am, wait," said the T-Mobile worker just as I was about to step back into the cold.

"Yes?"

"I can put a special promo on your phone. It's a one-month trial for international service. We can backdate it to the first day he called you, then, it'll extend out for thirty days. You just need to cancel it before that thirty-day mark, and it's like none of this every happened."

Now he was speaking my language.

"Let's do that," I said, handing this man my phone and thanking god for the Hail Mary.

~ ~ ~

The night of Schwa Round-Two had come and it was such a strange paradox. Half of me knew exactly what I was in for, but half had no idea where things would go this next time we were together. Our time with each other was both natural and real; two qualities I forgot could even exist in a dynamic between two single, attractive people. And beneath it all, I felt something I can only describe as "luck." Luck that I had ever met him, luck that I was eating at my second Michelin-rated restaurant in one week, luck in knowing that I was the only girl in the entire city who had all of this to look forward to on just a random Wednesday night.

I got out of work later than usual that night, about 6 PM My hair had gone flat, my skin a little greasy. The makeup I had thoughtfully applied earlier that morning had either faded away completely, or got stuck in the creases of my eyelids. I looked tired and felt defeated. With only one hour to both get ready and head over to the meeting spot, I decided beautifying myself was a job for a professional.

There are times in life when it's best to put your appearance in other people's hands. Classically, this is your prom, your graduation, and your wedding day. With no nuptials in sight, it was obvious that I needed help getting ready for something else—dinner with Floris.

I popped into a salon just two doors down from my work. This place specialized in one thing and one thing only: blowouts. I never understood the allure paying someone to wash your hair and then dry it.

This was a pattern of behavior I was comfortable executing myself for the last twenty-four years of my life without spending sixty dollars a pop. But the folks at Blo-Dri managed to change my perspective entirely.

"Hi. I know this is short notice, but do you have any availability tonight?" I asked, walking into the salon for the first time.

"When were you thinking?" the receptionist asked.

"Now. Ish." I said.

"Perfect. Katie is available for a wash and blow-out."

Katie, my savior.

I shut my eyes as I sat down and tilted my head back into the washbowl. Obviously, I wasn't riding the Hancock up and down, but I had a moment much like Floris's. I was carefree and thought to myself, what if he was meant to be more than just someone who got out of a cab so that I could get into it? What if he was more than just someone who would explain to me what eightysixed meant. What if he was part of something more?

"You can step over to the second chair on the right," Katie said, snapping me out of the daydream.

"So, what are you thinking?" she asked, combing out my tangled hair.

"Nothing too fancy; just a standard blow-out with a round brush, I guess."

"Well, are you doing anything special tonight?"

Going out for dinner wasn't special. That I knew. It was with whom I was going that made all the difference. She wouldn't understand this. I barely did.

"I'm actually heading to dinner at a place called Schwa," I told her.

"Hmm, I haven't heard of it."

Join the club.

"Well, it's apparently very fancy and it's my second date with the guy who is taking me, so I just want to look...nice."

"A fancy restaurant on the second date? Who is this guy?"

I wish I knew.

Katie got to work.

As she treated each strand of hair with the utmost care, Katie made a lot of small talk. She talked a lot about her own love life, and complained mostly about it. The guy she was dating for a year decided to move to New York City to pursue an art career. He barely called, he never texted, they hardly visited each other. The list of issues went on and on. For once, I was so glad this wasn't me. I wasn't the victim. My boyfriend wasn't ignoring me. I wasn't getting fucked over. For once, I was doing pretty okay.

"How do you like it?" she asked, running her hands through my hair one final time for a little additional volume and sass.

"It's perfect," I said. And it was.

After refreshing my make-up in the bathroom, tipping Katie, and grabbing an Uber to Wicker Park, it was time to take on Schwa. Assuming they'd take us in.

~ ~ ~

Contrary to the last time when the cab pulled up to Schwa, I saw lights on, which was certainly a good sign. Another good sign was Floris sitting alone at a table for two by the window anxiously awaiting my arrival.

Unlike Bonsoiree, the restaurant had no front-of-the-house staff. No reservationist, no maître d', no waiters, no sommeliers, and no women. What they had, however, were bearded men in aprons hustling in the tiny kitchen, running throughout the dining room, and impatiently sprinting back to the kitchen after each wild spiel.

Bonsoiree was small. Schwa was smaller. Noticeably smaller. There were plain black tables, tightly packed on top of shiny wood floors. The ceiling was tin and the music, heavy metal, was loud. This place had a Michelin star? Two, I reminded myself.

As I walked in, I heard a phone ringing and saw one of the cooks grab it and tuck it under his sweaty chin. Moments later, it slipped from the greasy residue that was visible on his skin, after which the cook then shouted, "Motherfucker!" to no one in particular. It was no wonder that this place had some engineering difficulties and we were unable to successfully tackle eating here the first time.

Just then, I tabled the negative preconceived thoughts that were crossing my mind and let my eyes lock with Floris's. Seeing him was like hitting the ultimate reset button.

It was an ordinary thing, a man sitting in a restaurant awaiting his date's arrival. But the sheer fact that I would not have this moment with this man again made me soak it in for much more than its face value.

It had been a long time since I had looked at something in the kind of light I saw him in. With adoration. With appreciation. A smile cracked across my lips and I didn't fight it. I couldn't.

He must have noticed the extra effort I put into the evening, for when I walked toward him to take my seat, he looked at me as though I was celebrity or something. He kept an intense gaze on me as the corners of his mouth flared with delight. He was speechless. I think he was happy to see me.

"Emele," he began, per usual, accompanied by three kisses on opposite cheeks. "You look like a princess or something! Please sit down. May I take your jacket? Can I show you the kitchen?" Though it came across as a classic case of ADHD, I knew that those two offers were of equal etiquette to Floris. Clearly, he had arrived early to ensure they were open and had already made himself at home in these dilapidated digs. He simply wanted me to kick off my shoes with their crew, too.

"Wow, Floris. We're in. This is great!" I said.

"We are in," he confirmed, momentarily taking hold of my hand from across the table in excitement, as if we were about to start a rollercoaster ride.

Just then, Michael Carlson approached our table. The man, the myth, the…maniac.

Little did he know, I had already conducted a pseudo background check on him and knew about his crazy life and his team. They were culinary wonders, sure; but, they also got their jollies off by inhaling CO_2 from whipped cream canisters in the back as a way to get high while on the clock. And while you might think we couldn't have been more different from Mr. Carlson—Floris, a foreigner, and me, the "deer" in the headlights—Carlson got right to work at making us feel at home.

"So, dudes. Check it out. We are soooo sorry about the other night," he said, sounding almost like a surfer with a raspy smoker's voice. "We normally aren't open on Mondays, but wanted to do something special for you seeing that you're joining us from Alinea. As you saw, we just couldn't swing coming in on Monday after all. My apologies."

"Not to worry," Floris said.

"But we are pumped to have you and your lady in tonight."

His lady.

"Are there any food allergies or can we get started?" Carlson asked.

Floris looked to me to give the green light.

"Take it away, chef."

Floris had brought with him that same little black notebook to record flavors and textures. With that making another appearance, and a mechanical pencil resting discretely on top of it, I knew we were in for another culinary treat.

"Remind me to take extra good notes tonight," he said.

"Why's that?" I asked, staring down our freshly dropped amuse: a single ravioli noodle filled with a runny quail egg yolk and oozy buffalo ricotta.

"You're going to want to keep your mouth entirely closed when you eat this," Carlson's sous chef instructed. "Otherwise it'll spew everywhere." He quickly returned to the kitchen, leaving us alone again. Uncouth, yes; but at least I could understand precisely what he meant when he used terms like "spew." I liked this place.

"As I was saying, remind me to take good notes because Mr. Michael Carlson doesn't write anything down. These dishes appear once on the menu and that's it. They disappear, he reinvents."

"That sounds like a lot of work; coming up with something new every day," I said, placing the ravioli in my mouth and tightening my lips.

"Well, he thinks it's more work to actually write down recipes," Floris said.

Describing the ravioli as an explosion was equal parts colloquial and spot-on. I will never forget the feeling of that gush: unexpected, tasty, and playful.

"How did he get so good at cooking? He's such a bad boy," I asked Floris. While his appetite for destruction was clear, I wondered about Carlson's path to success.

"He worked at Trio. That's where Grant Achatz was chef before Alinea. They were close."

So, this Achatz guy apparently had the Midas touch with cooks. Under his counsel, people learned. They grew. They excelled in all things culinary.

We were making progress with our meal, and unlike Bonsoiree, where all the dishes were a perfectly-done take on fine French fusion, Schwa was raw, non-traditional, and all-natural. It was delicious, skillfully prepared, and exciting to eat. The very cook who had prepared each dish brought it out himself. Even though everyone who worked there looked like they had just done a line of coke off a spatula, it didn't matter. Their passion came through on the plate, and we fed off it as we feasted on it. A three-star experience, as Floris would say.

As quickly as the cooks could rattle off whatever it was that we were eating, I glanced at Floris who was feverishly trying to take down bits and pieces of the disorganized spiel. Braised short rib this. Jellyfish and quail that. All topped with pureed roe and flakes of shaved black truffles from Australia. Everything was a mouthful. Literally.

"What do you taste, Emele?"

Let's not play this game, I thought. I knew my palette was laughable, if it was even existent at all.

"Oh, Floris. I don't . . ."

"Just close your eyes. Pause. Slow down. Then think: what do you taste?"

Pause.

Slow down.

Those were two things I never did. I couldn't. Because if I did, I was afraid of what that silence and loneliness would do to my emotional state. But with Floris two feet away from me, I felt secured. I could let go. I could stop the clock.

So I closed my eyes and thought, "Here goes nothing."

"I taste...I taste...chocolate?"

I couldn't be right. We were only on course four, definitely still very much in the savory portion of tonight's fare.

"Very good!" he exclaimed.

"What?" Apparently, I surprised myself and demanded answers.

"This is botarga. It's a fish roe."

I was lost already.

"It's paired with polenta, which is a base of cornmeal, and chocolate. Very good, my little sous chef," he joked.

I rolled my eyes and smiled as I wiped my lips with my napkin.

"I still can't believe you know so much about this stuff," I said to Floris. "It's like . . ."

"Science," he completed my thought.

"Yes, exactly. It's like science." Which I failed in high school, btw.

"That's what I like about it. What do you like about writing?"

For the second time in mere minutes, Floris was encouraging me to pause and think.

"It's a transporter," I said without much hesitation. "I can go from one place, feeling one way, thinking about one thing, and take myself somewhere completely different in a matter pages. It's an escape from my life, which isn't always all that exciting believe it or not."

"How do you mean?" he asked for clarification.

"Like, take this situation. Shit like this never happens. One minute I'm going to work, having bad dates with bad guys, and fighting my roommates for the microwave to heat up something I can pass off as dinner. The next? I'm sitting in Schwa having an Eat, Pray, Love-moment with a stranger I barely even know."

"What is eat, pray, love?" he asked.

Ironically, I had never read the book nor had I seen the movie. I knew it was good, a best-seller in fact, and a hit at the box-office. That was part of the reason I skipped it. I knew I was capable of doing something just as good. I, like the author, was a broken, lost woman, and I wanted to write about it myself before I read about it from someone else. That said; I didn't have a solid explanation for Floris.

"It's a book about a girl who eats really good food with a hot European guy." That's all I knew and all he needed to know, and at the end of the day, I think it worked.

Floris and I grew closer throughout the evening, both physically and emotionally. The perfectly paired champagne may or may not have had something to do with it.

In between courses, we found ourselves holding hands as much as we were holding conversation. Again, we covered our range of topics, never once running out of things to say. For every story I told, he countered. For every fun fact he gave me, I gave him one of my own. It was hard to believe that we had gone from "acquaintances" to "infatuated" in such a short amount of time, but it was real. I can assure you of that.

"What's your dream meal, Miss Emele?"

"I don't want to answer that."

"Why?" Floris asked.

"Because you'll laugh. It's nothing like anything you make. It's not beautiful or complex. It's not fancy schmancy. It's silly. It's stupid," I explained.

"Well, what is it?"

"Do you really want to know?" I asked.

"Yes!" he blurted.

"Steak."

"Steak?"

"Steak. A nice, medium-rare filet mignon with a baked potato, some green vegetable of some sort, and a giant glass of delicious red wine. That's it. That's my dream meal. Happy now?"

Floris gave a few clicks to his mechanical pencil and took to his little black notebook, annotating the following: "Steak. Medium rare. Potato. Vegetable. Giant glass of red wine." He put down his pencil and shut his book.

"Got it."

We stayed silent for a few moments, staring into each other's eyes with tiny little smirks on our mouths.

"So what are you going to do with that?" I finally asked, in reference to his note taking.

"Emele."

"Yes?"

"Miss Belden."

"Yes?"

"I promise you that sometime in the next two years, I will cook you dinner. I will cook you a special dinner and it will be just that. Your dream steak dinner."

I blurted out laughing. My "dream steak dinner" was so beneath him and I knew it.

"Floris, that's silly."

"No, it's not, because you will have to do something for me in exchange. It will be a trade," he explained.

At that, I took a large sip of champagne, while making the come-hither motion with my hand, inviting him to give me more details.

"You will have to write for me, and you will have to read to me."

"Excuse me?"

"I want you to write something. Anything. I'm sure it will be beautiful, whatever it is, and I want you to read it to me. I cook, you read. Do we have a deal?"

I knew my words would pale in comparison to anything he could whip up in the kitchen, even if it was just a basic, gluttonous, American slab of meat and potatoes. But, regardless, I liked this bargain.

"Deal," I said with a squeeze of his hand.

Eight courses had gone by, plus a few extras from the kitchen staff, probably as a way to apologize again for the Monday night snafu. Famously, we had stayed until the restaurant was clearing out and the cooks were cleaning up. It was just us, the chefs, and a little Metallica holding things down. And just as the last cook brought out our final dessert, he caught us in a tender moment. Looking at our linked hands and locked eyes, he said in reference to the courtship, "Aww, you guys. I like this. I really like this."

I liked it, too. A lot.

~ ~ ~

After another blissful three hours with Floris, the team at Schwa had more than made up for shutting us out the first time. On top of the stellar service and memorable meal, Michael Carlson came out with one final surprise.

"This is on us tonight, you guys," he casually said.

"Absolutely not," Floris said, refusing to let them comp the meal.

"Yeah, that's not necessary," I added, reaching for my purse.

Michael put out his hand and shook his head.

"Please, if you leave us anything on the table, we will fold it up in the table linen and throw it away. I promise. Now do either of you need help with getting a taxi?"

My phone was dead and Floris didn't have Uber on his. So, we both required transportation. Sadly, that was in the form of two separate cars to take us back to our two separate lives and drive us apart. Again.

"Yes, please. Two," I said bashfully.

The first cab pulled up and I insisted Floris take it. I needed a few extra moments to gather myself and plus I needed to pee. Floris kissed me on the cheeks and hopped in the backseat of the taxi.

Between Bonsoiree and Schwa, I had ingested about twenty different courses, four bottles of champagne, and a million little moments with a man I should have never met. And still, the most we had done was kiss on the cheek in groups of three.

And then there were two. Me, and Michael Carlson.

"So, I really can't leave you anything?"

"You can leave me with one thing," Carlson insisted. "A promise you will come back."

As reality would have it, I discovered another good guy in disguise. This was becoming my new favorite hobby.

CHAPTER NINETEEN/LESSON NINETEEN

- Stick it to the non-believers

My next opportunity to see Floris was late Friday night, as Grant Achatz needed him on the line for dinner Friday and Saturday to help with the expected rush from the weekend business. From conversations with Floris, I learned that the earliest the restaurant could accept a reservation was about three months from the potential patron's call date. A ninety-day wait-list? I had no idea what could warrant such a thing and couldn't even fathom the idea of it. Why anybody would wait a quarter of a year to have dinner at some random place was beyond me. Alas, I respected that this was his place of work and that working mornings-only was not an option for the next two days.

"Emele," Floris said as I picked up his call just before 5 PM that Friday. "I cannot talk long, we are about to start service. I just want to make sure we are on for tonight."

I didn't know what the plan was going to be. I just knew that I had to stay awake until at least 2 AM to see it through.

"Yes, of course we are."

"Wonderful. I miss you. I will call you after I am done. We can meet up then, yeah?"

"Looking forward to it, Floris. Have a good shift."

A shift? Could one even call it that? He was getting ready for battle, about to man a single station that was responsible for mass-producing one of 22 courses at the best restaurant in America. His entire tenure at Alinea revolved around learning and perfecting a single task, and then repeating it flawlessly for 200, sometimes more, covers a night.

"Have a good shift" just didn't seem to cut it, not by a long shot. "Good luck, and goodnight" was more like it.

Knowing that I didn't have to get up for work the next day was a major motivating factor in agreeing to start my night at 2am, but truth be told, it had been a while since I afforded myself the luxury of staying up past midnight for anything that wasn't "bad date with a loser guy."

To keep myself from going to bed, I made plans to go out beforehand with my gay friend, Justin (remember him?). We picked a high-energy club in an area close to the restaurant.

"So, what time does he get off?" Justin asked, shouting over the Lady Gaga-Madonna mash-up.

"Two," I screamed back.

"Jesus. What does he do?"

"He's a chef!" I shouted.

"A what?!" he asked again, louder.

"CHEF!" I screamed.

"Oh…sexy!" Justin said, raising his gin and tonic for a cheers to that.

He was right. It was sexy. Super damn sexy, in fact. And why? I couldn't quite pinpoint it. Was it that food is the way to someone's heart and Floris had that whole thing mastered? Was it that the level of cooking he did showcased a skill set found in about one in one-hundred thousand people? Was it that he was a sexy foreigner with a killer accent? Or that he owned his own business, drove his own car, and knew all about expensive champagne? Or how about the fact he didn't want to get in my pants, he just wanted a seat across the table from me at some of the nicest restaurants in the world? Obviously, attributing the sexiness thing to just one aspect of this "chef" would be impossible because the truth was—it was all of it. It was everything I just mentioned and so much more.

The irony was not lost on me knowing that I had gone from knowing nothing about the food industry, to dating one of its best cooks, and eating in not one, but two Michelin-rated restaurants in a matter of just days. Even though I was a newbie, I was already starting to feel like a seasoned foodie.

I knew full well people went through hell and high water to score resos at the restaurants I just so happened upon earlier that week. They saved up for months to spend a few hours eating at these places. And so far, I had spent nothing, made zero special phone calls, and slipped not a single, crisp twenty to some shirt-skirted hostess to make any of this happen. The only thing I did was simply get into a cab that a certain somebody was getting out of, and that was it. That was all it took, and suddenly I had the in of all ins with a man named Floris, who just happened to be good in the kitchen, and possibly in bed, although I was under no pressure to figure that out.

If the food world was some sort of exquisite fantasy land, and it sure appeared to be, well then I couldn't have aligned with a better tour guide to take me through it and explain what exactly it was that we were seeing to our right and tasting to our left.

I snapped back to reality when the lights came back on in the club. I then realized that was my warning. Lights went up at 15 minutes to closing time, which meant it was 15 minutes to 2 AM, 15 minutes left in Floris's shift, and 15 minutes for me to figure out where to tell him to meet me when he was released from his post.

"2 AM already?" asked Justin as he squinted his eyes from the light.

"Quarter to," I confirmed.

"Where are you meeting Florence?"

"Floris."

"Whatever."

"I don't know," I said. "I need somewhere that we can hang out until the sun comes up."

"Um, how about your place? Duh," insisted Justin with a good old elbow nudge.

"It's not like that," I retorted. "We aren't hooking up."

"Well that's unfortunate," he said before leaving me for the men's room.

I know he was disappointed, but the truth was, it really wasn't like that with Floris. Sure, he was dreamy. There wasn't a single part of him that couldn't be classified as "amazingly sexy," but our dynamic wasn't one that lent itself to being naked under the covers together. Would it eventually? I didn't know. I just knew that making out together was far from a priority, so long as talking together was still an option.

Call me crazy, or just plain prudish, but I insisted we find a public venue for this late night rendezvous. After all, the most we had done so far was kiss on the cheek—and that was simply his preferred way of saying hi and bye.

Justin and I left the club in search of a good after-hours spot. Failing to do the appropriate venue research, I quickly realized that our only option in the area would be a goth-themed metal bar down the block called the Flat Iron, which was a big hashtag-no in my book.

As such, somewhat of a logistical nightmare had presented itself. And so had Floris, whose number was popping up on my call screen yet again.

"Emele, I am in taxi cab. Where shall I tell him to go?"

With not much of a solid answer to give him, I looked up at the nearest street sign and told him the intersection:

"Milwaukee and North. There's a sandwich shop called Jimmy John's. I'll be inside."

"Milwaukee and North, how far?" I could hear Floris ask his cab driver.

Although these moments were few and far between, I liked when cabs were bringing us together.

"Ten minutes, Emele. I will be there in ten minutes, my lovely."

~ ~ ~

Lo and behold, the Jimmy John's sandwich shop—the venue for our romantic chat—was relatively empty at 2:15 in the morning.

"Are you guys open?" I probed the cashier.

"Yeah, till 5 AM"

"Do you mind if I just sit in here for a bit with my friend and talk?" I asked.

"Go right ahead. But let me warn you, you'll be the only sober ones in here till close," said the cashier who looked like he had just stepped off the set of a VICE News documentary on weed. "And I mean, the only sober people," he reiterated as if to imply him and his mayonnaise-spreading cohort were taking pulls of Rumplemintz in between chopping cucumbers.

"That's totally fine."

"Will you buy something before you leave so my manager doesn't get pissed I let you loiter?"

Was I really facing a potential loitering charge for being sober inside a Jimmy John's in the wee hours of the morning?

"That's totally fine," I said again, as I perused the chip selection.

I saw Floris' cab pull up. He stepped out in a snowboarding jacket and had on a backpack. I knew he was thirty-four years old, but everything about him had a youthful glow, especially his enthusiasm to see me so late at night after a grueling shift at Alinea.

"Hello, gorgeous," he said as he dished out three kisses.

"Hi there, how are you?" My cheeks erupted in a smile.

"So this is what you look like when you go out?"

We both looked down at what I was wearing. I had forgotten I had just come from a club and actually put effort into looking like I was still young enough to be a cast member on The Real World.

"Yes. I suppose it is," I said of my black leggings, low-cut black V-neck top, high-heeled boots, and a slouchy hat to accentuate my barely curled hair. Not bad, I thought. Not bad at all.

"I love it. You are so natural, so beautiful. Like a chameleon changing colors." I was convinced that was said in reference to whatever eyeliner I had applied that night running down to my cheekbones, but I tried my best to accept his compliment, and not be self-conscious after dancing around in a sweaty pool of gay men for the last two hours.

"And you. Is this what you look like when you go to work?" I asked as he unzipped his jacket, revealing a white chef's coat with a small bit of food splatter on it and a signature pair of Dansko kitchen clogs.

"Yes it is, Emele. I wear this every day in the kitchen."

Things were starting to come together for me. It was the first time I had seen this chef dressed for battle, which was giving me the context I needed to place him as a cook, and not just an incredible dining partner with impeccable taste in bubbly.

His uniform was by all accounts remarkably plain, exactly what you'd expect of someone who is preparing food in a fine dining institution. What hadn't yet dawned on me, however, was the fact that the precise chef coat he was wearing was the uniform of choice for so many aspiring culinary artists. It was issued by Grant Achatz. It was worn in Alinea. It was dressing to the nines, kitchen style. But the stark reality of it was that despite the millions who'd aspire to one day wear just that, only a small percentage of men and women would ever have the honor.

Alas, there we were, Floris and I, smack-dab underneath the harsh fluorescent lighting in the middle of a random Jimmy John's, starting a conversation that was bound to be fruitful. All the while, all of the people within a five-mile radius of us were either raging on or sleeping in. Again, it was the most peculiar set of circumstances stemming from a chance encounter that could never intentionally be repeated. Where I was, who I was with, what I was doing—I wouldn't have traded any of it. Was it the most romantic venue, especially when scantily clad bitches came in to ask for the bathroom key so they could throw up and then proceed to order a Beach Club? Of course not. But, again, it was a moment that I knew we could never have again—and that, in and of itself, was a fairytale.

"What is this place?" asked Floris. I neglected to realize how unordinary this must have been for him, and found it rather charming. For a moment, I wondered what the Dutch version of this mass-produced sandwich shop would be, and struggled to think how I would begin to explain the beauty behind a mayonnaise slathered sub sandwich to man whose food knowledge stemmed from the Michelin guide.

Our conversation about sandwiches didn't last long. Instead, it segued into something I secretly hoped, but never expected, we'd circle back to: a life together.

I know, this sounds crazy considering it was only the third time we had shared the same space, and it was all apparently going down in a sandwich shop known for being freaky-fast, but nothing felt like a more natural fit than the way we were together. In my heart of hearts, I knew there were married couples in the world that weren't as "in love" with each other as Floris and I were in that moment. In every sense of the word, he was my man. And I wanted to tell the world, regardless of time zone, language barrier, age, or level of sobriety. Never in my life had anything evolved on a trajectory like this, but I wasn't scared. I didn't try to pump the brakes or pull out in the least.

"Emele," he began.

"Floris," I responded, grabbing his hand, awaiting the fate of his words.

"I have to tell you what I was thinking about tonight while at my station. I was thinking about you coming to Holland."

"I would love to come to Holland. It's been a while since I've been overseas. A vacation sounds lovely," I said excitedly and without any hesitation.

"Well, good, my dear. But traveling for a visit is not what I mean."

What did he mean?

"I mean, you coming—and you staying—in Holland. With me."

On one hand: Take me now, God. Take me now.

On the other: "Floris, I…I have a job." The hesitation was kicking up. "I…I have my family. I have an apartment. And what about . . ."

"Emele, I have thought about that. All of that. You can work in my restaurant. You can manage the books or work front of the house. Or you can just be a hostess a few days a week, you have such a warm personality, the guests would love you."

"What would I do other than that? I don't know anyone there."

"You will write when you aren't working. And you will have me."

Wow, he had really thought about this.

"Floris. My family…"

"My friend," he interrupted, putting his hand on top of mine, regaining physical control of our dynamic at the table. "My friend works for KLM. That's the airline between here and Rotterdam. I spoke with him today. He said he could fly you for $200 each way: you twice a year back to the United States, and then your family twice a year to us. It'll be less than a thousand dollars each time."

It was happening again, an Eat, Pray, Love moment. And even though I hadn't seen the film, nor read the book, it was obvious that I could identify with a woman who couldn't seem to resist a smooth-talking foreign man, especially when he was combining his powers with delicious food and beverage.

"So what do you think?" he asked.

What did I think? How about: this is ridiculous, absurd, and asinine for starters?

But then again, not really.

Why was this all sounding so right?

A higher than average phone bill I could explain. But how the hell was I going to bridge this topic with my mother? I saw how she reacted when I decided to stay in Nebraska for my ex-boyfriend, Trent. She'd for-sure flip out if I told her I was moving to Holland for some guy I met in a taxi who refused to believe there was an "i" or "y" in my first name.

Regardless of whether or not I was going to pack my bags and put in my two-week notice at work, I was glad that this simple, sober moment proved that whatever was going on was no longer just a silly, one-sided teenage dream. He, too, was aware—very aware—of what was happening between us. Moreover, he accepted it, acknowledged it, and was making plans about it.

Floris could see the wheels turning in my head. And even though the thought of uprooting me in a big, gigantic way would require some serious processing, he didn't want to sit in silence. Silence was not characteristic of us—of our time together. We were accustomed to making the most of things. We were used to witty banter, to honest engagements, to enriching two-way conversation. Those were things fueling this interaction—this addiction—making it more authentic than any other relationship either of us had ever had thus far in our lives.

So, he switched the subject and began to tell me another story.

"Guess what else," he said.

I had to laugh at how much he had come out of his shell from the first time we met. Just a few days ago, this man kept his distance physically and emotionally from me, and now he was rapid-firing preposterous romantic inklings and cute little quips. Either way, I had no problem being the target of all this story-time and gladly replied: "What, Floris? Please tell me."

"I really got to know the woman across from my station tonight."

"Uh-oh, another woman…" I said facetiously.

"Not to worry, she's moving."

"To Holland?" I asked.

Floris chuckled.

"No, to Denver. Could you just listen?"

Were we already married? Cutting each other off, finishing each other's sentences, giving each other a hard time, flirting, frolicking, smiling. I must have been so jet-lagged that I missed our wedding.

"I'm sorry. Go on, go on." I recovered.

"It was her last night at the restaurant and we spoke all night. About everything."

Surprise, surprise. Limitless conversation was Floris's M.O.

"And before she left for good, she gave me this."

Floris pulled out some fancy, silver contraption from his backpack. It looked like a cross between a Phillips-head screwdriver and a dental mirror.

"I'm not sure what that is, but that's great!" I said with as much fake enthusiasm as I could muster.

"It's her spoon!" he exclaimed.

"That's a spoon? Let me see that," I said, snatching the device.

"Yes. All cooks carry a chef's spoon in their jackets so they can taste their food, spread sauces, stir things, whatever. It's very personal. Lots of restaurants will tell you what clothes you have to wear, what shoes you have to own, what knives you must work with. But the one thing you can always make your own is your chef's spoon. Hers is very ergonomic; it fits nicely in your hand. Here, hold it like this."

Floris reached over to guide my fingers as I awkwardly held this strange woman's "spoon" like a wooden pencil. Floris worked to guide my hand around it a little more appropriately, but he couldn't break my vice grip and gave up.

"You are a writer," he said of my flawed spoon-holding style.

Poking fun aside, he knew I understood the story, which was all that mattered.

"So why'd she give it to you?" I asked.

"Well, in the culinary world, it's tradition to give your chef's spoon away to someone in the industry that has inspired you. Someone you respect, trust, and learn from. Someone who changed the way you view your craft and pushed you to be better, to do better. It's a complete and total honor. And she gave me hers. I couldn't believe it. We only talked a few hours."

"So who at Alinea are you going to give yours to? Grant?"

"No. No one. Emele, you have to listen when I say it's the highest honor outside of a Michelin star or a James Beard award, you don't just give your spoon away to anyone. Don't get me wrong, I'm honored this woman gave me hers, and I will treasure it fondly, but I'm just far more protective of mine. That is all."

"Fair enough," I said sliding the spoon back his way.

"Uhhhh, sorry to interrupt," said the stoner sandwich maker. "But we are about to close and I really need you to buy something."

"Number twelve, no cucumber, cut in half, wrapped separately, to go," I rattled off like a well-rehearsed monologue.

"Well, Floris, we should probably pack up before they charge us rent, what do you think?"

"What time is it?"

"It's four-thirty in the morning, Floris."

"Oh my god, I have to be back at work again in six hours," he gleefully lamented as he zipped up his jacket.

"It's your last day though, isn't it? Tomorrow?" I inquired, zipping up mine.

"Yes, it is. Then Sunday I have off. I have plans to eat as a patron at Alinea that night, but I'd love to spend the day with you before my reservation at 9pm."

I was more than okay with the timeshare, and even more glad that he hadn't phrased us seeing each other again as a question this time. In fact, after letting him paint a picture of our lives in Rotterdam, he must have learned that there really wasn't anything I'd object to if he looked me in the eye and said it sweetly.

"Here's your sandwich, guys."

I paid the hipster ten dollars and told him to the keep the change.

"What is this?" Floris asked inquisitively.

"Just eat it on your way home. It's a sandwich, and it's amazing."

And at that, we left each other. Even as the happiest girl in the world, I couldn't help but feel sad that we were getting good at this whole separate-cars thing.

CHAPTER TWENTY/LESSON TWENTY

- It really is "the little things" in life

The pressure was on to make Floris's last day here unforgettable. I racked my brain for countless hours trying to plot out the perfect day. I had made phone call after phone call, racking up one coveted brunch reservation after the next. I researched everything from the Navy Pier Ferris wheel hours, to the cost of a VIP package at the Shedd aquarium, to the exhibits at the planetarium. But for as many options as I had, none of these Chicago staples screamed "I'm going to remember this day forever" quite like I wanted it to.

I decided on one thing for sure—and that was a surprise brunch at the Trump Tower. This glorious building was situated in the heart of the city and the buffet was served from The Terrace on the sixteenth floor. If anything, I knew the service would be flawless, the food would taste nice, and the view would be incredible. Not a bad start to the day, right?

I called ahead to prepay and reserve a table up against the window. I wanted an unobstructed view of the city in which we met and went on to make our playground for the last five days. On that, I refused to budge. I also didn't want them to drop a check at our table at any point during our meal. Part of me just wanted to limit the time a stranger spent lingering around our table, but the other part of me wanted this to be my treat completely. After all, the only meal I'd paid for since our casual relationship with Michelin-starred restaurants had begun was a brief outside affair with a Jimmy John's sandwich. And because this was going to be my treat, I decided to make it a surprise.

I arrived at the Radisson Inn off Michigan Avenue about an hour before our brunch reservation. Walking in to the hotel, I checked my appearance on every shiny reflection there was. The last date was just as important as the first, and I wanted to look good. More importantly, I wanted to look memorable.

As I walked through the lobby toward the bank of elevators, I took an index finger to every surface. The chairs near the foyer, the banister to the stairs, the reception desk. So, this was where he spent his nights dreaming of our life together in Holland, huh? It was certainly strange to see the place where this man had been living the last seventeen days, and I wondered how many other "Florises" there were tucked away in humble hiding spots waiting to find their "Emeles."

I arrived to his room on the nineteenth floor. Everything about it, besides him, was utterly uninviting. But even more unsettling than the tiny bathroom or the archaic television were his suitcases that were half packed. I ran my hand over his luggage tag and tried for a moment to pronounce the street name written on it, but couldn't. He really wasn't from here. He really was leaving.

"My dear Emele," said Floris. I dropped the luggage tag like a hot coal. After all, it was too soon to get emotional. I absolutely had to cherish every minute of this day, as it was the last one that would end with us being on the same continent.

"How are you?" he asked hugging me tightly. This time he skipped the kisses and just held me close in the nook of his chest.

"I'm good, how are you?"

"Did you see Nicole?"

Who was Nicole? Another woman giving her spoon away to my European lover?

"Nicole at the Front Desk," he clarified. "She's my friend and she should know you by now."

"What do you mean?" I asked, uncertain how I could know a woman who I had evidently never met before.

"Every night since I've met you, Nicole has been at the desk. I would stumble in happy as could be. She thought I was enthusiastic."

"Enthusiastic?" A language barrier had clearly presented itself.

"Uh, uhhh. Hmmm," Floris said, looking to the ceiling to find the right words. "Enthusiastic, like, had too much champagne . . ."

"Drunk, Floris. She thought you were drunk."

"Ah, yes, she would treat me as if I was drunk. And I'd say, 'No! I just had another fantastic night with Emele.'"

Oh dear, bless her heart.

"So, I told her everything about you, about us, about all of our adventures. She couldn't believe it."

She couldn't believe it? What about me! I was the leading lady in a real-life romantic comedy that was never supposed to happen and I couldn't believe it.

With that, I looked at him and smiled, saying: "Come on, silly. Are you ready to eat?"

We departed from the hotel and started walking down Michigan Avenue. The January chill was relentless, yet familiar for us. Floris was taking a lot of photos; everything seemed to impress him from the size of our banks to the amount of people waiting for the walk-signal to change. Had it been anyone else, I would have slapped the camera out of his hands, and told him to stop being such a tourist, but with Floris I didn't care. I didn't care that he stopped every other minute to take pictures of snow-covered branches, street signs that said "Honorary Oprah Winfrey Parkway," or a taxicab advertising deep-dish pizza on its roof. I wanted him to soak in everything that would help him remember this city, and the special girl he met when he was here.

But, he was making us late for brunch. I will say that.

After nearly filling up his memory card on skyline snapshots, I decided to divert our route and head down Wabash, a lesser-known north-south street. There wasn't much to see besides a small Thai restaurant that was closed, and the back entrance of a Nordstrom department store, but I knew what impressive thing would be making an appearance after the road straightened out, just a block ahead.

The Trump Tower is one of the most beautiful buildings in the city. It rivals the Hancock Center in terms of height, but is unparalleled in terms of design. It's chic and modern, yet still timeless in comparison to Trump's other gaudy creations. There is no gold, no glitz. Just glam.

From the bellhop to the manager of their one-Michelin star rated restaurant, Sixteen, the level of customer service is reminiscent of what you'd expect from a stewardess on a trans-Atlantic flight in the 1960s— friendly, responsive, and pristine. The Trump building, located on the Chicago River in the middle of the city, was where old school met new money. From the inside out the place was a wonderland, and I knew once Floris saw it from around the bend, he'd go absolutely nuts.

"Oh my gosh, Emele! Look at that building. What one is that?" Floris asked as he pulled out his camera once more and began capturing the moment.

Thankfully, he wasn't looking at me, or my smirk would have definitely given away something. So, as he continued staring through the lens, I did my part in playing tour guide, telling him everything I knew, and whatever else I could make up, about the ever-so-fascinating Trump building.

"That, my friend, is the Trump Hotel & Condominiums," I began.

"People live there?" he asked. "No way."

"Yup, they started building this sometime around 2007. I remember when it was just going up. Now, it's all finished, and as you can see, it's perfect."

As we became parallel with the front entrance, I made a tactical point to mention just how gorgeous the interior was, hoping that I could get him salivating a little more before the big reveal.

"High ceilings, incredible artwork, marble everything: the place is an absolute gem. You would hardly believe it."

"Man, I wish I could see the inside," he said, not taking his eyes off the gorgeous façade or his hands off the camera.

Grabbing onto his arm, I give him a quick pull and abruptly changed our direction. He was caught off guard.

"You wish to see the inside? Well, you will. Because this—this is where we are having brunch today."

"Are you kidding?" Floris was shocked.

"Kidding? No. Late? Yes. Our reservation was at eleven."

Floris looked down at his watch, then up into my eyes. Not only was it the first time we had made eye contact since leaving the hotel, but this was the first time for something else—it was our first kiss on the lips, unsolicited by someone's coming or going. This one was different. This one was fueled by happiness and romance bubbling over at 11:10 AM on a

Sunday in the cold city of Chicago. As he gently pulled away, he smiled at me. As quick, sweet, and innocent as it was, I had no idea why we waited so long to do that. But like everything else that had unfolded with this man, I wouldn't have changed a thing.

"Good morning. What brings you in today?" the doorman politely asked.

"Good morning. My lady and I are eating brunch in Sixteen today," Floris instructed.

His lady.

On the entire ride up, to Sixteen, I couldn't stop thinking about our kiss—that teeny, tiny, little kiss. My first kiss was when I was seventeen years old in a hotel on a journalism field trip in Washington D.C. But my first real kiss was here: seven years later, standing outside the Trump building in the freezing cold weather with a gorgeous Dutchman ten years my senior from across the ocean. What are the odds?

Coming off the elevator to the sixteenth floor, the crew was expecting us.

"Good morning Miss Belden. Good morning, Chef Floris."

They did their homework. They'd listened when I told them I had a top-chef in from Holland. They'd listened when I told them that he'd busted his ass all week in Grant Achatz's kitchen, and that we wanted to have a leisurely lunch with a gorgeous view. They'd listened and they delivered. That was Michelin-star-level service. How did I not know this world existed before meeting Floris?

"How's this for you, Miss Belden?" the Barbie-doll maître d' asked of the table she planned to put us at. We were isolated compared to the rest of the dining room, typically a faux pas by any trained hostess who knows how to control the pacing of her dining room, but it was perfect for us. The four-top table, set for two, was facing out above a snowy city on a simple Sunday. I was beyond pleased.

"It is perfectly lovely, thank you," I confirmed.

Soon our waiter arrived with complimentary champagne and welcomed us. He departed just as quickly as he descended to allow us the opportunity to toast in private. I appreciated this, as Floris took it upon himself to do the honors.

"This is to you, Emele. To you—for this incredible day, this incredible week, and the incredible amount of life you have helped me live over the last few days. You have no idea what you've done for me, and I thank you. To you, my dear, deer." Then, he teared up.

"Too early for tears," I said with a smile, clinking my glass against his, before taking my first sip of the beautiful bubbly.

I have to admit, for a man whose first language was not English, his subtle toast was perfectly said. I couldn't imagine more touching words coming my way by a man who I truly respected.

Our server re-approached the table and proposed a tour of the robust brunch selections. We followed him with no expectations; however, what we saw surpassed even Chef Floris' wildest dreams.

"You will start by grabbing one of these plates," the waiter explained, pointing with an open palm to a large stack of bright, white china.

"Then, you will make your way to any of a number of food stations behind me. As you can see, there is everything from custom breakfast staples like omelets and pancakes, to gourmet grilled cheeses with tomato soup, to mounds of sushi, a mountain of fresh, iced king crab leg, and an array of desserts. Do you have any questions?"

Our eyes lit up at the epicurean wonderland. From what the server was saying, I gathered that you could literally start anywhere and end nowhere. It was the perfect setup to reflect our very own dynamic.

"No, I think we're good," I replied, feeling free to get started.

Floris and I started with a lap around the stations, sans plates. We wanted to see just what it was we were about to get ourselves into. Looping around back to the beginning of the line, Floris proposed an enthusiastic, "Shall we?" as he eyed the fine china that was beckoning us like a pile of blank canvases.

"Oh, yes. We shall," I answered.

Floris picked up a plate and handed it to me first. Then, he snagged one for himself and preceded to toss it in the air like a highly breakable, super-expensive pizza pie. Next, he got cocky and flipped the dish around his back, toggling it from one hand to the other as we walked back through the corridor towards the mecca of food.

"I bet Grant Achatz can't do that," he said, looking back at me with a wink.

I smiled and shook my head in absolute awe. At that moment, I wasn't just brunching with the man of my dreams, I was following around a 15-year-old boy trapped in the body of a thirty-four-year-old man. It was nothing short of an utter joy to watch him frolic. I had never known what it was like to be behind this kind of exuberance. Clearly, I had just made someone's moment, and it felt wonderful.

Another difference in our cultures became highly visible when I beelined it to the grilled cheese and mini-burgers station while Floris approached the king crab table and circled it like a shark. It was like he was admiring Michelangelo's David, the way he looked at the mountain of ice and fish in admiration. He commented to the steward of that station that they were some of the nicest pieces of fish he had ever seen.

About five minutes later, we met back at the table, our plates were remarkably different. Mine was full of greasy finger food and bite-sized gourmet desserts, while his was loaded with intimidating pieces of seafood.

"I don't know how you eat that," I said condescendingly as I shoved a burger in my mouth.

"What do you mean? It's good," he defended.

"No, like literally. How do you eat that?" I said in reference to the king crab leg.

"I'll show you."

For the first time since our meeting, I was finally able to see Floris work with some food. Granted he wasn't preparing anything from scratch over an eight-burner oven, but rather picking apart some king crab leg and arranging it perfectly with his hands. His gaze was fixated on the plate, and mine was on him. If his concentration on creating the perfect forkful for me was any indication about his passion in the kitchen, I suddenly knew this man was doing exactly what he was supposed to in life. I understood precisely why he had given up most everything to pursue this career, this demanding way of life.

A solid 60 seconds later, Floris finally said, "Open." I didn't realize he was bestowing first-bite privileges upon me, especially for a delicacy I was convinced I was going to hate. But like everything having to do with him, I relinquished control and surrendered my taste buds, praying he wouldn't lose respect for me when I spat the crab back out in his face.

Needless to say, there was no big reveal on this one. I loved it. And I loved the man feeding it to me. I really, truly did.

"Not that bad?" he asked.

"Not at all."

Floris continued to share bites with me, politely declining my attempts to give him some of my gourmet grilled cheese. However, more impressive was his defense against me steering the conversation towards the inevitable: the fact that he was leaving. Not only would we not get to relive this lavish moment again, we wouldn't even be able to enjoy the most casual encounters without first flying over an ocean or switching to an international phone plan. I couldn't help but feel dejected; as if everything I had put towards making this day special was futile, because it was for sure fleeting.

~ ~ ~

"Emele, I have a present for you."

I perked up. A present?

Over the white linen tablecloth, Floris slid me a flat wrapped package from his backpack. I unwrapped it carefully and could tell it was a book. Which one? I had no idea.

It was called The Physiology of Taste and I immediately opened the hardcover book and fanned its pages; it smelled new. The type size was likely a maddening seven-point font, and the pages were an unwelcoming shade of beige. I briefly caught words such as "molecular" and "gastronomy," and I knew there had to be something more to him giving me this monstrosity, which might as well have been a foreign language textbook.

"You won't understand any of this," he stated with confidence. Thank god he was giving me a pass already.

"But this is the book that made me fall in love with cooking, and I want you to know that every time I read it, it takes me to a place of passion and life. It takes me exactly to where you take me. Think of this like a little time machine. We both open it, and we come back here. To this table. How does that sound?"

Beautiful. Absolutely beautiful.

Floris then took out one more wrapped book and placed it on the table.

"What's this?" I asked coyly.

"One more for good luck," he said. Little did he know, I already had good luck: the best luck, in fact. Either way, I obliged and opened it softly.

It was Eat, Pray, Love. Though neither of us truly knew the story, we both knew enough about it to know we were having our own little version of the best-seller right there at a table by the window at Sixteen.

"You said you had an Eat, Pray, Love moment with me. I don't ever want you to forget what that moment feels like. So, here's the book.

Do you know what the best part is? You won't have to read it to have it take you back to our dinner at Schwa. You can just look at it on your shelf, and you'll be there. We'll be there."

I had no words. How could a man who knew me for just one week be able to capture who he was, who I was, and who we were in book titles? They were, largely, the most appropriate gifts I'd ever received.

It was my turn to reciprocate, if I could even contend. Luckily, I had the same thought as him to bring a gift to this final meal together and as corny as it sounds, I wanted to get him a souvenir for his maiden trip to Chicago: something by which he could remember this beautiful city, and everything magical about it.

After searching high and low for something, I came across a clothing line started by some young, male entrepreneurs who called themselves "Chi Boys." Perhaps something for Chicago by Chicago would do the trick? In combing through their designs, I stumbled upon a black t-shirt with an artistic iteration of the John Hancock building. If my memory served me correctly, that's the location where he first stopped and thought that perhaps I was someone he was "supposed" to meet on his trip. The shirt, and what it symbolized, was perfect for the occasion.

"For you," I said, sliding my gift his way.

"Emele . . ." he said, as if I shouldn't have but it was okay that he did.

Floris opened it and immediately put it on, layering it over the soft, oatmeal-colored Henley he'd picked out that day. I was so flattered that he wanted to literally be inside of this stupid t-shirt.

"The Hancock building! The second loveliest thing in this city! I absolutely love it."

At that moment, with him in his Chi Boys tee, and me with my pile of books, Floris grabbed my hand and had a proposition for me.

"Emele, I want you to come to Alinea with me tonight."

What?

Or rather, WHAT?!?!

Asking me to dine with him at Alinea was almost as outlandish as planting the why-don't-you-move-to-Holland seed in my head.

I knew that he had a reservation there, and I knew he wanted to take intricate notes about everything and anything related to the dining experience. And I respected that he wanted to plow through the 24-plus courses and write down all there was to know about the complex dishes being served from the best restaurant in North America. After all, reservations take at least three months to get, and they were willing to accommodate him late on a Sunday night as a solo diner. That in and of itself was unheard of, let alone asking me to come along for the ride.

Absolutely nothing about me tagging along and going, "Wait. How do we eat this?" over and over was conducive with experiencing a true oneness with Grant's menu, and I understood that. And yet, he still insisted that I come along. Was he really willing to risk my presence disrupting this once in a lifetime opportunity?

"Floris, I don't know if I can. I mean, I want to, I really want to. But, Alinea is a whole other level. Even I know that..."

"No. I want you there. Wine pairings will go great with the food, but you will go perfectly with the entire night. I need you there. Will you please, please come with me to Alinea tonight?"

Alinea was $225 per person. It was more than double the price of Schwa, which was comp'd, and Bonsoiree, which I didn't pay for. Saying yes meant not only would I have to promise to keep quiet during the dinner, but I'd have to pay out of pocket for this astoundingly special treat. Could I afford it was not the question. What do I have to cut out of my budget next month to make this happen, was.

"Yes, I will go."

How drastically my life had changed. From frozen tortellini and hazelnut gelato at the corner store, to multicourse dining at places even the foodiest of foodies couldn't get close to. And then men who were behind both of those meals, how different could those two be, right?

Back to reality, we still had the rest of the day on our hands. Not expecting Alinea to be part of the equation, I had done my research and presented several viable options for Floris and I to have "the best Chicago day ever." Navy Pier, the architectural boat tour, shopping down Michigan Avenue—believe me: I could have worked for the tourism bureau with what I was bringing to the table.

"So, what of those would you like to do?" I asked Floris.

He looked out the window and pondered, letting out an audible, hmmmmm before saying, "I think I just want to feed the squirrels."

WTF. What squirrels? Was there some squirrel exhibit at the Museum of Science and Industry that I didn't know about? How could I have missed that in all my research?

"It's just that we don't have squirrels in Holland," explained Floris, as he finished his glass of champagne. "So if at all possible, I'd like to find some squirrels...and then feed them."

My biggest hold up on this was not his choice to feed rodents all afternoon, it was that I honestly did not know where in the city one goes to find a squirrel that wasn't freshly run over by a Land Rover. Alas, the theme of the day was to make Floris' day, so to his request, I said: "Well then, I suppose we should go get some nuts."

~ ~ ~

It was a Sunday afternoon at Trader Joe's, and for as packed as it was with yuppies getting chocolate covered pomegranate seeds and Two-Buck Chuck, I can guarantee you that Floris and I were the only ones there staring at the nut selection trying to figure out what variety would best suit a squirrel.

"So...what ones should we get?" I asked.

"I like macadamia," said Floris.

"Me too. Salted or unsalted?"

"Unsalted.In case they don't have water readily available," he replied definitively, snagging a pack that fit the bill.

As we headed to the checkout line, Floris pulled me into the produce section. He clutched a lemon and held it to my nose.

"Smell this."

I inhaled deeply. He then pulled it toward his nose and did the same.

"Mmmm, that's my favorite smell."

"A lemon?"

"Not just a lemon. The Meyer lemon, Emele. It's the best lemon out there. Mmmmm," he sniffed again. "Soo good."

It was taste that he said never let him down, but scent must have done something else for him, too. His spirit was lifted yet again, as we got in line to buy the squirrel food. I could not get over how delightfully and literally foreign this all was to me.

Floris and I took an Uber to Lincoln Park. It was cold and snow boots were sadly not part of my wardrobe for the day. But all my white girl problems evaporated when I saw Floris, a thirty-four-year-old man, bolt out of the cab in pursuit of more childish joy: feeding squirrels. As I watched him skip around, I felt a sense of sweet peacefulness. When I was with this man, my biggest and only worry was what kind of nut a squirrel would prefer. Maybe living in Holland with Floris was more paradisiacal than I had imagined.

We fed the squirrels until the sun went down and intermixed the zoology session with sweet kisses and warm embraces. To anyone else that may have seen us from afar, we were boyfriend and girlfriend, stepping outside our Lincoln Park apartment to feed stale bread to the birds. How ordinary. But to us, up close, ordinary couldn't have been further from the reality. We weren't boyfriend and girlfriend, but we were in love with each other. We didn't live in Lincoln Park, but I did. And we weren't feeding birds; we were exclusively there for the squirrels. By all accounts, we were on a once-and-a-lifetime adventure, never to be repeated again. In other words, it was a day—a date—like none other. And the best part was it wasn't over yet. Not by a long shot.

Coincidentally, the squirrel-feeding territory was only a few steps away from one of Chicago's most iconic hotels and residences—the Belden-Stratford Inn. On the ground floor was L2O, the only other three-Michelin starred restaurant in the city. This was from where Floris had first called me to ask me out to dinner at Schwa.

"The interior is absolutely my favorite that I have ever seen," said Floris of the restaurant as we walked toward it. "There are textured walls of soft velvet, and everything is so warm and elegant. Have you seen it?"

As it had turned out, no. No, I had not experienced the interior of a $200-a-person restaurant in the heart of "bougie" Lincoln Park.

"Well then let's take a tour!" exclaimed Floris.

While I appreciated his enthusiasm toward putting me within arm's reach of a velvet wall, I didn't want to burst his bubble when surely the door would be locked at 3 PM on a Sunday. There was no question that they didn't waste their time or resources doing a lunch service and equally as certainly they were busy getting ready for the 5 PM dinner hour, both of which led to one thing: a locked door to the entrance of L2O.

Floris and I were no strangers to being locked out of nice restaurants, but this time he wouldn't take no for an answer. He knocked on the large wooden door and did what he could to align himself in between the crack of it, angling himself just-so to see that there was in fact staff in there polishing and prepping for their future patrons.

After a moment, a waiter put down a glass, and made his way to the door.

"Someone's coming," he whispered excitedly.

Our cultural differences had yet to embarrass me, but that didn't stop me from cringing at the inevitable: we were going to be turned away. Rudely. And that'd be the point Floris would learn the hard way that Americans are neither warm nor inviting if it doesn't mean money in their pockets.

"Yes, may I help you?" said the gentleman, whose tone of voice indicated he was already on a short fuse.

"Yes, hello. We need a tour of the restaurant and the kitchen immediately for this lady. Surely you have been introduced to her by now, correct?" asked Floris, pointing at me standing next to him.

What was he talking about? I just finished telling him I had never set foot in this luxurious building, let alone had a reservation in their restaurant's ultra-elite dining room.

"No, I don't recall we've met. Forgive me for being rude," said the waiter. "But who might she be?"

"This is Miss Belden, of the Belden-Stratford family. Miss Belden, will you show the man your I.D. for verification purposes?"

Oh. My. God.

Without much hesitation, and zero say in the matter, I dug deep into my wallet and produced the "proof" for which Floris was beckoning and showed my driver's license to the server.

The waiter took hold of it and squinted his eyes. He read the name listed on it, "Emily A. Belden," and looked at the picture, then up at me, then back at the picture. A moment later, he handed back my I.D. and said, "Right this way Miss Belden. Welcome to L2O," as he propped open the door a tad wider and invited us in for a tour.

Impostors. Alone in a pristine dining room with velvet walls indeed. Floris simply smiled at me as we took a lap in what truly was the most gorgeous interior I'd ever seen. I had to give him credit: his humor and wit were really coming into their own. I had trained him well.

"Miss Belden," said the waiter. "The chef is ready for you in the back. He would like to say hello."

Next thing I knew, we were walking into the kitchen. It was as perfect as the dining room but in a far different way. The chef had cleaned up for us, shook our hands, welcomed me—"the heiress"—into the facility and asked if there was anything he could get for me. A reality check was all I needed, but I spared the ask.

~ ~ ~

When our Catch Me If You Can-moment ended, Floris and I departed Lincoln Park in pursuit of my apartment, which wasn't too far. As I went to call an Uber, a bus pulled up on the curb in front of us.

"Can we get on that?" Floris asked.

"The 36? Well, we could. It does go by my apartment. But it makes a lot of stops, are you okay with that?"

"I want to do what you do every day. I want to live, even if it's just for a moment, the way we would if we were together. Can we please get on the bus?" he insisted.

At that, we filed on and I paid our fare. It was back to my apartment by way of a dirty, smelly Chicago Transit Authority bus for the two of us. And it was more romantic than one could ever imagine.

Once we pulled up to my apartment, decrepit front porch and all, I became somewhat embarrassed: I knew Floris owned his own place, I saw pictures of it. It was a mansion compared to the shit-hole I was living in. I was afraid it would serve as yet another reminder of how far apart our lives—figuratively and literally—were. To my delight, he made no comment about my living space, as we headed inside, so that I could change into proper attire for the dinner to which I had been so graciously invited.

I had asked myself this a few days earlier, but this time I really meant it: what does one wear to the best dinner of her entire life?

As I pondered that question, Floris was laying down in my bed. He let out a sigh. I hardly noticed, nor was I taken aback at him occupying such a precious piece of real estate. I continued fanning through my wardrobe, determined to stumble upon something halfway suitable for the evening.

He let out a sigh again. This time asking, "Am I really in your bed?"

"Excuse me?"

"Am I really in your room, laying in your bed, looking up at your ceiling right now?"

"Yes, I believe that you are doing just that."

Please ignore the water damage, my internal dialogue added.

"Funny how I traveled all this way, all these thousands of miles, thinking I was just to end up at Alinea, cooking for Grant Achatz. But this journey, I truly believe, was meant for me to get here. To Emele Belden's bed, so I could stare up at her ceiling."

Of course, that's not why he booked a ticket. But there was something to winding up in the oddest of places, amongst the most random of people, and cutting into a parallel world that you never even knew existed. There was something to him having a moment that was so normal to me, yet so out of reach for him. But alas, that's all it was—a cut-in. Every moment we spent together, every event we shared, that's all they were—cut-ins to what the master plan was for us. Sad, yes. But I appreciated the gentle reminder to never take a routine thing for granted.

After applying mascara before she darted, Katie, my roommate, ran into Floris in the dining room. I overheard him introduce himself to her, and of course, a conversation about culinary wonders ensued. Katie was a foodie, abreast on the restaurant scene in Chicago and beyond. I had mentioned Floris to her previously: I even showed her a picture of him. I remember her being less taken aback by his beauty, and more impressed by the fact that the picture showed him with Joël Robuchon, apparently another master chef who, at the time, I had never even heard of.

"Ready?" I asked coming out of my bedroom donning a navy pencil skirt and gray blouse. I hadn't looked this put together since my eight grade graduation. Both Katie and Floris were shocked at my evening attire.

"You look absolutely wonderful," said Katie.

"Yes, what she said," Floris concurred. With a special look in his eye and the extension of his hand, we were ready for Alinea.

"Be my date for dinner at Alinea tonight?" he said as he grabbed my hand and gave it a kiss.

"I suppose," I replied facetiously.

CHAPTER TWENTY-ONE/LESSON TWENTY-ONE

- YOLO: no, really, YOLO.

Our car ride to Alinea was the last we'd share together. Cabs brought us together, but they also took us apart—night after night. Cut-ins, like I said. They were all just cut-ins.

When we told our driver the destination was Alinea, he knew exactly where to take us without needing any further direction. This restaurant was that serious to true Chicagoans.

When we pulled up to its unmarked, humble façade, I knew right away that, no, I was, in fact, not worthy. Not of this food, not of this man, not of the fate that brought it all together. But I walked inside like a champ, because this all was so totally out of my control, and surrendering and just owning it was the trick to doing it right.

We entered through a dark walkway. Two steel doors suddenly opened on my left. A team—an army—of men dressed in fine suits greeted me and took my coat.

"Welcome to Alinea," they said. It was truly as if they had been expecting me for months, even though I was merely a last-minute invitee.

As we were being guided upstairs to our table, I caught a glimpse of the kitchen. About thirty people dressed in all white were hunched over various countertops. Their faces were just inches from the dishes they were so intimately working on perfecting, before blasting them off to the dining room. I imagined Floris as one of those soldiers, one of those chefs.

In total contrast to what was going on downstairs in the brightly lit kitchen, upstairs, we were seated in a dark, quiet dining room. It dawned on me (aside from being in the number-one restaurant in the nation) that I was across from the number-one dining companion in the world. I was the luckiest girl alive.

We were seated in the corner of the restaurant with the wall to our left. I sat in the cushy banquette facing Floris. Service started with a waiter changing out our linens to match what each of us was wearing. I say "a" waiter instead of "our" waiter because a team of about ten people per table per night conducts Alinea's service.

As we settled in, it was time for that famous question: "Are there any food allergies at the table?"

Giving the waiter the "all clear," he proceeded to discuss the wine options.

"We have prepared a wine tasting to go alongside tonight's 24-course menu. The selections are rare, fabulous, and beautiful. Or," he paused, "You can feel free to peruse our wine-by-the-bottle list."

My view on dining like this had officially changed. I declined to see the wine book and pick out whatever the cheapest option was. Instead, I wasted no time at all intrinsically opting for the pairings. Experiences are meant to be rich. Me after this dinner, not so much. Regardless, I had come this far and I wasn't going to start skimping on things now.

"Fantastic choice," our server concurred. "I will be right back to get you started."

Moments later, our server tagged-in his counterpart and another young man swooped to our table. On it, he placed two glasses of champagne.

"Good evening," he said. "Grant had me bring these up for you. While he is busy in the kitchen, he would like you to know that he knows you are here. And that he, along with the rest of us, are happy to have you. Floris, thank you for all your hard work these last two weeks. Cheers to you both. Enjoy."

And so it began.

"Can you believe we're here?" I said, asking the obvious.

"It's incredible. I knew all along I was going to eat here, but I never thought in a million years it'd be with you."

Well that makes two of us.

Before we could make any significant headway on our champagne, the amuse was brought out. On a bright white plate were square colored gelatins. I could not tell you, upon first glance, what they were. Thankfully, a translator stepped in.

"Welcome, again. Here you have solid cocktails. Each one is meant to be a one-bite, and they are each a take on a classic cocktail. There is alcohol in all of them, and you will likely be able to tell exactly which libation each one is a mockery of. Enjoy."

Layman's terms: a plate of very expensive, very scientific, Jell-O shots.

As I placed each cube into my mouth, the texture was what got me. I'm chewing something I'm supposed to be drinking, I thought. I had swallowed an entire Manhattan in one bite. How was that even possible? Little did I know, that would be the first of many times that night I'd ask that very same question.

Service continued just like that, course after course. A member of the team would deliver a dish, explain what the hell it was, provide any necessary instructions for consumption, and then disappear. Everything was paced perfectly. The communication between all of the men and women was stellar. The wait staff was more like an acting troupe in the way that they dramatically and believably presented each plate and wine pairing. For example, when a dish that was based off of something British royalty would eat in the 1800s, our server spieled with an English accent, projecting a regal flare. It wasn't cheesy—it was a time machine. I was paying to step foot into a time machine.

Furthermore, the level of service was beyond any of my wildest dreams. I swear, they could literally predict exactly when I would need to use the restroom, and would flock to pull out the table for me to get out easier. When I returned, they would unfold my napkin and rest it back on my lap, as if I couldn't have been bothered to do it myself. And when they noticed my lipstick accruing on the glassware, they conveniently swooped in to switch out my water glass and give me one free of lip print pile-ups. I was being treated like a VIP, when really, this all was just part of the package: the $225 per person package.

As each course arrived, true to his form, Floris jotted down notes in a little black book. He marked down how things were structured on the plate, drawing pictures and diagrams of the layout. He noted the architecture of the service pieces, most of which were custom designed for the restaurant itself to fulfill Chef Grant's vision of service. He also wrote about the smells and tastes associated with the dishes, and key words that the servers used as they spieled what we were about to ingest. He was a kid in a candy shop being on this side of the fence for once and it was amazing to see him finally relate to the fruits of his labor for the last two weeks.

Our server dropped off two large puffed up pieces of cloth. Almost like an airplane pillow but filled with air instead of foam. I saw nothing edible about it.

"Here we have a dish that is evocative of the country. Everything you'd expect from a day of prancing through the meadows. In one bite, you will taste what we mean, but to start here is a pin."

What did prancing through the meadows taste like? I had to laugh; this was so silly. Until I popped the pillow, and it all became clear.

Immediately as the air seeped out, I could smell dewy grass. I don't know how, I don't know why, I just know that in that moment, I was not sitting in Alinea. I was running through a field somewhere in the middle of nowhere.

Under the pillow was one bite. Helium. Green apple. It made no sense, but magic never does.

Each course was more unexpected than the last. Even if I wanted to gab Floris's ear off, I couldn't. I was utterly entrenched in what we were eating at that moment, while somehow still not being over the last thing, we had put into our mouths. And yet, despite being entirely overwhelmed, I somehow still managed to be very aware of the moment, and very grateful, as every part of me geared up for the next dish in anticipation of its arrival.

In many ways, this ensemble was starting to resemble my interactions with Floris: it was totally obscene that I was even at Alinea, just like it was outlandish to think he and I would ever have met. I had no idea what I'd be presented with next by the server, just like I had no clue where Floris would steer our relationship. Regardless, I was happy to wait on whatever would come my way—and even happier for the chance to participate in it—to feel alive with it. I didn't realize it was possible, but I was losing myself in a meal—among other things.

"Pardon us," said a server, as his counterpart began to swap out our place-settings. The silverware and china were getting replaced with something that looked like what French colonials in the 1500s would use. Our wine glasses were switched to gold goblets. Again, Chef Achatz was making me feel like I was in a different place and time. How was I able to do this from just a corner table in an unmarked Lincoln Park restaurant? I hoped Floris was writing it all down.

Grant threw in a couple of bonus courses to signify his gratitude to Floris and his guest of honor. By that point, I had lost count of how many plates we'd gone through—somewhere between 20 and 30? After around 22 courses, I sensed the savory beginning to subside; we were finally transitioning into dessert. Ironically, I wasn't "full" either. In fact, I was completely and utterly satisfied on every level—physically and emotionally.

I glanced at my phone to check the time: half-past midnight. We were heading to the three-and-a-half-hour mark at Alinea. Even though we weren't done yet, I kept thinking: "I don't want to leave. Don't make me leave."

"How has everything been so far?" asked our service captain.

Lovely.

Amazing.

Mesmerizing.

Astounding.

Take your pick—all of them were understatements.

"Great to hear. Grant is insisting he make dessert for you tableside, but he is just finishing closing out the kitchen. Would you mind a 15-minute break until he is able to make it up here? Otherwise one of the sous will come up and do the honors."

The honor was Grant. There was no substituting that. So, if the question was, could we wait 15 minutes to seal in the memory of a lifetime, the answer was—yes. Absolutely.

"So, now that we have some time, I have something to tell you," I said. "Actually, I have something to read to you," I corrected.

I reached into my purse to pull out four pages of handwritten words. I was making good on my promise to Floris. I wrote something for him, about us, and there was no better time than that moment to read it to him.

"Emele, what is that?"

"It's my part of our deal. Better start thinking about how you're going to marinate my steak," I said.

I unfolded the paper and began reading him an excerpt from a quick passage I had written about our time together.

A week from now, Floris will be thousands of miles away, cooking in his kitchen, driving his Audi, hugging his niece. Meeting and dining with him in the nook of a tiny Chicago restaurant will be like a momentary blip on the radar of my life. I will no longer have the luxury of sitting across from him, watching the excitement in his eyes as he attempts to explain just how exactly he is feeling in a language that is not his own. I will no longer have the honor of dining opposite a top chef moments before he indulges in a delicacy that this cheeseburger-and-fries girl has most certainly never even heard of. And I will no longer have the privilege of being near someone who is as in love with life as he is. Such is life—my life, at least.

I can tell already that I will miss him, but I also know that the void will pale in comparison to the luck I feel that I was even able to meet this incredible man.

Bon appétit.

I looked up and Floris was crying. I had said before that it was too soon for tears, but now it was the time. It was okay to cry, so I joined him.

"You don't know what you've done for me, Emele," Floris said, sniffling and wiping the tears from his eyes. I knew this was in reference to him being brought down in recent months by the depression of his former lover. He was a grown adult trying to run a successful restaurant, be a good family member, a loving uncle, and all the while a supportive boyfriend in a relationship that was crashing and burning before his eyes. It's no wonder he felt dejected, unable to keep up with the expectations of living a rock star-chef life, and having it all.

"I wish you everything you deserve." He took a deep breath and tried to compose himself. "You have restored my faith, my passion, my hope that things in this crazy world can sometimes just work out. Thanks for being there that night. Thanks for being you. And thanks for helping me find myself."

I didn't know what was crazier, the fact that I did that for someone else, or that someone else had just done that for me. It was in that moment that suddenly I realized I could let go of everything, and everyone, that had wronged me in my past. I was no longer bitter about the Trent situation, frustrated by the bad apples, or embarrassed about the Jacob blip. Those people and those situations didn't define me. They didn't define my worth. And they certainly didn't define my future. I was free at last. Free from the pain and free to be me. And damn, did that feel good.

"I'm going to really miss you. You have no idea," he affirmed.

And just as I tried to form a response, any response, a ghost floated into the room: The man. The myth. The actual legend. Grant Achatz.

He was average in height but noticeably lanky. His signature swept hair was tucked behind his ears, and a long white apron covered his pants. He walked the way anyone who just finished working 15 straight hours would: slowly, carefully.

Floris stood up to shake his hand.

"Chef, everything has been absolutely wonderful. You have no idea. It's the best in the world, the best I have ever seen."

"Thank you, Floris. You've done such great work. We are going to miss you."

That makes two of us.

"Sit down," Grant insisted. "Let me do your dessert."

Besides sitting with Floris, the absolute highlight of the night was this dessert. Server assistants appeared from the woodwork yet again, asking if we wouldn't mind moving to a larger table, so that Grant could have more room, and both Floris and I could sit in a banquette and watch whatever was about to happen from the same vantage point. It was funny, every seat in the house—when we arrived—was taken. And now we had our pick of front row seats to the main event. And for the record, no we didn't mind moving.

Once settled in, they laid down a silicone mat, making sure the table was covered from corner to corner, end to end. Another server assistant wheeled out a cart. On it, were several bowls and cups all relatively small in nature, and each containing a spoon.

"Thank you," Grant said, politely shooing away the help.

The look on his face was inquisitive. He stared at our blank table and said nothing. Did nothing. We were all silent in anticipation. Even Grant.

Eventually he grabbed one of the bowls and got to work. Grant was spooning out an assortment of chocolates in several different forms— liquid, melted, frozen, etc.—and he painted them on the table. It was like watching da Vinci do the Mona Lisa. Again, just in a different time and place.

Swirls, dots, globs, repeat. White, dark, milk, repeat. Using a combination of colors and textures, spoons and spatulas, Grant created a masterpiece right on our table. I wanted to take pictures. Hell, I wanted to film the whole thing. But I couldn't, as doing so would have been too tedious for such an authentic moment. I wanted to see it through my eyes, not a camera lens. It was the only way I could believe it all myself.

After about ten minutes of artistry, Grant invited us to enjoy his creation. He thanked both of us for coming in and gave an extra warm thank you to Floris for his hard work over the last two weeks. It was, indeed, a very special moment.

"Okay, I've managed to keep this in all night," I began. "But now, I mean it: how the heck do we eat this?" I asked one final time.

"Any way you want," said Floris, as he dug in, claiming the first bite.

And there we were: two little kids playing with our food. It did not seem unnatural to have such fun with Floris. But I was having difficulty wrapping my head around the fact that we somehow managed to make our playground a three-Michelin starred restaurant. Then again, how did we manage any of this? Apparently, I was having difficulty wrapping my head around a lot of things.

Alinea was not a restaurant: it was a museum. We didn't arrive hungry to scarf down food: we came to pay admission, wander through each exhibit, and learn something—experience something. We came to put the final touches on one of the greatest serendipitous encounters of all time.

Four hours after we arrived, we finally got up to leave the restaurant. Floris had closed us out without me knowing. He had treated me to another once-in-a-lifetime experience that tallied over a thousand dollars once the wine pairings, tax, and gratuity were added. What did I do to deserve that? Did it honestly come down to the fact that I was in the right place, at the right time, for the right person?

It was just after 1 AM and it dawned on me: I had work the next morning; and Floris had a flight home. Fuck.

Prior to leaving, Grant had autographed our menus for the evening, which were customized to include the wine pairings and bonus courses sent up by the kitchen. There I had it: proof I was there. Proof that we were there.

"Until tomorrow," Floris said with me in his arms.

"Yes, until then."

"You're still coming by my hotel to say goodbye, right?" he asked.

"With lunch and a smile," I confirmed.

With a sweet kiss on the lips, and a warm hug, cabs took us apart in this city for the final time.

I have no concrete explanation regarding why I didn't go back to the hotel with Floris that night, or why I didn't invite him to my place after we disembarked. In fact, I have no concrete explanation as to why those thoughts never even crossed my mind. Perhaps he was my first real taste of an emotional connection, and I was now smart enough to know that the physical stuff would be the fastest way to mess it all up. Whatever the reason, I'll leave it up to the book clubs to discuss, because let's face it, your guesses are as good as mine.

But what I knew for sure was that the next day was going to be different. I already felt the pain of the hardest goodbye I'd ever have to say looming in the horizon.

CHAPTER TWENTY-TWO/LESSON TWENTY-TWO

- Always make it come full circle

I woke up the next day knowing my fairytale was ending. It had been a great run, a perfect run, but it wasn't immortal. Our experience was not excused from the reality that it would end.

I thought about taking the day off. Not only was I merely exhausted from a four-hour dinner that went into the wee hours of the morning, but also doing so would have warranted me a few more hours with him. But I ultimately determined that the sooner I got my life back to the way it was pre-Floris, the better. And that started with not making any more exceptions for this exceptional human being.

So, the best I could do was take my lunch break early, pick up some food, and meet him at his hotel. From there, we'd eat lunch together and say goodbye before he made his way to the airport. For as simple and routine as it sounded, my heart never felt heavier.

I grabbed a pizza and a salad from a nearby restaurant and made my way over to his hotel. Pizza and a salad? Really? After Alinea? Should I have packed some peanut butter and jellies from home, and called it a day? Let's get real; my concept of good food had been blown up sometime in the last 12 hours and would never be the same.

"Emily?" I heard as I walked into the hotel. The voice was coming from the desk.

"I'm Nicole. Floris told me you were coming."

Nicole? Nicole? I racked my brain until it clicked: Nicole, the front desk agent at the hotel who worked nights, and always heard Floris talk about me, about us.

"It's so nice to place a face to a name," she said.

"Likewise."

"I normally work nights, but I've been hearing about you for a week now, so I put myself down to work a double so I could catch a glimpse of the famous Emele."

"Oh, you didn't have to do that!" I exclaimed, somewhat embarrassed that this woman was working overtime just so the story could come full-circle for her. Then again, discounting the value of coming full-circle wasn't fair. It was what I was there to do, after all.

"Anyways, have a great lunch. I'll make sure Floris gets to the airport on time."

"Thank you, Nicole," I said walking toward the elevator bank.

~ ~ ~

Floris was in his room waiting for me. He was nearly all packed. I couldn't help but think that each piece of luggage stacked against the wall was a reminder that he was from a far-away land. He did not live here, he was not staying here, and everything was temporary. Everything was a cut-in.

The mood was quiet. It was somber. We picked around at the pizza until he finally moved the box off the bed entirely.

"Lay with me," he said.

He held me, and we talked casually, doing our best to ignore the inevitable.

I don't know what reminded me of it, but I recalled the tattoo I had seen through the hole in his jeans on the first night.

"Can I see your tattoo?"

"My tattoo?" he asked, surprised.

"Yes, I know you have one. I saw it through the hole in your jeans in the car to Bonsoiree."

Next thing I knew, his pants were off.

No, this is not going where you think it's going. It was simply easier for him to show me his ink without his pants on. His entire leg—quad to calf—was covered in dark, black tattoo representative of another culture. It meant something spiritual to him, and I would never have guessed that it as there.

He pulled his pants back up and resumed his place next to me in the bed. He kissed me. Yes, we had kissed before, sweetly on the lips, as I said. But until that moment, we had never kissed—not like this. I never wanted it to stop. Who would have?

A moment later, we broke away, and looked into each other's eyes. A part of me wondered why we hadn't done that sooner, but a part of me knew we weren't supposed to. This was never about sex, or physicality. And if you want to be technical, it was never about food, either. It was about reminders: that something true and beautiful can happen to anyone, whether you "think" you deserve it or not. Something true and beautiful can happen, but only when you let go, and let it.

I had to get back to work. Floris had to get back to Holland. As such, I started to gather my belongings.

"Emele," he said, "I have one more thing for you."

He had already given me a collection of books that would have a permanent place on my bookshelf in every apartment or house I'd ever live in. What more was there?

Floris dug around in his kitchen bag and pulled out his chef's spoon. He held it in his hand and walked over to me.

"Do you remember me telling you that you give your spoon to someone who inspires you; someone who you respect?"

Yes, I remembered that quite well.

"That person is you," he said, as he handed me the spoon—beat up, passed down two generations, and from an ocean away.

I was speechless. How could I accept this? More puzzling, how could I not? This was my piece of proof that this whole week wasn't just a pop-up fantasy. Now, no matter what, I was connected to a parallel world. The one that belonged to this brilliant, beautiful man. Any day, any time, I just had to look at—touch—the spoon, and I'd be there. I'd be in another time, and place.

I started to cry, hard and uncontrollably, and that was my cue to leave. I had never known perfection, and with most things, I doubted it existed. But this, the ending to our story, was perfect.

I tucked the full-length four-page essay I wrote about him into his carry-on and left his hotel room. I took a left out the door toward the elevator bank and pushed the button to go downstairs. He was sobbing, I was sobbing. I watched the lights above the elevator doors click to each progressing floor. The impending arrival of the car was haunting me.

I refused to make eye contact with Floris, who I saw in the corner of my eye waiting in the doorway of his room until the final moment I had to leave. Well, that moment came, and it came all too soon.

At that moment, I looked up at him for the last time ever. He said something to me in Dutch, in his native language. I don't think it is outlandish of me to suppose that it was: "I love you."

~ ~ ~

On the bus back to my office, I was a crazy lady. I was sitting there, crying in the back row, clutching a metal sauce spoon. No one would understand, because it wasn't for anyone else to understand. All I knew, was that I held in my hands what would always be my most prized possession— my imperfect proof that perfection really does exist—my spoon from Floris.

I received a call from him before he took off. I could barely understand him through his choked-up voice and tears.

"I can't get on the plane. My foot," he complained.

"Floris, are you okay? Slow down. What's going on? What's wrong with your foot?"

"It's heavy. I can't lift it onto this plane. I don't want to leave." His foot was fine. His heart was not.

"You have to leave, Floris. You have to leave."

I sat on the line with him as he cried a little longer. No words, just tears. I was trying to be strong and not lose it completely, but this moment was almost as hard as leaving the hotel just an hour before.

"Floris," I said calmly and finally, "You have to leave."

"I know."

He had to leave. This story had to end. And it did.

~ ~ ~

Floris got on the plane and went home. He was jet-lagged for approximately two days. After the second day, I received a phone call from him to let me know he landed safely. It was 8 AM my time, 3 PM his. I was on a crowded city bus navigating through heavy morning traffic. He was in his restaurant, banging pots and pans, prepping for dinner service in his kitchen. The reception was terrible. We could barely hear each other. And for the first time, our interaction did not feel natural. It did not feel right. I knew then that our story had ended. It had been eightysixed.

CHAPTER TWENTY-THREE/LESSON TWENTY-THREE

- Never close the door on closure

I let go of Floris. I never tried to call back at a less chaotic time. I never sat by the phone thinking the next incoming text would be from him. And, I never tried to find him on Facebook. I did, however, sit and wonder what he might be doing at certain moments throughout the day. I wondered frequently if he thought of me like I thought of him. When I really missed him, and believe me I did, I'd grab the spoon, or I'd sit in my bed and stare at the ceiling in the exact spot he did on the night we went to Alinea.

Sometimes, I'd take out a piece of blank stationery and start to write a letter, thinking I could just buy an international stamp and mail it to his restaurant if I really wanted to reach him. But reaching him was not what I wanted.

What I wanted was the courage to be the new me—by myself. Floris was my ticket to another time and place. Every time I was with him, I somehow became more aware of who I was and what I wanted. When I was with him, I was the woman I aspired to be all my life: confident, daring, loving, playful, carefree, classy. I needed to learn how to feel and be those things independently of him—or anyone else for that matter—before I could chase down any sort of long-term relationship. My biggest fear was regressing back into a life that others defined.

So off to work I went, maintaining authenticity in everything I did. Surprisingly, I wasn't as hung up on Floris as I thought I'd be. After all, my life had no choice but to snap back to reality. It wasn't like I'd be solo dining at Alinea anytime soon, or taking tours of fancy kitchens in which I so clearly did not belong. So, for me, it was back to eating one-course meals from the microwave and seeing only American area codes pop up on my phone. Being okay with the downgrade was part of the bargain. I had to accept that everything—as it was—was okay. I had to trust that like that cold January night, I was where I was supposed to be, doing exactly what I was supposed to be doing, even if the reward was not as obvious.

As time went on, I continued to think about him and our week. The poignancy of my memories was becoming diluted, but the experiences we had remained rich—I could feel the aftereffects.

I stopped dieting. I spent less time worrying about how I looked, and what I wore, and more time focusing on me, and what I wanted to do. I quit drinking when things bothered me. I took an interest in the Chicago food scene, and eventually found friends with that same desire. Once a month, we'd go out to eat and splurge a bit on the experience. While I didn't keep a Moleskin full of notes, I certainly paid attention to flavors, service, and ambiance, in ways I never had before. Again, it wasn't about the food. It was about life. An awareness, a mindfulness, gratefulness for all the little things that make something great.

Undoubtedly, in the months leading up to our chance encounter, I was in dire need of recharging my batteries and restoring my faith—not in dating, not in men, but in myself. I had lost sight of my value, measuring my worth against things and people who didn't matter. I had been depreciating my closest friends and family and forgetting what joy it was to be my true, authentic, simple self. Floris, for however temporary it was, had brought this to the surface.

With that, I had reached an epiphany that helped explain why I wasn't emotionally debilitated when he left, as I had been with every other guy who'd come and gone in my life. Floris was never the man for me. He was the mindset, and then the memory, for me.

~ ~ ~

Six months later in July, I turned twenty-five. I spent my birthday enjoying a glass of champagne at a restaurant in Little Italy, celebrating the big quarter of a century milestone with some friends. Taking a quick inventory: I was happy, healthy, single, employed, eating well (albeit cheaply), and enjoying the beautiful summer weather.

After plenty of wining and dining, the iPhones came out, and the bill calculation commenced. Even though I was exempt from contributing, I took out my phone as well, catching up on whatever birthday wishes I might have missed over the last few hours.

There were four missed calls. All from the same number. All from Floris.

Six months had gone by in silence. Six months. Any residual wondering and wishing had long since faded into an abyss as our flash-in-the-pan romance boiled down to just a lovely little blip on my life's radar. And now a call? Four of them, to be exact? Why?

A voice-mail icon suddenly appeared I checked it just as quickly. While it was difficult to make out what he was saying amidst a crowded restaurant, the gist was that he wanted to "congratulate" me on my birthday, which he'd written down in his notebook after the first night we met. I powered off my phone after hearing his message, my arms covered in goosebumps.

I could have called him back when I got home to my apartment. I would undoubtedly have much to ask him. But I didn't. Because not many people get a perfect week in life, and I did. If you're one of lucky ones, you might be able to look back at your life and pick out four or so moments that really mean something to you. And even then, they're probably milestones such as childbirth or marriage. Rarely can we extract a casual string of time from our lives and say, "Hey, everything about that…was great."

I wanted to leave it our string of time together at that. I wanted the lessons I had learned, and the memories I'd acquired, to be my souvenirs at the end. Nothing about meeting him took effort. There was no confusion, no questions, and no quarrels. He played his part in the story of my life, and it was time to move on.

~ ~ ~

When I climbed into bed, I grabbed my phone and turned it back on. Not to call him after all, even though he was still on my mind, but to do something else—to go to his restaurant's website.

I skimmed through the pages of his site. It was all in Dutch and I couldn't make anything out. That didn't stop me from looking in the photo gallery, seeing his familiar face, and even downloading a PDF of his most reason seasonal menu.

Nothing on it was written in English, but I did recognize one word. It was course five, the main one: "Emele" was the title of the dish.

I presumed "Netto—Aardappel—Spinazie," listed below the name, were the ingredients. "Merlot" was the wine it was paired with. I quickly punched this all into Google Translate.

"Emily: Filet—Potato—Spinach. Merlot."

Though he never came through on his promise to cook for me "sometime in the next two years," perhaps this was his way of showing that he, too, felt the lasting effects from our chance encounter. This was my sign that it really was a two-way street with us. He hadn't just swept that one week in the winter under the rug. He had clearly created a dish based on my favorite meal, and he named it after me. People an ocean away were eating something that Emily Belden was responsible for and I had confirmation that our story had come full circle.

EPILOGUE

People always say relationships are hard. If I've learned one thing through my go at them, it's this: they're only hard when things aren't aligned. Whether it's the wrong person, wrong place, or wrong time, no amount of fussing or fighting will fix it. You just have to break free and wait for the right match to come along. The perfect fit will set you free.

Relationships don't require a near constant battle of wills. For a long time, I was simply so accustomed to fighting for every inch of ground that I neglected to realize a good relationship doesn't require strife at all. It's just that all the crap can cloud us into thinking that that's all we deserve—which we don't.

And to that, I say, take the next opportunity to let someone prove that to you.

When someone comes along who understands you exactly the way you want to be understood, treats you like a legend, and loves you like there's no tomorrow, do yourself a favor and embrace it. It's not the norm, and it's unlike anything we twenty-somethings have struggled through before, but it's precisely how things should be.

Sure, it's uncomfortable to have things flow so well, and be so easy, when you're used to a constant state of panic. But, when you're in the right place, at the right time, with the right person—well, then you can eighty-six the panic and feast for a lifetime on the stuff that's good for the soul.

Bon appetite.

ABOUT THE AUTHOR

Emily Belden is a food journalist, social media marketer, and storyteller. She is the author of the novels *Hot Mess* and *Husband Material*, and of *Eightysixed: A Memoir About Unforgettable Men, Mistakes, and Meals*. After she tiled her bedroom floor in over 60,000 pennies – all heads up for good luck – she was a guest on The Today Show and her story was covered by media outlets across the country. A Chicago native, Emily lives with her husband, Matt, and spends all her free time volunteering with rescue dogs and thinking of ideas for her next novel.

Read on for an exclusive excerpt from the novel HOT MESS by Emily Belden, available via HarperCollins.

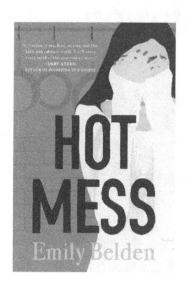

Twentysomething Allie Simon is used to playing by the rules—until Chicago's most sought-after, up-and-coming culinary genius, Benji Zane, walks into her world and pulls her into his. The only thing more renowned than Benji's mouthwatering masterpieces and equally luscious good looks? His struggle with addiction and his reckless tendency to live life on the edge, no matter the havoc he wreaks along the way. But loving someone means supporting him no matter what, or so Allie tells herself. That's why, when Benji's offered the chance to light up foodie hot spot Randolph Street with a high-profile new restaurant, Allie takes the ultimate risk and invests her life savings in his dream.

Then one day Benji disappears, relapsing to a place where Allie can't reach him. Left with nothing but a massive withdrawal slip and a restaurant that absolutely must open in a matter of weeks, Allie finds herself thrust into a world of luxury and greed, cutthroat business and sensory delight. Lost in the mess of it all, she can either crumble completely or fight like hell for the life she wants and the love she deserves.

With razor-sharp wit and searing insight, Emily Belden serves up a deliciously dishy look behind the kitchen doors of a hot foodie town, perfect for fans of Sweetbitter and The Devil Wears Prada.

CHAPTER ONE

"Are you going to be okay?"

His question gives me pause. Will I be okay? Was "okay" a hypothetical three exits ago?

All things considered, I'm hurtling through time and space with a guy whose recovery from a serious cocaine addiction matters as much as the rise of his chocolate soufflé tonight. So I answer honestly.
"I don't know." My voice sounds far away.

"Well if you're not sure, change. You'll be walking at least five miles between ushering people to tables and the bathroom and running back and forth from the kitchen."

"Oh, shoes. You're asking if I'm going to be okay in these shoes." I glance down at my black platform wedges.
"Yeah, babe. What the hell else would I be talking about?"

He grabs the bottom of my chin and plants a quick kiss on my lips before he rinses a whisk in the sink.

The shells of seventy-five hardboiled eggs are in the trunk of a car I rented to shuttle all the shit required for tonight's guests, I took an unpaid day off from work to be here to help, and my parents are about an hour away from arriving to this special "comeback dinner," which will be the first time they've seen Benji somewhere other than the headlines in the last thirty days.

And he's worried about my shoes?

"I'll be fine," I say sweetly, knowing now is not the time for a true audit of my emotional well-being. Tonight is about Benji's big return and my confidence that all—including my shoe choice—will go as smoothly as the housemade butter at room-temp that he's just whipped up.

I find my reflection in a nearby cryo-vac machine and take out a tube of my go-to matte pale pink lipstick from my makeup bag. I sweep it across my bottom lip, then fill in just above my lip line on the top for the illusion of a slightly fuller mouth. After all, I know at least half the guest list is here to see what the woman behind the man looks like.

Speaking of lists, I can see Benji in the reflection as well, leaning over a stainless steel counter consulting the prep list for tonight's dinner service. He takes a black Sharpie from the pocket of his apron and puts a quick slash through each item as he recites them out loud to himself.

I come up behind him and cast my arms around him slowly; my touch puts him at ease. He curls his left arm up to hold my arms in place and continues to mouth ingredients one by one to make sure he hasn't forgotten anything. It sounds like sweet nothings being whispered to me a romance language I barely understand.

Benji crumples the list, a sign he's successfully on track with everything from the dehydrated goat's milk to emulsified caramel, and I snap out of my schoolgirl daydream. He turns to face me, shuffles a few steps back in his worn kitchen clogs, and bends down to shake out his longish dark hair.

I know what he's about to do. And for as ordinary as it is, especially to girls like me who *routinely* wear their hair like this, watching Benji shimmy a hair tie—my hair tie—off his right wrist to tie up his mane into a disheveled topknot is like the start of an exotic dance. For anyone who says the man-bun trend isn't their thing, they're lying.

The hair tie snaps when Benji tries to take it for a third lap around his voluptuous bun. "God dammit!"

"Relax, babe," I tell him as I zip open my makeup bag and pull out a spare. Crisis averted, I think to myself as I put another mental tally in the "Saves-the-Day" column.

He re-ties his white apron for the umpteenth time over a tight black T-shirt that shows off his tattooed-solid arms. I know for a fact he doesn't work out (unless you consider lifting fifty- pound boxes of pork and beef off the back of a pick-up truck getting your reps in…) but somehow he's been blessed with the body of a lumberjack. The only thing missing is the ax, which has been appropriately swapped out for an expensive Santoku knife custom engraved with some filigree and his initials: BZ.

No doubt he's got the "hot and up-and-coming chef" thing down: tattooed, confident, exhausted, and exhilarated. Hard to believe this isn't a casting event for *Top Chef.*

Harder to believe this is the man I get to take home every night.

"FUCK! Are you kidding me, Sebastian? Where the fuck is the lid to that thing?" Benji's words effectively snap me out of the trance I was in danger of being lulled into. It takes me a minute to realize what happened: his sous chef Sebastian has pressed "pulverize" on a Vita-Mix full of would-be avocado aioli, except the lid to the blender is nowhere to be found. Green schmutz has gone flying, marking up Benji's pristine apron like the start of a Jackson Pollock piece.

"Sorry, chef. I got it on now." Tail between his legs, Sebastian gets back to work as Benji furiously wipes at the streak with his bare hand. He's making it worse.

"Benji. Breathe." I grab his half-drank can of LaCroix and pour a little onto a clean kitchen rag. While tending to the stain in the hot kitchen, I look directly into those deep brown eyes and give him a reassuring smile. He smells of cigarettes and sweat, garlic and onions. It's intoxicating.

"I know, Allie. This is just…huge for me. Huge for us. The press is going to be here tonight." He wipes some sweat off his brow.
"And my parents," I whisper.

"Oh god, them too." He releases the tension by cracking the bones in his neck. A poor substitute, I imagine, for his true preference: a shot of whiskey.

But even a slug of 120 proof wouldn't take the edge off the fact that Benji's pop-up dinners are the new It Thing. People salivate at their screens just waiting for him to tweet out the next time and place he'll be cooking. Why? Because he's the hottest chef in Chicago and you can't taste his food at any restaurant. So when he announces a dinner, it's a mad, server-crashing race to claim one of only twelve spots at the table. And when everyone wants to see how the reformed addict is faring, they'll cancel all their plans for the day on the off chance they'll be one of the first to submit a reservation request, followed by prompt pre-payment—which all goes to me, the fan-favorite girlfriend of Benji Zane.

I can't blame his followers for the obsession. Our flash-in-the-pan love story was covered by the most read food blog earlier this spring, and since then, there have been myriad articles chronicling his love-hate relationship with hard drugs and high-end cooking. Between his unlikely relationship with me, his checkered past, and his unmatched kitchen skills, Benji's managed to divide people like we're talking about healthcare reform or immigration.

Half see him as a prodigy in the kitchen who was given a second chance when some no- name poster child of millennial living suddenly inspired him to get clean. The other half of Chicago views him as an all-hype hack who uses the media attention to rob his patrons of their hard-earned money so he can get his next score.

Fuck those people. Because the Benji that I know, that I live with…well, he's a stand-up guy whose brunch—and bedroom—game happens to be on point.

"Listen, babe," I say. "What did I tell you? I'm not going to let you down tonight, okay? I'll pace the seating however you need me to. I'll greet the press and spot the critics, too. We got this, okay? I believe in you." And I do.

I don't always agree to help Benji at his pop-ups—usually I just accept the reservation requests and keep the books straight. But tonight is different. Benji told me yesterday that he's got an outstanding dealer debt to pay off and so he's oversold the dining room by about twenty- five chairs to try and make a little extra cash. Without me here to help host a guest list of this size, this highly-publicized dinner would look and feel more like a dysfunctional family reunion. Something I'm sure the piranha-like press would love to write about.

I wanted to be pissed about this little "oops" moment. How careless could he be? Now, by over-inviting a hoard of overzealous foodies, and in the past, by racking up a $2,000 coke bill. But he assured me it's just one of those things that *needs* to be handled in order for him to move on with his sobriety. And that's what I signed up for by being his girlfriend: unconditional support and a back that would never turn on him.

He's even arranged for Sebastian to be the one to hand over the cash tonight after the last diner goes home. Consider it just another example of how hungry people are to work alongside Mr. Zane. The same set of hands is willing to debone fifty squab *and* pay off gang-banging drug dealers from the south side, all in the same night.

I don't blame Sebastian, though. There's something about Benji that makes you want to strap in for the ride. It's like rushing a sorority: you'll do what you need to do to get in, because ultimately, you end up part of something bigger than yourself. I just don't think any of us know what that *something* is yet.

At least that's the way I see it from my vantage point, which is currently the groin area of a brand new apron that was marked with an unsightly stain until I stepped in.
"See babe?" I say. "All clean."

Benji pulls me in for a kiss, his hand cupped around the back of my neck. With my French twist fragile in his palm, I feel the stress in the kitchen disintegrate. I'm no superhero, but if I were, my power would surely be managing to make it all okay for him, every time. It doesn't even matter that there's garlic burning in a sauté pan, my lipstick is now smeared, or that my work email is probably blowing up with a hundred notifications an hour.

"You're my rock, babe," he tells me, tucking a few strands of loose hair behind my ears. I love hearing that I'm doing a good job, because it's not always easy.

"Okay, so here's the final guest list," he says, getting back to business. Benji hands me a piece of paper from the back pocket of his charcoal-gray skinny jeans. At the top, "Aug. 20 Pop- Up" is underlined in black marker. I give the list a quick once-over.

"So the first round of seating is at 7, second is at 9. Simple enough," I say.

"Well, it's more than just ushering people to their chairs." He tenses back up. "After everyone's seated, I'll need you to run food and bus tables if we get in the weeds."

"Weeds?"

"Busy as shit."

"Ah. Okay."

"And water. Constantly. You should be carrying the pitcher and filling any glass that's lower than two-thirds."

"Got it."

"Pay attention to what people are saying. Any issues, come find me immediately." "Obviously."

"And as we're wrapping, make sure you call a cab for anyone who's too drunk to drive. The last thing I need is bad press about a deadly DUI from someone I fed."

"Anything else, your highness?" I jest to lighten the mood. I get that he's on edge, and rightfully so. So am I, to be frank. This mini-romper won't be forgiving in the derriere area should anyone drop a fork while I'm rehydrating them. I also barely know the difference between kale and spinach, and am about to play hostess to a room full of people who are jonesing to fire off a photo or two of this year's culinary George and Amal to their judgmental social sphere. It's a lot.

"Very funny. And yes, there is one more thing. Mark and Rita just texted me. They can't make it tonight. Couldn't find a sitter for Maverick or something."

While it would be great to finally meet Benji's sponsor, Mark—and his wife Rita—I'm okay with the last-minute cancelation. Two less comp seats means more profit and less work for Benji. It also means two less people who I need to impress on the spot. Especially people whose job it is to spot bullshit. They'll be missed by Benji, I'm sure, since they're basically the parents he never had from what I gather. But hopefully he'll just shake it off.

"I'm sorry, that sucks. It's tough with kids," I say like I know.

"Yeah, it's whatever. I told them we'll see them next weekend. Anyways, can you just promise me something?"

"Of course."

He looks me dead in the eye and says: "Promise that you'll fuck me after this is all done."

Blood rushes to places it hasn't since I lost my virginity on Valentine's night my freshman year of college. I know, I know. That's totally cliché. But what was your first time like? Okay then, let's not judge.

Speaking of clichés, now would be a good time to mention that I fell for the bad boy. And being "that girl" doesn't end there: just imagine a more basic version of Selena Gomez with a day-old blow-out tucking her leggings into Uggs when the temperature falls below 70 degrees. Give or take a Pumpkin Spiced Latte and a *Real Housewives* viewing party, and you've just about got me—Allie Simon—pegged. I'm the last person someone like Benji Zane would want to date and the first person the food blogosphere has been able to confirm he actually is dating. I give him a wink and turn toward the dining room. I've got a little time before our first guests are set to arrive and I need to get my game face on. I need to feel less like someone whose super-hot boyfriend wants to ravish her across the very counter the amuse-bouches are being prepped on and more like someone who knows on what side of the plate the fork goes.

Tonight's pop-up is in a small indoor ballroom on the 45th floor of a high-rise luxury apartment building way up on the north side. For a Friday night, it'll be a bit of a clusterfuck for anyone who lives in the heart of Chicago, The Loop, or out in the suburbs like my parents, to get up here, but the views of the boats on Lake Michigan and the sunset reflecting off the buildings in the skyline will be so worth it. This summer evening is the kind of night Instagram is made for.

How Benji secured the venue this time is a doozy. He put an ad on Craigslist: "Party Room Needed." Said he couldn't pay money for the space, but would leave all his leftovers behind *and* the secret to "a roasted chicken guaranteed to get you laid." Thirty minutes later, some teenager whose parents live in the building dropped off the keys to the penthouse floor. It never ceases to amaze me the things people will do just to feel like they have a personal connection to the Steven Tyler of the food world. Alas, here we are.

I push on the balcony door handles fully expecting they'd be locked. But they pop down with ease and the warm summer wind hits me in the face. I grab the railing, close my eyes, and suck in that city air.

I don't breathe enough. Not like this, deep and alone. I have to admit that being Benji's girlfriend sometimes feels like sitting in the passenger seat as he drives 110 miles per hour on the freeway in a jalopy with no seatbelts. It's easy to get overwhelmed, but I remind myself that Benji came into my life for a reason. Every douchey, going-nowhere guy I dated before him was worth it because they led me to him: a beautiful genius who knows exactly who he is and what he wants. A guy with talent, charisma, and nothing but pure adoration for me. So what if he had a flawed start? All that matters is that I stopped the top from spinning out of control and now we're good. We're really fucking good.

Just then my phone, which I have stashed in my bra (hey, no pockets, okay?), buzzes with a text. I dig around in my cleavage and read the message from Benji.
"2-top off elevator. It's time, babe."

~ ~ ~

My feet are aching and I'm sweating, but as far as everyone can tell by the smile on my face, I'm having a grand old time filling water glasses. By now, we're more than halfway through the service and so far, Benji's only used the bottle of bourbon in the back for a caramely glaze on the dessert course, not to ease the kitchen chaos. In fact, in the ten or so times I've popped my head in to check on him, he appeared to be keeping his cool entirely.

"And how are you two enjoying your evening?" I say, hovering over a couple at a round top table I haven't checked on yet.

"There she is." My dad wipes his mouth as he stands up to give me a hug. My god, he's wearing a wool suit and a silk tie. Overdress much? "What do you think of the food?" I ask.

"It's outstanding, Allie. Say, can we get another one of those Siracha Jell-o cubes?" "Goodness Bill, don't embarrass me like that. Just ignore him, Allie. Although, yes, the
Siracha cube was..." My mom, Patti, closes her eyes, puckers her lips, and explodes an air kiss off the tips of her fingers. I think that's mom-code for

amaze-balls.

"I'm really glad you guys could make it," I say. And I mean that. It's not easy to accept the fact that your daughter is dating the most talked-about, tattooed chef in the Midwest, let alone show your support by attending a BYOB makeshift dinner party on the far north side.

"Wouldn't miss it for the world. And hey, I couldn't figure out how to get the flash on this dang iPhone to work, but I took a bunch of pictures," my dad says. "You'll have to explain later how I'm supposed to send them to you."
I'm positive they will all be blurry but it's the thought that counts.

"Is Benji going to come out?" my mom asks, playing with the pearls on her necklace. Her question captures the attention of strangers sitting across the table and now everyone's eyes are on me.

"We'll see," I say, knowing that answer isn't good enough. Not for anyone in the room who paid to be here. "You'll have to excuse me. I've got to keep checking on other tables. Love you guys."

As I make my rounds, everyone seems to be gushing over the fifth and final course of the night: grilled fig panna cotta with a bourbon, honeycomb drizzle over vanilla bean gelato. I hear one person whisper it was better than Alinea's dessert. Another says she just had a foodgasm. At that, I set down the water pitcher and offer to clear a few dirty plates back to the kitchen. When no one is looking, I dip my pinky into some melted gelato and run it through a glob of the bourbon honey before quickly licking it off my manicured finger. Heaven. Pure heaven.

Even though there's no negative feedback to report to the kitchen and everyone is stuffed, I can tell people are saving room for one more culinary delight. They want to see Benji Zane.

Put it this way: sure, the tenderness on the squab was on-point. And yes, the scoop of gelato was spherical as fuck. But as rock-star as his dishes may be, these people are here for something else entirely. They've ponied up to get up close and personal with Benji Zane and not just because he's easy on the eyes. To them, this is the Reformed Addict Show. It's their chance to witness first-hand if he's turned over a real leaf this time, or if he's just moments away from the downfall more than a few food bloggers think is coming. My money is on the former.

Does that make me a naïve idiot? Maybe. But these people don't know Benji like I do.

The one thing I'm sure of is that I am Benji's number-one supporter. If I waver from that, I know the chances of a slip are greater, so it's not something I'm willing to do. Especially not since we live together. I mean, *you* try staying ahead of the curve when your roommate has a kinky past with cocaine.

"Benji?" I say, cracking the kitchen door open a few inches. "Can you come here a sec?"

He puts down his knife roll and heads to the doorway, tapping Sebastian on the way over and telling him to take five.

"What is it? Everything good?" I can see the anxiety in his eyes. Whether it's an audience of one or a roomful of skeptical diners, Benji cuts zero corners when it comes to his cooking. He wants tonight to go seamlessly and if he's not pulling a huge profit in the end because of some dealer drama, well then, his reputation among these unsuspecting people needs to be the thing that comes out on top.

"Everything's great," I whisper. "But are you going to step out? I think people want to applaud you. They loved everything. Honestly, it was the perfect night."

Benji's not shy. Not by a long shot. But I can tell he's delayed making his cameo until I offered up the reinforcement that people really are waiting in the wings like Bono's groupies.

"Really?" he asks.

"Really. Look at Table Eight. Bunch of food bloggers who wet their panties when they ate the deconstructed squash blossoms. I'm pretty sure they'll have a full-blown orgasm if you just come out and wave to them."

He peers over me to check out the guests. Table Eight is all attractive blondes with hot pink cell phone cases who must have taken a thousand photos so far. I'd worry, but when your reckless love story has been chronicled on every social media platform since its hot and heavy start, that makes it pretty official: Benji Zane is off the market, folks. Has been since the middle of May.

"Alright, fine. Give me a sec."

Benji ditches his apron and grabs my hand. Together, we walk into the dining room and all chairs turn toward us. I feel a bit like the First Lady, just with a trendier outfit and a more tattooed Mr. President by my side. I bite back the urge to wave to our adoring fans.

"I just want to thank everyone for coming out tonight. I hope you enjoyed the food. It was my pleasure feeding you. Feel free to stick around and enjoy the view or see Allie for a cab if you need one. Goodnight, everyone." Benji holds our interlocked hands up and bows his head.

The crowd goes wild—well, as wild as forty diners who have all just slipped into a serious food coma can go. It's a happy state, the place Benji's food sends you. Kind of like how you feel after a long, passionate sex session. When done, you've got a slight smile and glow on your face, but just want to lie down for the foreseeable future and possibly smoke a cigarette.

I spot my father standing in the back, filming on his phone as my mother claps so hard, her Tiffany charm bracelet looks like it's about to unhinge and fall into what's left of her dessert. Seeing them both smile proudly across the room at who their daughter has wound up with warms my heart. It's been an uphill battle, but I'm confident we've won them over.

Benji whisks me back to the kitchen and before I can congratulate him on a successful evening, he pushes me up against the walk-in fridge. His tongue teases my mouth open and I am putty in his hands. With his right hand, he pulls down the collar of my romper, exposing my black lace bra. He frees my breast and kisses my nipple. My neck turns to rubber and my eyes roll back.

"Benji," I pathetically protest, very aware that all that separates us from a roomful of people who are currently picking a filter for a photo of the two of us holding hands is a swinging door that doesn't lock.

He continues kissing my neck, my breast still exposed. "I couldn't have done any of this without you, Allie."

"Oh, really?" I say, recognizing that the natural high he's on is most certainly fueling whatever is happening here. He slips a hand up my thigh.

"You made everyone out there have a good time tonight."

"I know," I playfully agree. He pulls my panties to the side. I know where this is going. "And now it's my turn to get in on it."

Before I know it, he's inside of me and we're officially having sex against a cooler with forty people standing fifteen feet away, two of whom are my doting parents.

Sex between me and Benji has always been explosive. It's like he knows exactly what I need and where to touch me without me having to give a lick of instruction. Sex has never been like this in my entire life. Granted, I've only got about five solid years of experience, but nothing rivals what Benji has introduced me to in the last three months. There's virtually nothing I'll say no to with him. Pornos, toys, and now public places. Who am I? I'll figure it out *after* I get off. A few hushed moans later, and I'm there.

"You did so good tonight," he whispers in my ear as he helps adjust my outfit. "Now I need you to go back out there and get everyone to leave so I can fuck you again over that balcony with the view of the lake in the background. Okay?"

I come back down to earth and reply, "Yes, sir."

Back in the dining room, I brush shoulders with Benji's sous chef, who's on his way back to his station. I give Sebastian a nod and return to my post, trusty water pitcher in hand.

There are a few stragglers left in the dining room, including my parents, finishing the last sips of their BYO selections. From what I can tell as I clear empty dishes and put the tips in a billfold, people liked dinner. They *really* liked it. The average gratuity being left on the pre-paid meal is about $50 cash per person.

After subtracting the dealer's cut, it's looking like we'll walk with about $2,000 cash for ourselves and I can't help but feel like a bit of cheat. I know nothing about this world—this high- end foodie club that I got inducted into overnight—yet people are emptying their wallets of their hard-earned cash to show their gratitude for what we've done. Do they realize just hours ago, the black squid ink from course two was being stored on ice in my bathtub? Regardless, we need the money. Benji may have kicked his expensive habit, but I'm the only one with a steady job right now and being a social media manager for Daxa—yes, the organic cotton swab brand made famous by Katy Perry's makeup artist on SnapChat—isn't exactly like being the CEO of Morgan Stanley.

"Excuse me, where is the ladies' room?" a tipsy guest asks. Benji might not have taught me how to sous vide a filet mignon, but he did tell me you always walk a guest to the bathroom when they ask. I promptly put down the dirty glasses and the wad of tips and walk the boozy babe to the loo.

Upon my return, I nearly collide with another guest, this one quite a bit soberer.

"Allie." The prim-looking thirty-something woman with a bleached blonde pixie cut says my name matter-of-factly. I stand up straight; this chick has "CRITIC" written all over her face.

"Yes, ma'am. Can I help you? Do you need a taxi?"

"No, thank you. I just wanted to give you a tip."

"Oh, that's so kind of you. You can actually just leave a gratuity on the table."

"No, I meant, like, some advice."

I tilt my head to the side and try not to lose my grip on my smiley service. She's five-foot nothing, but her demeanor is as bold as her bright red lipstick.

"I'm not sure Benji would be cool with you leaving a billfold with what I'd guess is about $2,000 in it just sitting on a table in a room full of drunk people who don't know that it's time to go home. It would behoove you to keep an eye on your shit."

She jams the check presenter into my chest and proceeds to walk right past me to the elevator bank.

And just like that, I've officially been felt up twice for the night.